Praise for *Legal Upheaval*

"We, lawyers, are normally trained and prepared to provide technical legal advice. However, our role in corporations and firms requires an additional set of abilities, including a wide range of skills, behaviors, and a broad mindset. *Legal Upheaval* guides us into the future with a road map to legal innovation and culture change." **Marco Araujo, General Counsel, Global Commercial Banking & Regional General Counsel Latin America, HSBC**

"*Legal Upheaval* comprehensively captures, in one book, all the current moving parts and challenges of the most seismic shift in how legal advice will be innovatively sourced and delivered in the 21st Century and beyond. The book also provides helpful workshop structures and an action plan to stimulate the reader into taking immediate action. Its overarching message, which should be ignored at the reader's peril, is that the time to act has arrived. Do it Now!" **Richard Barlow, General Counsel and Chief Regulatory Officer, Domestic and General plc**

"Innovation" is one of the most misused and misunderstood terms in Law-Land. Much characterized as innovative isn't and even more is neither useful nor practical in terms of customer delivered value. In *Legal Upheaval*, Michele DeStefano utilizes interviews, critical analysis, and humorous, conversational writing to provide a practical roadmap to actually innovate—but it requires behavioral change, commitment, and rigor. Those that can create and work in that innovative, collaborative, creative problem solving environment will sharpen skills, open minds, and change the way they work to delight their customers." **Jeff Carr, SVP General Counsel & Corporate Secretary, Univar Inc. and Former SVP General Counsel & Corporate Secretary, FMC**

"Michele DeStefano really understands the challenges facing the legal profession and in her book she offers powerful yet practical insights about how these will need to be met—essential reading for those leading firms through the most turbulent of times." **Peter Cornell, past Managing Partner Clifford Chance; Chairman, Lexington Consultants**

"Powerfully persuasive. This book will convince any lawyer of the critical need to think about and to try their hand at innovation. Open *Legal*

Upheaval with a positive attitude and be prepared to be challenged." **Robert Cutler, Chief Executive Partner, Clayton Utz**

"Be the change or face disruption. If you are ready for the most rewarding journey of your professional life, *Legal Upheaval* will open the door for you. Dive into the adventure of innovation." **Dr. Guenther Dobrauz-Saldapenna, Partner & Leader PwC Legal Switzerland**

"Everyone talks about the importance of law firm innovation—but how do you actually do it? Michele DeStefano, chief architect of LawWithoutWalls and visionary of law's future, has the answer in her essential new book *Legal Upheaval*. Loaded with powerful insights yet also accessible and engaging, *Legal Upheaval* guides the reader step-by-step through the innovation process, from honing new lawyer skills and mindsets to creating an innovation culture to designing an implementable roadmap to innovation every firm can use. Especially valuable for the law firm reader will be excerpts from exclusive interviews with more than 100 C-level executives in law departments and law firms that collectively describe a legal marketplace in irreversible transition. This book is not just for the enthusiastic legal innovator—it's especially meant for the skeptical or reluctant lawyer who's not sure why she should care about all this. Michele DeStefano's book makes an outstanding case for caring, and acting, right now to lead your legal enterprise to new heights of service and effectiveness through the systematic adoption of legal innovation. Add *Legal Upheaval* to your collection of must-read resources today." **Jordan Furlong, Legal Market Analyst, author of *Law Is A Buyer's Market***

"*Legal Upheaval* makes a compelling argument for why we must enter the "Innovation Tournament" and, more importantly, provides easy tips about how to play once we are in the innovation game." **Michael Hertz, Chief Marketing Officer, White & Case, Co-Founder, Pro Bono Net**

"This is a remarkable book on why innovation is the key ingredient for successful lawyers and how law leaders can drive a culture of innovation in their workplace. I learnt a lot about technology, creativity, leadership, and practical do's and dont's. It is thoroughly enjoyable reading, well researched and informed, wise and witty." **Peter Kurer, former**

Chairman, UBS, Chairman Sunrise Communications and author of Legal and Compliance Risk

"*Legal Upheaval* addresses the core questions for most about innovation in the legal industry. What it is? Why does it matter? The depth of research combined with the breadth of industry insights gives the most skeptical reader a guided road map from curious bystander to a creative problem solver that clients' value. Innovation in law is a contact sport, and Michele DeStefano captures—in an accessible and practical way—the rules of engagement." **Michelle Mahoney, Executive Director Innovation, King & Wood Mallesons**

"We are all talking about innovation but who is really doing it? DeStefano shines a welcome light on the topic, showing us the way to the Holy Grail while revealing who is doing this for real or simply faking it. For those getting this right, the rewards are high; this book will show you how." **Moray McLaren, Partner and Founder, Lexington Consultants, Associate Professor, IE Law School**

"Michele DeStefano's *Legal Upheaval* is a powerful and practical guide to a new kind of client service: one that changes your mindset, your skill-set, and how you interact in an evolving global landscape." **Juan Carlos Mencio, Senior Vice President of Legal Affairs and Compliance, LATAM Airlines Group**

"This book is a fantastic reference point for students, legal disrupters, academics, investors, legal psychologists, legal engineers, legal coaches, legal project managers and—yes—lawyers and especially law firm leaders!" **Alastair Morrison, Head of Client Strategy, Pinsent Masons LLP**

"Everybody knows that the economy has become topsy-turvy with change. And nowhere are the forces more ferocious than in the legal profession. Michele DeStefano draws on a wealth of interviews across the world of law to help you navigate these choppy waters. If you're looking to get more out of your own legal practice, or improve the performance of your own legal team, this book is a smart and practical guide." **Daniel Pink, author of *WHEN* and *DRIVE***

"Michele DeStefano expertly bridges the divide between innovation theory and practical application by picking the brains of in-house counsel—the people innovating and demanding innovation from their firms." **Chas Rampenthal, General Counsel and Corporate Secretary, Legal Zoom**

"The first step in fixing any problem is to acknowledge it exists. *Legal Upheaval* makes it easy for those in the legal profession—lawyers and alt lawyers—to identify the age-old practices of an age-old industry which, if left unaddressed, will marginalize law firms and their lawyers. Like the utility industry and power distribution, Michele DeStefano explains how the delivery of legal services is at an inflection point, and rather than fight the market forces driving this change, law firms must rethink and reinvent what it means to deliver the legal products their clients demand." **Eric Satz, Director, Tennessee Valley Authority and CEO, AltoIRA.com**

"In *Legal Upheaval*, Michele DeStefano shows how and why lawyers benefit from infusing creative problem solving into their practice. She provides tangible techniques that can be used within a legal organization and collaborating with other professionals." **Tina Seelig, Professor of the Practice, Stanford University School of Engineering**

"For much of the history of our Republic, the ideal for lawyers who would be leaders was the lawyer-statesman. Today it is the lawyer-innovator. Michele DeStefano offers a practical, accessible, far-sighted manual to get you there." **Anne-Marie Slaughter, President & CEO, New America**

"Michele DeStefano's research shows that collaboration towards innovation is the new value equation in law that will make relationships with clients stickier and more profitable. *Legal Upheaval* explains why you need to light an innovation bonfire in your organization and how to go about doing it." **Mick Sheehy, General Counsel, Telstra**

"A decade ago, no one would have believed that "innovation" would be the hottest buzzword in the legal profession of 2018. But over a decade ago, Michele DeStefano was already leading the way through her creation of LawWithoutWalls, the world's first—and still only—global legal innovation network. *Legal Upheaval* is a critical book at a critical time because it brilliantly describes where our profession has been, where we are and where we're going, but also provides proven, helpful tools to drive innovation and creativity in legal organizations. Michele DeStefano has no rival in the realm of generating energy and hope and unlocking the creative potential of lawyers." **Scott Westfahl, Professor of Practice and Faculty Director of Executive Education at Harvard Law School**

"Michele DeStefano doesn't just identify the critical need to inject an innovation mindset into the legal profession, she provides three simple rules that will help you ensure that you are not left behind!" **Mark Swatzell, Leader of Learning and Development for Corporate, External, and Legal Affairs, Microsoft**

"When you're not paying attention, it's called disruption . . . it's called transformation when you are paying attention. Clearly, Michele DeStefano is paying close attention to the changing legal ecosystem. If you would rather have your organization be transformed, then *Legal Upheaval* is required reading." **Robert Taylor, VP Senior Corporate Counsel, Liberty Mutual Insurance**

LEGAL

upheaval

A GUIDE
to Creativity, Collaboration, and Innovation in Law

MICHELE DESTEFANO

Cover Design by Tahiti Spears/ABA Design

Printed in the United States of America.

22 21 20 19 18   5 4 3

ISBN: 978-1-64105-120-0
e-ISBN: 978-1-64105-121-7

Library of Congress Cataloging-in-Publication Data

Names: DeStefano, Michele, author.
Title: Legal Upheaval: A Guide to Creativity, Collaboration, and
Innovation in Law / Michele DeStefano.
Description: Chicago : American Bar Association, 2018. | Includes
   bibliographical references and index.
Identifiers: LCCN 2018018955 (print) | LCCN 2018019821 (ebook) | ISBN
   9781641051217 (ebook) | ISBN 9781641051200 (hardcover)
Subjects: LCSH: Lawyers--Effect of technological innovations on--United
   States. | Practice of law--Technological innovations--United States.
Classification: LCC KF318 (ebook) | LCC KF318 .D47 2018 (print) | DDC
   340.068/4--dc23
LC record available at https://lccn.loc.gov/2018018955

Discounts are available for books ordered in bulk. Special consideration is given to state bars, CLE programs, and other bar-related organizations. Inquire at Book Publishing, ABA Publishing, American Bar Association, 321 N. Clark Street, Chicago, Illinois 60654-7598.

www.shopABA.org

CONTENTS

Introduction

This book is written to inspire lawyers and legal professionals to embrace innovation practices, even if their business model isn't "broken." In the process of innovating, lawyers hone the mindsets, skills, and habits that clients desire—and, in the future, that clients will require. The book is divided into three parts and each part can be read on its own.

Part I: Why Lawyers Should Hone the Mindset, Skill Set, and Behaviors of Innovators

Part I details what is at stake and why all lawyers should adopt the mindset, skill set, and behaviors of innovators even if their business model is not broken. Informed by extensive interviews with more than 105 general counsels and chief executives, heads of innovation at law firms, and law firm partners from around the world, this part describes the upheaval in the legal marketplace—the explosion of innovation that is occurring in the law marketplace and is changing the needs of clients. It explores the gaps that exist between what clients say they want from their lawyers and what lawyers are delivering. It concludes by demonstrating that the New Value Equation in Law is innovation. In the process of innovating, lawyers adopt new attitudes and behaviors and create new cultures that transform the relationships between lawyers and clients and how they collaborate to solve problems. The bonus: this kind of collaboration (toward innovation that adds value) is a client leadership edge opportunity.

Part II: The Three Rules of Engagement: Creating a Culture of Creativity, Collaboration, and Innovation

Part II describes how lawyers can approach the upheaval in the legal marketplace. It provides Three Rules of Engagement for creating a culture of creativity, collaboration, and innovation for lawyers: having an Open Mind, an Open Heart, and an Open Door. These rules are important to learn even if—or especially if—you are a lawyer leader and you yourself do not want to innovate. They are important because the only way to lead this type of culture creation among your team, department, or firm is by exemplification. Moreover, the focus is changing from what lawyers do to how they do it. Thus, following these Three Rules of Engagement will help you change how you collaborate with others, especially clients. In turn, this new collaborative way of providing service will help you build stronger and more durable relationships.

Part III: The Innovation Possible: Putting Together the Theory, Practice, and Proof

Part III takes innovation from concept to action by putting together the theory (the frameworks of innovation) with the practice (a method of innovation for lawyers) and the proof (this innovation method works for lawyers). It is designed to help make innovation possible regardless of the size or location of your firm or legal department. It introduces the Seven Essential Experiences that all lawyers must master to achieve innovation and the 3-4-5 Method of Innovation for Lawyers, designed specifically for lawyers who want to transform how they collaborate with clients and create innovative solutions to problems at the intersection of law, technology, and business. This part concludes by mapping out a journey of a lawyer-led team through an innovation cycle to provide proof that these experiences combined with this method work.

This book is for anyone invested in changing the future of legal services, be it someone tasked with transforming his/her practice, someone looking to approach his/her work in a new way, someone looking for a fresh approach to client relations to garner competitive advantage, or someone new to the field interested in a forecast of the world to come. As such, each chapter concludes with points of reflection designed to help you determine the best approaches for your team, department, or firm. Exercises for each chapter are included in my forthcoming book: *The 3-4-5 Method of Innovation for Lawyers: A Handbook of Exercises and Best Practices.*

Why Lawyers Should Hone the Mindset, Skill Set, and Behaviors of Innovators

> *"Start with why."*
>
> —Simon Sinek, *Start with Why*[1]

Your business model isn't broken. The sky is not falling. So why should you learn how to innovate? Even if you agree that lawyers could use a refresher on creativity and collaboration, you might still be skeptical or even shaking your head and asking why you should learn how to innovate. The answer to that question is explained in Part I of this book.

Part I is designed to explain why in a way that will convince you to at least *try* to hone some parts of the mindset, skill set, and behaviors of innovators. Through the voice of your clients and professional colleagues, Part I demonstrates that the focus is changing from *what* a lawyer's work is to *how*—how lawyers currently work and how clients want lawyers to try new ways of working.

So Part I is dedicated in Simon Sinek fashion to "starting with why"— the reasons you should try to innovate, to collaborate, and to creatively problem solve—even if your business model isn't broken. The next five chapters will take you through the following five whys:

1. Because the world is changing and these changes are creating legal upheaval in the law market. This chapter identifies three key forces behind the changes.
2. Because there *already* exists an innovation explosion in the way law is delivered, priced, packaged, sourced, and defined.
3. Because our clients' needs, worries, and demands have changed. Clients are asking lawyers to help manage this change, to leverage technology differently, to learn new skills, to partner together to collaboratively and creatively problem solve. This chapter identifies the Lawyer Skills Delta, those skills (above and beyond legal expertise and legal advice) that today's lawyers need to provide full-service client service, and the Innovation Disconnect that exists when they don't.
4. Because lawyers are getting in their own way. Their temperament and training serve as a pair of crutches inhibiting (but not preventing) the development of the mindset, skill set, and behaviors that clients desire. Understanding how we might be handicapped by our attitude and education can make all the difference.
5. Because the New Value Equation in Law is innovation. Lawyers' clients are asking for and rewarding innovation, even if in the form of simple incremental changes that add lasting value. This chapter presents the ABCs of Innovation: attempting to innovate changes our *A*ttitude about innovation; it changes how we *B*ehave; and over time, it changes the *C*ulture that suffuses our teams, our departments, and our firms as new kinds of relationships are formed.

CHAPTER 1

Three Forces Impacting
the Law Market Today

> *"Certain things they should stay the way they are. You ought to be able to stick them in one of those big glass cases and just leave them alone."*
>
> —J. D. Salinger, *Catcher in the Rye*[1]

People like to say that the legal profession hasn't changed. As someone who has spent the last eight years leading LawWithoutWalls, an experiential learning and development program that brings together lawyers, businesspeople, and students to hone new skills, behaviors, and mindsets to transform how participants creatively problem solve, collaborate, and cultivate relationships, I can tell you unequivocally—that isn't true. But you don't have to take my word for it. For this book, I have interviewed more than 100 subjects: general counsels (GCs) from large, international corporations, heads of innovation at law firms, and law firm partners all over the world. They all report how much the legal profession has changed over the past 10 years. And it is continuing to change—even if some lawyers would prefer that things stay the way they are.

One of the reasons legal markets have changed and will continue to change is because the world is changing. According to the World Economic Forum's recent report on the future of jobs, we are now entering the fourth industrial revolution[2] that has been driven in part by the technical revolution along with other forces continuing to transform global industries and occupations.[3] This chapter presents an overview of three of those forces:

technology, shifting socioeconomics and demographics, and globality/ glocality, all existing both outside and inside the law marketplace. Of course, books could be and have been written on each of these subjects. The following, however, provides some highlights that all lawyers should know. If you are one of those lawyers that already knows this stuff, I recommend you skip to Chapter 3 because that's when things get really interesting in this Part of the book.

Technology

From artificial intelligence to Microsoft's HoloLens to blockchain, Infinity AR, and Watson, the past 10 years have seen mammoth advances in technology and its usage. Indeed, some claim that new technologies are disrupting everything from jobs to industries to government.[4] Mobile internet and cloud technology has enabled more efficient delivery of all types of services and increased workplace productivity. This combined with the IoT (the "Internet of Things") and our ability to use remote communication capabilities in objects of all kinds has changed how people work, interact, and respond in terms of location, speed, and kind. Unsurprisingly, a recent World Economic Forum's survey reported that 74% of respondents identify mobile internet and cloud technology, computer power and big data, and/or the Internet of Things as a top driver of change.[5]

And this doesn't just mean that we can get our burgers and our coffee from kiosks.[6] Today we can chat instantaneously with someone who speaks a different language.[7] We can self-diagnose if we carry a disease.[8] We can print our kidney on a 3D device[9] drive in a driverless, autonomous pod (aka car)[10] that automatically reduces our insurance costs as it gets safer[11] and perhaps one day escape death[12] or at least live beyond 120 years old.[13] And unbelievably, sometime in the near future, we may even be able to remember what we cannot remember.[14]

It is predicted that within 10 years, computers will surpass the capacity of the human brain.[15] This power combined with AI (artificial intelligence) and machine learning advances has led to a computer program named Alpha Go that recently became the best Go player in the world[16] and to a computer system named Watson, identified as the #1 chess player, the #1 Jeopardy player, and, most recently, the #1 doctor in the world.[17] If Dentons and ROSS Intelligence have any say in the matter, one day Watson will also be the #1 lawyer. Dentons owns NextLaw Labs, a global innovation incubator designed to develop and invest in new technologies and processes to change legal practice, service, and solutions.[18] Dentons is collaborating with ROSS Intelligence, a start-up, to develop a legal adviser app powered by IBM Watson that is designed to answer natural law language questions at rapid speed.[19]

Two different futurists have predicted that in the next 10–15 years, we will reach "technological singularity," the point at which artificial intelligence is capable of continually rebuilding and improving its software and hardware to make it more powerful and smarter autonomously—without the need for human assistance.[20] As early as 1965, theorists such as British mathematician Irving John Good have hypothesized about this moment, calling it the "Intelligence Explosion"—when AI surpasses the cognitive ability of humans.[21] Even now, we have entered the era of being impacted by what is coined the "law of accelerating returns." This means essentially that in terms of technology, innovation begets innovation. Disruptive technology is being discovered faster and faster because existing technologies are used to improve the latest technology inventions and to create new ones. Technological inventions are reaching the mainstream faster, and innovation in technology is not graphed as a linear movement forward, but as exponential leaps.[22]

AI is everywhere. And not only that, AI is now being used in a way to personalize the user's experience. Think Apple's Siri, Microsoft's Cortana, and Amazon's Alexa. In our homes, we are now able to connect many of our electronic devices—our lights, our doorbell cameras, our alarm systems, our cable television. And then we can ask our friendly, almost human-sounding AI to manage them for us. Alexa, turn off the lights. Alexa, set the alarm for the house in 15 minutes. Alexa, give me options where I can eat breakfast close by. Alexa, play songs by Fleetwood Mac. Alexa, write that contract for me? It might not be that far from our reality.

More and more professional services firms, including law firms, are utilizing AI every day to help with compliance and due diligence and to help automate contract analysis and exchange, conduct legal research, and do document review.[23] AI is also being used for litigation analytics and outcome prediction. Companies such as Premonition sell you just that—a premonition based on that type of case, country, court, lawyer, and judge (and yes, it takes into account race, religion, and gender). In other words, Premonition sells you a prediction of whether you will win.

Right now we are seeing AI doing some task replacement by augmenting legal practice—in other words, by the lawyer and AI working together. But a big impact from AI is likely going to come from bots. Bots have been predicted to replace apps as they help us in the moment where we are and they help us do almost anything. So instead of using your TripAdvisor app to book a trip, you will simply chat with a bot that will then mine the data and information that TripAdvisor has and give it back to you the way you want it. Similarly, instead of calling or emailing your attorney, you might chat with Billybot, a virtual assistant designed to direct individuals to solicitors or barristers or to tools such as LISA (Legal Intelligence Support Assistant), an AI tool founded by Chrissie Lightfoot, powered by Neota Logic.[24] And maybe, just maybe, it will be as predicted in the book *Ready Player One*. Maybe, like Parzival, who programmed his virtual personal assistant Max to personify a late-80s talk show host,[25] we will decide what our bots look and sound like. The question people keep asking is not whether bots will assist us but whether they will replace us.

The one saving grace for lawyers in this seemingly scary futuristic landscape is that tech is not human and can't provide the human element. But with augmented reality and its ability to create products that look and feel, if not human, at least "alive" and empathetic, like a therapeutic robotic baby seal,[26] or Sophia, the first robot citizen,[27] that saving grace appears to be disappearing. Robots are already better at "feeling" our emotions. Robotic sensing machines are now able to detect emotions and moods. Researchers from MIT's Computer Science and AI Laboratory (CSAIL) have developed a device that uses wireless signals that measure heartbeat and breath to determine whether you are happy, sad, angry, or excited.[28] Richard and Daniel Susskind predict that machines will be able to display more empathy than humans and that people will eventually prefer to tell their most personal secrets to machines.[29] Machines don't judge, right? Combine looking alive with the ability to gauge moods and emotions and with feeling via haptic technology (also referred to as kinesthetic communication)[30] and the future of the law is bound to be impacted as surely as fields such as medicine and the military—perhaps even more so given the legal profession's commitment to trust, confidentiality, and ethics (and the legal rules related to property, crime, privacy, and fraud). Identifying and regulating the contours of those principles as it relates to AI and robots (which may end up in the hands of lawyers) will be as difficult a task as drafting the Magna Carta.[31]

Shifts in Socioeconomics and Demographics

In addition to the technological revolution highlighted above, socioeconomic and demographic shifts are changing the nature of how we work, where we work, and with whom we work. If we were going to boil all of that down into one highlighted word, it would be *flexibility*. New technologies—especially those that provide video conferencing (e.g., Skype) and collaborative work platforms and cloud storage (e.g., Google Drive)—enable employees who generally work at a corporate office to work from remote locations at different times and in different types of spaces, whether from a home office, a shared office (hot desk), or even a coffee shop. 44% of the respondents to the World Economic Forum Survey and 63% of professional services respondents highlighted flexible and changing work environments as the most impactful socioeconomic driver of change.[32]

What people mean when they say they are "going to work" is radically different than it was 15 years ago. But in addition to that, those with whom we work are varied and have different relationships with our employers. According to the same report mentioned in the previous paragraph, the number of core full-time employees will get smaller and smaller. These small teams will be supported by external consultants hired on a by-project basis.[33] This new organizational attitude and structure impacts how clients—especially those within large global organizations—work with their lawyers and with whom lawyers must partner when servicing clients. Those organizations that have embraced remote working, flexible time, contractual versus full-time employees, and disaggregated work have new challenges[34] related to recruiting, managing, training, assessing, and retaining employees, and in creating a cohesive corporate culture—especially one that is ethical.[35] This is likely even more true for global organizations than local given the increase in cultural dimensions—and the reality that global companies must deal with globality and glocality.

The confluence of flexibility and diversity can be seen not only in terms of geographic swath but also within individual organizations that may employ up to five generations at once. Due in part because we are living longer,[36] we now have in the workforce traditionalists, baby boomers, Generation X, Generation Y (millennials), and Gen 2020 (also referred to as Gen Z—the digital natives).[37] Recent studies suggest that managing multigenerational teams poses new challenges because of the different expectations each generation has about work and the lack of comfort older managers have with younger employees.[38] Those organizations that best manage the multigenerational workforce will enhance employee retention.[39] Those that don't will experience conflict and be less efficient.[40]

Such diversity has a number of unforeseen wrinkles, such as the different skill sets that each generation possesses and the different mentalities they are heir to. For example, according to EY's recent multigenerational study, Gen Xers are substantially more likely to be perceived as revenue generators, relationship builders, brand ambassadors, problem solvers, team players, and entrepreneurial.[41] However, the new crew of millennials (the largest and most diverse generation to date)[42] infiltrating law firms at the associate and senior associate level have been shaped by technology. In keeping with that, they are more likely to be social-minded opportunists than boomers and Gen X.[43] Although like Gen X, millennials are viewed as collaborative and adaptable, they are also more likely to be perceived as "difficult to work with," "entitled," and "lacking relevant experience."[44] Indeed, this may be why there is more reported conflict between them and boomers than with the boomers and Gen X.[45] As discussed in more detail in the conclusion of this book, if millennials are empowered and provided quality feedback, training, and opportunities to grow, there could be a huge upside to law firms that have been challenged by costs associated with attrition and lateral movement. That said, if they are not provided flexibility along with opportunities to grow, learn, work on teams and enjoy life, they will switch employers and/or careers.[46]

Globality and Glocality

The third major force impacting the law market today refers to how the world has gotten more global and smaller at the same time—global and glocal. The effects of the force of globality are felt in some expected and unexpected ways. Survey upon survey of senior executives, GCs, and chief compliance officers at global corporations across varying industries (from financial services, to healthcare, to insurance), report that their top concerns are (1) regulatory risk associated with increased regulations and regulatory scrutiny, and (2) the extraterritorial nature of our global economy (i.e., applying jurisdiction and regulations outside a country's borders).[47]

Let's take these two in order. In the past 15 years, the number of U.S. regulations has grown exponentially from Sarbanes-Oxley Act of 2002 (SOX)[48] to the Dodd-Frank Act.[49] In addition, the level of scrutiny by the government—and ensuing litigation—has risen. For example, in the fall of 2015, Deputy U.S. Attorney General Sally Yates announced a new policy on white-collar crime to target individual corporate executives in addition to corporate entities.[50] The number of SEC enforcement actions based on FCPA violations has risen almost 30% in the past 10 years.[51] The risk and impact of increased regulations becomes amplified when globalization is considered, and parties mount enforcement actions against foreign entities—the U.S. versus other countries or vice versa. Essentially, as the United States has increased its regulatory reach and influence outside its borders, other global economies have followed suit, enacting regulatory and legal changes to increase transparency and enhance compliance with the law.[52] Both the United States and the European Union have enacted far-reaching international sanctions against countries such as Iran, North Korea, Russia, Sudan, and Syria.[53] Use of third-party vendors from around the world that are all held to different standards of compliance depending on the organizations/NGOs they follow causes unique challenges. The regulatory and extraterritorial forces of change impact how corporations are structured and the role the CEO, board, lawyers, compliance officers, public relations officers, and other senior leaders play at corporations.[54]

Legal Upheaval: Changing World, Changing Pressures

All of this is causing legal upheaval in the marketplace and challenging the traditional, historical business model of the law firm. It is challenging the idea of bespoke work, it is challenging leverage and rate increases, and it is challenging the make-buy decision matrix as corporate clients adapt to the changing legal marketplace by insourcing. The lore has been that we have entered an era of "more for less." With technology and changes in socioeconomics and globalization, clients are expecting more from their service providers—especially legal service providers— at a lower price. Although that may be true, a more apt conclusion may be that we have entered an era of "more is more." Our clients want more of us more of the time.

"The one thing I've noticed that's changed a little bit in the past five to 10 years is increasingly demand . . . Rather than advice or assistance on a particular matter, we are often after a lawyer to be devoted to us in respect to a particular project . . . whose sole focus is helping us . . . We don't have the numbers or the staff to deal with that and we need someone there day in day out for the next three months to be on call to go to meetings immediately and to work through urgent work immediately to be available to us. That's the one trend that's always been there but becoming more pronounced." —GC, Government Department of Australia[55]

Given the forces of change, there are more channels for law, more places that law impacts, more opportunity for lawyers, more competition, and more risk.

Speaking of risk, when clients are asked what keeps them up at night, it is all about risk—new and strange risk, the kind of risk that can only come from a dizzying rate of technological advancement and unexpected and seismic shifts in regulatory realities across the globe. Clients today report new problems that are VUCA, as in *v*olatile, *u*ncertain, *c*omplex, and *a*mbiguous. This term was first used by the U.S. Army War College to describe the impact that the Cold War had on the world. In the past few years, this term has been used to frame the issues facing GCs: the increasingly global world we live in wherein regulations in places all over the world impact how corporations operate. VUCA issues are related to cross-border compliance, the vast reach of internal investigations, the threat of bribery and corruption, cybersecurity and data privacy, and catastrophic, systemic risk—all of which have been made more complex by boundary blurring.

> *"Can you imagine the pressure a general counsel is under? The complexity of the law combined with the lack of expertise in certain areas and the fear that they are being taken advantage of by their law firm lawyer. Take something like the brand new GDPR (General Data Protection Regulation). GCs are doing it for one company and for the first time. I am too but I am doing it for 35 companies. You have to trust me. I know a whole lot of a tiny area of law. But if you ask me a real estate or employment question or corporate question, I'm worse than a law student. If I was a GC and had to snap my fingers and know this stuff tomorrow? That would be terrifying."* —Partner, New York City–based law firm[56]

So how does a legal department keep up with that? In a word: innovation.

◖...Reflection Point Take a moment to jot down how you have changed, grown, or innovated on your own or due to pressures from clients, your organization, or the marketplace.

◖...Reflection Point Lead a discussion among your team to generate ideas of how clients might demand change and/or innovation in the future. Discuss why this frustrates or energizes the team.

CHAPTER 2

The Innovation Tournament in Law: Transforming the Way Law Is Delivered, Priced, Sourced, Packaged, and Defined

> *"Be not afraid of growing too slowly.*
> *Be afraid only of standing still."*
> —Benjamin Franklin

There exists today what I call an Innovation Tournament in Law (i.e., an explosion of innovation in legal services that has evolved to counter and/or leverage the three forces impacting the market today: technology, socioeconomic and demographic shifts, and globality). The type and level of this innovation is increasing across multiple dimensions: the way legal services are delivered, priced, sourced, packaged, and even defined. The entire landscape is already vastly different than it was 20 years ago.

"If I look at the firm now, 27 years later, there is not one thing in common aside from aspects of the culture. The premises are different. The work is different. The way we do the work is different. The way we interact with clients is different. The clients are different. Everything is different. And we can expect in the next 10 to 20 years that this will happen again and again. To stand still is to go backward and to go backward is to go out."—Managing Partner, midtier Australian law firm[1]

And the law market is not going backward. The Innovation Tournament exists and is not going away. That said, there does not appear to be a Spotify in the law marketplace that is akin to disruptive innovation. And there won't be if lawyers continue to embrace change and adopt new technologies along with new ways to deliver, price, source, package, and define legal services.

Delivery

The way legal services are purchased and delivered is different than it was before. Now the average consumer or mid- to large-size domestic company can purchase its legal services online from companies such as Legal Zoom, Rocket Lawyer, Novo Lawyer, and Avvo—many of whom make it more efficient to file for a trademark or patent protection then utilizing a firm's own in-house counsel.

Take it from me. When I sought the trademark for LawWithoutWalls, I did it on Legal Zoom for under $1,000 in 2010. I had sought the trademark because my experience in marketing and working as a Special Master on patent law cases after law school taught me the importance of owning your brand and protecting it. Later, after I transferred my ownership of the LawWithoutWalls trademark to the University of Miami, I created LWOW X, our all-virtual offering, and I knew it should be trademarked too. But because this wouldn't be in my name, I called our in-house legal department to set it up. Essentially, I was told it would cost a lot more for UM to seek the trademark for us and I should just do it via LegalZoom even if it meant doing it in my name and then seeking reimbursement and then transferring it again to UM's name.

The point is, there are some types of legal services today that just make more sense to be delivered online. A report by the Boston Consulting Group and Bucerius Law School (the first private law school in Germany and one of the schools participating in LawWithoutWalls) predicts that innovation is here to stay. Like Richard Susskind and Professor Dana Remus, it predicts that technology will continue to automate standard legal tasks—which is exactly what the alternative legal providers and LPOs (legal process outsourcers) are leveraging. These groups also predict that tech will slowly start to take over some of less "standard" legal tasks. That doesn't mean that there isn't room for people with a law degree to help create or utilize new tech-fueled products and services.

In the previous chapter, we discussed Dentons's business accelerator, NextLaw Labs, whose mission is to invest in the development and deployment of new technologies to transform how lawyers practice. One of its projects is with ROSS Intelligence to develop an IBM Watson–powered app that provides legal research answers when asked in natural language. The idea is that you could open the app and say into it "ROSS, I want to rent out my guest cottage. Can I do that? What does my lease need to include? And can I take first and last months' rent and a security deposit?" ROSS would read and examine the law and case law, make some inferences, generate hypotheses, evaluate strengths and weaknesses, and then return an evidence-based answer.

If this sounds unbelievable, it is not. Evidently, Watson can store more medical information than doctors and, importantly, provide evidenced-based answers that are free from cognitive biases, including those that come from overconfidence. So it has the potential to be the ultimate lawyer in one way, one that saves the client time and money. Even if real lawyers are never replaced, an ever-increasing amount of legal advice and services surely will be delivered online in the approaching future.

Price/Structure

The law market is seeing huge shifts in billing and pricing, as well as in the structure of law firms. Some changes we may never have imagined have already arrived, such as some clients (e.g., Deutsche Bank) that are refusing to pay for first-year associates,[2] and others (e.g., UK-based law firm Radiant Law), which are refusing to hire junior lawyers as part of a fixed-fee pricing strategy.[3] Not coincidentally, this has caused some law firms to structure themselves differently. AccuLaw trains juniors and lends them to firms as secondments. Axiom, arguably a "law firm light," is part law firm and part technology company. Its founder, Mark Harris, pivoted the original business model in 2011 to completely transform the way legal services are delivered to the large companies. Like Lawyers on Demand, Axiom lawyers can work from anywhere and are hired on a project basis—they are essentially contract attorneys for the companies that hire Axiom. Because their status is not officially as a law firm, this enables Axiom to sidestep rules preventing outside investment in law firms (a rule that exists in the United States but no longer in the United Kingdom or Australia). And indeed, Harris has successfully raised more than $65 million from investors. Axiom's original focus was on what might be called "bread-and-butter legal work" such as small mergers and acquisitions, technology licensing, investment advisory work, customer and supplier contracting, and hedge fund formation—services that free up company lawyers' time to focus on bigger picture matters. In addition, Axiom offers innovative technological software, providing clients with increased transparency on processes that are routine in order to enhance efficiency. Recently, the firm signed a $73 million multiyear contract with a big global bank to process the bank's standardized contracts. Axiom, profitable since 2003, appears to have met its mission as it now has more than 500 lawyers and revenue at more than $100 million from some fairly big companies, including Cisco Systems and Unilever. Further changing the structure and pricing landscape are the lawyers providing law-related and legal services within a Big 4 accounting firm such as Deloitte, EY, KPMG, or PwC. Calling these firms accounting firms is a misnomer. Deloitte Legal has more than 1,300 lawyers and practices law in 56 countries.[3] EY has more than 2,000 law professionals across 75 jurisdictions.[4] And PwC just announced it was opening a law firm in D.C. [5] Although it will not provide counsel on U.S. law, it will provide counsel on foreign law while present in the United States. In addition to legal services, PwC will provide integrated, multidisciplinary, and one-stop shop professional services related to business, tax, real estate, digital security, data protection, corporate restructuring, and mergers and acquisitions, to name a few.

Sourced

Recent developments have prompted a big change in how legal services and lawyers are found and hired. This means that how lawyers and law firms are sourced and source business has changed dramatically for both individuals and corporations. We can begin with what could be called law firms inside some of the big corporations. Some of the largest corporate legal departments would be larger than some of the largest firms if they were law firms. For example, GE and Microsoft each have more lawyers than some of the largest law firms.

For some law firms, their sourcing has changed—or perhaps I should say reverted—to a strategy that didn't work in the dot-com bubble era: swapping legal services for equity.[6] The way swapping works is that the law firm defers payment for its legal advice and services to the start-up in exchange for a percent stake of the start-up if the start-up goes public.

Wilson Sonsini LLP reports in the WSJ that it has utilized this strategy for ages and actually had major success in the 1990s dot-com bubble, investing in 35 companies that went through IPOs in 1999, three of which were valued together at more than $80 million at the close of the IPOs.

Dentons is banking on the same risk. It recently invested in WeWork, a shared office space concept designed for start-ups that leverages the start-ups' need and desire to collaborate with other start-ups. WeWork is touted for creating a culture of interaction and collaboration amongt those who pay the monthly memberships. According to Dentons, likely the largest law firm in the world with 6,600 lawyers, its Venture Technology group will hold office hours for WeWork members at five locations in New York City locations.[7] Evidently they will provide a suite of advice and services including legal as well as market insights, advice on how to raise funds, and general business consulting. They will also host events with investors and offer extra for-pay services, including start-up packages, IP assessment, and advice on positioning for IPO, exit, or sale.[8]

Such swaps come with some risk and caution for law firms. First, there are some risks around conflicts of interest, ensuring that the interest is not adverse to the client, and protecting the attorney-client privilege and confidentiality as it relates to the law firm playing the role of investor and lawyer. These risks have been compared to that with taking a percentage in a contingency fee, but they are surmountable. Second, unlike venture capitalists who invest (and swap money for equity) for a living, many lawyers lack the experience in evaluating start-ups, as this is not their main business.[9] Third, research indicates that generally about 20% of new businesses fail in the first year.[10] Obviously, Dentons thinks it is worth this risk. And they will be right if the next Fitbit or Ring rents space at WeWork.

As I have written about extensively in various law review articles,[11] litigation funding (also called alternative litigation financing and claim funding), is another "new" but old strategy that is changing how work is sourced in the law market. It is also another form of swapping. Essentially, in exchange for the funds, the funder is given the promise of recovery of the principal plus a percentage of the profit (often 30%–50% in commercial litigation funding)—if (and only if) the claimholder prevails. If the claimholder loses, the litigation financing company foots the bill, eating the entire loss. Similar to contingency fees, litigation funding is not considered a loan, although there has been debate about that.

Historically, there have been other types of litigation funding, such as non-recourse loans, insurer-insured agreements, transfer of claims in bankruptcy proceedings, transfers of patent law claims, commercial claim funding, and contingency fees. And hedge funds, commercial banks, and investment banks have been part of the litigation funding industry for ages. But litigation funding is *new* in three ways. First, more and more litigation funding companies are being started and run by lawyers. True, the client contracts directly with the funding entity and retains its current lawyer. Therefore, the funder is not being hired to provide "legal advice or services," which lowers the risk of infringing on the lawyer-client relationship, the lawyer's independent judgment, and U.S. rules about fee splitting. However, it is also true that these lawyers-turned-funders help not only with finding and vetting the claim but also managing it. Second, technology and data are helping to drive decision making, and more and more new start-ups are providing help to these litigation funders. For example, Legalist uses algorithms to analyze millions and millions of court cases to find and vet commercial litigation that is a good investment for commercial litigation funders. The company, Mighty, provides funders with cutting-edge technology and legal funding software to help assess funding opportunities, determine the right level of investment, and track the litigation and assessment through the litigation process.

Litigation funding companies are an innovation in law that taps into what is talked about in Part II, Chapter 8: Open Door—they tap into the beautiful migration that happens when people from different disciplines work together on a case. The client gets the benefit of not only its lawyer's legal advice and services but also an array of professionals with law and business degrees that are looking at the case from multiple perspectives and have a large financial stake in losing. In one of my articles on litigation funding, I argue that it is an example of the type of innovation we need in the marketplace because it enables what lawyers pejoratively call "non-lawyers" to influence lawyers. Instead of too many cooks in the kitchen, this combination results in the beauty of stone soup—discussed further in the Open Door chapter.[12]

Packaged

We are also seeing a big change in how law is being packaged and sold to clients. We are seeing unbundled legal service providers packaged together as "one" (e.g., HiveLegal, founded by a group of law firm partners from large law firms in Australia).[13] And we are seeing law firms packaging together legal, law-related, project management, and tech services akin to how other professional service firms, such as advertising agencies, have historically done. In advertising—at least when I was in advertising in the 90s—a big account (with advertising budgets of $50 million or more) would have multiple people at multiple levels with various backgrounds servicing the account: an account director, an assistant supervisor, a senior account executive, an account executive, an associate account executive, a media director, a media supervisor, a media buyer, a media planner, a creative director, an art director and copywriter, and an event planner. Crazy to say, but this team grew even bigger when we were actually in production mode for a commercial or new packaging development. To save money and to provide better service, the client's main contact was the account executive—not the more senior execs or the creatives. The account executive's job was to manage the entire project—to pull together all of the various people/roles to make sure we were on strategy and on time. Moreover, the account executive made sure that we aligned the team with the client's needs and operation style. Only during the final strategy pitch or commercial storyboard did the client meet with the senior account director or the lead creative director. We also charged a flat rate back then. We charged a percentage (around 15%) of the total costs to produce the advertising and place it. So if the budget for the year was $30 million, we would get a percentage of that total as our fee. It was transparent and certain. That doesn't sound like a traditional law firm, but it does sound somewhat like a few new legal service providers today (e.g., Riverview Law or Carbon Law Partners).

To that end, the way I have heard both Karl Chapman and Andy Daws describe Riverview Law reminds me of how Leo Burnett structured its professional services teams. In the spring of 2015, I had the pleasure of being the keynote speaker at Richard Susskind's 23rd Annual Ross Priory Conference on the Future of Legal Services at the University of Strathclyde in Loch Lomond, Scotland. During the retreat, I heard Karl Chapman speak about his vision for Riverview Law. And although his vision is not an exact replica of the old advertising client service platform, it is similar in a few ways. First, Riverview Law appears to have a similar circular layered group of professionals servicing the client, and the main client contacts are not the most senior (and most expensive) professionals on the team. Second, Riverview Law offers the provision of additional services and tools (like the research and presentation decks offered by

Leo Burnett). Riverview Law offers technology and software and project management services. Third, there is transparency. In a future article, I will write more about how advertising and law are similar and different (if you look at what has happened to the margins in the advertising world, we should hope for the latter, that is, different). In advertising back in the 90s, billing was transparent—a flat percentage of the total bill. Riverview Law is all about transparency (as are many of the alt law providers such as Axiom and Elevate Services). Riverview Law is not the only firm to attempt tactics such as these. Traditional law firms are also trying to find new ways to provide a complete layered suite of services to clients by adding new roles (like the chief innovation officer role at many of the major Australian firms, or the role of strategic transformationalists in the U.K. Magic Circle firms) along with additional transparency and cost certainty.

Essentially, new law companies are redefining "legal" services and products, which is what the next section addresses.

Defined

The definition of a legal service or product continues to expand. Consider the following three facts.

1. There Is a Major Increase in the Number of Legal Start-Ups Around the Globe

Since the economic crisis in 2009, there has been a huge increase in legal start-ups around the world. The United States has witnessed fast growth in legal entrepreneurism. In 2009, only 15 companies were listed as legal start-ups on AngelList (a U.S. website for start-ups to raise money from angel funders), yet just four years later, in 2013, that number had risen to 305. By 2016, the number of legal start-ups in the law and tech arena more than tripled to 1,500. Companies such as Crowd & Co, Lawyers on Demand, Lexvoco, Law Choice Australia, LegalVision, and Unison suggest a similar trajectory in Australia. For example, Lawyers on Demand has grown more than 700% in Australia over the past five years.[14] Innovation in legal services in the United Kingdom is also on the rise, and consumers are taking advantage of it.[15] Globally, there are at least 650 registered legal-tech start-ups—although it is not clear why we call some start-ups legal-tech start-ups as all law-related start-ups today utilize tech in some way to enhance delivery and services. Legal-tech, as Dirk Naumann, deputy general counsel, Orange

Business Services, defines it, is "technology-based cost and efficiency opti-misation of legal processes and legal knowledge."[16] And investment in these legal start-ups is not minimal. In 2016, more than $155 million was invested across 67 deals with legal-tech start-ups.[17] Indeed, Avvo itself has received more than $70 million in outside funding.

2. There Is an Entirely New Sector of Legal Service Providers

There is an entirely new segment of legal service providers today that likely didn't even have a name 15 years ago: what was formerly called legal process outsourcing has now been coined alt legal, which is made up of alternative legal service providers (ALSPs).[18] Joe Borstein, global director, Thomson Reuters LMS (formerly Pangea3), and innovation columnist for Above the Law defines an alternative legal service provider as "a company (not a law firm) working to solve legal or quasi-legal problems by leveraging technology, a globalized workforce and business processes (although some law firms have worked to build their own, with mixed success)."[19] Included in this segment are companies such as Avvo (mentioned above), Neota Logic, Elevate Services, UnitedLex, and other law companies providing e-discovery and document review, M&A diligence, contracts automation, and regulatory compliance services. The important thing about the name and the sector is that it is called "alternative" not just additional—meaning that these firms are not just providing additional services like the traditional LPOs did. Instead, they are offering alternative legal services and hoping to do LPO work as well as what might be considered traditional legal work. A recent study by Thomson Reuters in collaboration with Georgetown and the University of Oxford Saïd Business School demonstrated that this is the reason clients are hiring them—because they provide specialized expertise not available in-house in addition to providing efficiency and transparency.[20] According to the report, the ALSP market is "not unsubstantial" and is con-tinuing to grow. Furthermore, the report finds that, approximately 60% of corporate legal departments use ALSPs, and it predicts a 14% increase in the next year.

3. There Is an Entirely New Sector of "Legal" Products

In addition to a whole new sector of service providers, we have a whole new sector of legal products. As Naumann explains in his article

"The Legal Tech-Train Is Rolling—Better Get on Board!" this legal-tech sector is increasing efficiency and changing culture in departments and firms that are using and/or creating products such as regulatory self-service portals, digital procurement contract management systems, automated template creation, semi-automated contracting, and tools for collaboration, matter management, and knowledge management.[21] Consider, for example, a seed-funded tech company such as Bodhala, which describes itself as "a data and analytics platform that uses machine learning algorithms and human intelligence to empower companies to source and manage their legal counsel in a sophisticated, data-driven way."[22] As mentioned above, Dentons' NextLaw Labs is working on the capability to extract insights on judges' and lawyers' specific performances on, for example, cross examination or ruling on motions so that in-house counsel can evaluate the legal strategy options that outside counsel provides and decide a course of action. Another output of Dentons' NextLaw Labs is Qualmet. Like its sister OCI, Qualmet uses data to track lawyers, but not related to hard factors such as hours and costs. Instead, it is a platform for clients to use in providing ratings and qualitative, subjective assessments of their outside lawyers that includes costs but tries to get at "value." Interestingly, outside lawyers and law firms can subscribe to receive the info and customized reports from their clients and of their rivals. So far, only clients have signed on.[23]

The Innovation Tournament Is Not a Black Swan

The Innovation Tournament exists. It is not a black swan—that is, it is not an unpredictable, unforeseen event with extreme consequences. It is predictable and foreseen and not yet extreme. It is producing new competitors, like LegalZoom for individuals to ALSPs and multidisciplinary PSFs offering integrated services at the intersection of law, finance, strategy, and project management for corporate clients. And many different players are playing different roles in the innovation tournament, including big law.[24] There is evidence of three types of innovation: First, intrapreneurship—the creation of innovation internally within a law firm or legal department. For example, in a 2016–2017 study of innovation by the legal profession in Australia by Vicky Waye et al., more than 75% of respondents reported that innovation was developed by

innovating internally and that the law firm was the most important facil-
itator of innovation activity.[25] Many of the projects recognized by Reena
Sungupta's Legal *Financial Times* Awards represent intrapreneurship.
For example, Clifford Chance won an innovation award for using Six
Sigma and Lean. Pinsent Masons was recognized for developing an AI
tool to help corporate clients identify Brexit risks in current and future
contracts. Even the development of new roles such as the chief innovation officer or pricing directors within a law firm could be considered
a type of intrapreneurial innovation. Second, entrepreneurship in law is
driving innovation. The legal start-ups discussed above (e.g., Agreement
24 and Neota Logic) and new law firm models (e.g., Riverview Law,
Elevate Services, and Fondia) are great examples. Third, we are witnessing extrapreneurship in the tournament for innovation. An extrapreneur
is the intrapreneur who not only chooses to apply those talents and that
energy to his/her organization to affect change but also to apply those
talents externally to other organizations to affect change and to bring
those experiences back to attempt to change from the inside out—and the
outside in—in a continuous loop.[26] LawWithoutWallls, BLP's Lawyers
on Demand, and Allen & Overy's incubator Fuse are great examples of
extrapreneurship.

The question everyone is wondering is whether there is a Spotify in
the legal market. Is there disruptive innovation in the law market in the
Clayton Christensen sense? In other words, are there new products and
services in the law market that can bring down big law such as U.S. Steel,
Xerox, and Digital Equipment were brought down?[27]

Everyone is asking whether the sky is falling, but no one is quite sure
whether we are in the story of Chicken Little (who, of course, is wrong
and overreacts) or the story of the Boy Who Cried Wolf (who thought
it was fun to see everyone rush to save him when there wasn't a wolf in
sight. Then later when there is a wolf, no one believes him when he calls
for help, and he gets eaten.). Many lawyers reading this book will have
heard my all-time mentor David B. Wilkins, Lester Kissel professor of
law, and faculty director of the Center on the Legal Profession, Harvard
Law School, discuss whether the legal profession is witnessing a "paradigm shift" or a "temporary correction."[28] And what he always says is that
neither is likely true. The global financial crisis simply accelerated the
fundamental changes that were already happening before 2008.

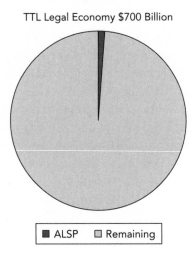

TTL Legal Economy $700 Billion

■ ALSP   □ Remaining

FIG. 2.1. Chart depicting alternative legal service providers' percentage of the total legal economy.

Many books and articles have been written about disruptive innovation and recently a slew of law review articles as well.[29] A quick sketch of Clayton Christensen's four-stage theory of disruptive innovation follows. First, new competitors enter the marketplace. Second, in response, the current market share holders (the incumbents) ignore the new competitors and/or flee to higher-margin work. Third, the new competitors slowly become entrenched in the middle of the market. Fourth, the market is turned on its head. Then the established players must compete with the new entrants because if they don't, they risk losing profits and even viability. Arguing that there is an Innovation Tournament in law is not the same as crying disruption or that the sky is falling—it is not. The sky is not falling—yet. Consider this: Out of the total global legal economy (approximately $700 billion), alternative legal service providers make up only $8.4 billion.[30]

Furthermore, much of the legal market innovators have gone after what could be termed low-hanging fruit: price-sensitive, less important work. Technology is automating standard legal tasks, which is what most of the alternative providers and LPOs and legal start-ups are leveraging. Essentially, what we are witnessing today is what I call the rise of the legal freegan. A freegan is someone who finds things that are valuable in other people's garbage. Many of these legal start-ups are eating many lawyers' (especially big law's) leftovers—parts of service that law firms didn't want to do because the margins were low. Legal freegans are offering new legal tech products or cheaper, faster service that is good enough.

However, I am not crying that the sky is falling because right now in 2018, that would be like crying wolf when the wolf is not there. I say this for four reasons:

1. The hype about AI is still a great deal of hype. Will it reach its potential? Let's hope. But it hasn't lived up to its expectations yet. This is even true outside the law market. For example, Watson isn't yet living up to its expectations outside (let alone inside) the law market. It is still learning how to decipher the different forms of cancer; only a few dozen hospitals have adopted Watson, and there have been complaints that Watson is actually biased toward Americans and the American patient care methods.[31]

2. When AI reaches its potential, I predict that it is going to make us better at our jobs, not take over all of them. And no matter how cute robots look, we are not going to trust them in the same way we trust people. We will likely trust them more in some situations and less in others. Kurt Gray makes a compelling argument in a *Harvard Business Review* article aptly entitled "AI Can Be a Troublesome Teammate."[32] Gray points out that trusting relationships are built on knowing that people care about you and about whether you live or die. Gray gives the following example: "When a platoon leader risks being shot by going behind enemy lines to rescue one of his soldiers, he is not making the optimal decision from a functional perspective. However, the very fact that—unlike an AI system—he will choose this 'irrational' course of action makes everyone in the platoon trust him more, which leads to better overall team performance." Furthermore, relationships are a two-way street with mutual consequences and vulnerabilities. Gray explains, "If humans mess up in a job, they can be fired . . . AI systems are gambling only with the fates of others, never with their own."

3. If we think of the law marketplace (all law and law-related work) as a pie, odds are it is going to continue to grow. True, some lawyers' piece of the pie might not grow at all or might not grow at the same pace, but overall, a bigger pie means opportunities for people with law degrees. It is not clear what is going to happen, and people have varying views:

"If the law firms don't do it, then these new entrants will. And then the law firms will become less significant and less relevant. So it is less about a conversation demanding that law firms innovate. Instead it is about the opportunity that law firms continue to miss out on because they are not being proactive in helping us in areas that they have not traditionally helped us in past." —GC, large media and telecommunications company in Australia[33]

"The handful of truly global players will pull away because they will continue to be able to differentiate, but the firms a tier down from that will be significantly impacted because there will be ongoing erosion and profitability challenges in some of their key addressable markets and then perhaps at the smaller end—boutiques and specialist, there is an opportunity to thrive . . . If we are talking the big law firm model using time based billing in practice in very large partnerships, I think it will become undone with enormous pressure and I think the next 10 years will look very different." —VP and associate GC, American multinational enterprise information technology company[34]

"At the top of my pyramid, there will always be a place for the traditional way that in-house and legal work . . . in the big ticket M&A transactions and the bet the company advice where you want the letterhead and and the judgement calls essentially. I think there will always be a spot here. Again, going back to the bottom, the big trends are digitizing this kind of work, having tools to augment the provision of legal services . . . to operationalize your know-how." —Head of Legal, large international airline[35]

More likely, the reality is an oxymoron, like Daniel Kahneman's "Thinking Fast and Slow."[36] The innovation tournament is not a black swan, and the sky is not falling—not yet.

4. We can prevent the sky from falling. And part of the purpose of this book is to be a part of that prevention movement—to convince lawyers and law firms not only that there is an Innovation Tournament but also that they should embrace it, enter the tournament, and *not* make the mistake inherent in Christensen's model of disruption, which is to ignore or flee. Some law firms are setting great examples and entering the Innovation Tournament.

Yet the only way to make sure that we are not the chicken or the little boy eaten by the wolf is to enter the tournament ourselves. This is the only way to make sure that Professor Wilkins's prediction is accurate (i.e., that we are witnessing neither a seismic change nor a temporary shift). In his book *Women in Love*, D. H. Lawrence wrote the following: "You can't stand holding the roof up with your hands, for ever. You know that sooner or later you'll *have* to let it go . . . And so something's got to be done, or there's a universal collapse—as far as you yourself are concerned."[37] And that is the message here. We "can't stand holding the roof up with our hands, for ever." And entering the Innovation Tournament is one of those "something[s] [that's] got to be done."

As will be discussed in depth in Chapter 5 of Part I, if you enter the Innovation Tournament and follow the Three Rules of Engagement, you will gain invaluable benefits. This isn't just about determining your competitive response; it is also about understanding the user of legal services.[38] This is about knowing what the competition knows and having the mindset, skill set, and behaviors of innovators so that you can be a leader in this marketplace and create a winning strategy to compete and maintain a leadership edge.[39]

The point is: Don't be a chicken. Don't ignore, flee, or chicken out. As Lee McIntyre, a research fellow at the Center for Philosophy and History of Science at Boston University explains, "You don't want to be a denialist and say, 'Oh, that's not a tiger, why should I believe that's a tiger?' Because you could get eaten."[40] In other words, enter the Innovation Tournament, and you will never be in the position of Chicken Little or the Little Boy Who Cried Wolf.

●...Reflection Point From where do you think innovation is going to come in the law marketplace? Consider the following three types of innovators:

1. An intrapreneur: someone who has the qualities and skills of an entrepreneur but seeks to create innovation internally—within the organization or company or firm in which she/he works;

2. An entrepreneur: someone who forges a solo path to build something new (e.g., a new legal start-up that is external to the organization in which she/he currently works);

3. An extrapreneur: an intrapreneur who not only chooses to apply those talents and energy to his/her own organization but also seeks to apply those talents externally to affect change and to bring the fruits of the external innovation back internally.

- Do you know lawyers in each of the three categories?
- With which of the three types of innovation (intrapreneurship, entrepreneurship, extrapreneurship) is your firm or department experimenting and why?
- What businesses in (or impacting) the law marketplace fall in each category?

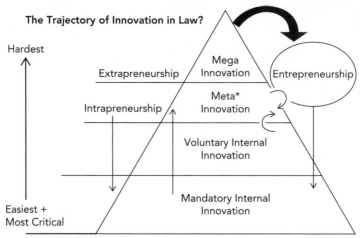

*Meta innovation impacts the legal profession; mega innovation impacts industries within and outside the legal profession.

FIG. 2.2. A chart proposing one potential prediction for the trajectory of innovation in law.

...Reflection Point How would you develop a graph to depict the trajectory of innovation? The chart above is a rough attempt to map out the potential trajectory of innovation in the legal marketplace. It rests on the hypothesis that most of the changes we will see in the short term in the legal marketplace will come from what could be called mandatory internal innovation wherein lawyers and/or law firms and legal departments innovate because they "have" to. An example of this type of mandatory innovation is when a client (internal or external) mandates a budget cut or flat fee or a new knowledge management system. This innovation is internal and is at the bottom of the pyramid depicted above.

The next step up is voluntary internal innovation—the types of innovations your firm or department might be seeking that are not mandatory but are designed to give a competitive edge. It could be something as small as taking one of Harvard Law School's Executive Education courses or participating as a mentor in a LawWithoutWalls innovation cycle. Or it could be creating a new role such as the chief innovation officer of the firm or a strategic transformationalist role. Or it could be developing new initiatives on multiple dimensions including data capability, knowledge management, client development, and project management.

Towards the top of the pyramid is meta innovation. This type of innovation impacts not only your firm or department but also the legal profession at large. Finally, there might be what we call mega innovation, which is innovation that is not limited to the legal profession alone. PwC's latest moves to broaden its legal practice(s) into the United States could be considered an example of mega innovation, impacting the legal profession and other professions. The Florida legal services start-up TIKD, which helps consumers contest routine traffic tickets online, could also be considered in this category. Mega innovation often happens externally (outside the pyramid) by extrapreneurs who might not even be lawyers. The founder of TIKD, Chris Riley, has an MBA, not a JD, from Harvard. For the legal innovator, the top levels of the pyramid are the ultimate goals—that is, finding an innovative approach that bridges the professional gap and provides innovative solutions that reach beyond the limited legal services market horizon. But for the average lawyer or law firm, intrapreneurship might fill the sails.

- Try to think of examples for each level of the pyramid and make a list.
- How would you revise this chart based on your own predictions of the trajectory of innovation in the legal profession?

●...Reflection Point List the reasons that most resonate with you as to why law might be ripe for disruption and why it might not be ripe at all.

CHAPTER 3

The Lawyer Skills Delta

"Law firms are not wanting to cooperate and help. We spent lots of money and time teaching our law firm lawyers how the business is done. But now, GCs need law firms to reach out to them and ask how can we help you. We need more space to talk between us, where we can connect and together figure out the best way to deliver legal services. We want something new. The law firms are willing to create something, to learn from us, but they are still doing the tasks the same way. They know they have to do something and they haven't figured out what it is yet. I want collaborative help from our firms but if it has to be a billed by the hour to have that conversation, then it probably won't happen."

—GC, the Chilean division of a French cosmetics company

The world is changing, and clients are asking their lawyers for help. Clients are asking their lawyers to utilize tech, to be more efficient, and to add value at every step, to cross-collaborate and partner with them and other legal service providers to solve problems, and to innovate with them. In other words, clients need lawyers with new and different skills. The goal of this chapter is to bring these needs and desires to life through the voices of the clients I have interviewed and by introducing a skills rubric for the 21st-century lawyer. The Lawyer Skills Delta depicts the skills that clients desire now and predicts those skills they will require over the next 10 years. However, gaps exist between today's present approaches to lawyering and the approaches that will help individuals and firms scale to the top of the Lawyer Skills Delta so that they help their clients the way they are being asked to help. This chapter starts by explaining the changing needs of clients. It then turns to the skills for future lawyering. It concludes by identifying three gaps that exist between the current state of legal services and that which is desired.

Cheaper, Better, Faster

I don't know a lawyer who isn't sick of hearing those three words. And the reality is that they aren't going away. Clients within corporations are increasingly sophisticated with more access to information. As a result, they are demanding more transparency from their legal departments on budgeting, outside spending, and prioritization. Clients of law firm lawyers are demanding the same—more transparency and certainty on project staffing, management, and billing. Clients are demanding that their law firms utilize tech to maximize efficiency. More than that, clients are forcing a more efficient unbundling and repackaging of services in an effort to move toward not only value billing but also value production. Clients want value produced every step of the way as the law firm journeys toward project completion—not just at the end.

Henrik Kniberg, a coach and consultant at Crisp, a consulting firm, developed the following chart about how to build a minimal viable product that illustrates the point.[2]

After they are briefed, law firm lawyers often see their job as solving the problem as depicted in the top example. The problem the client needs solving is transportation from A to Z. So the lawyer goes off and comes back to the client having developed the "car" and in the worst-case

Not Like this...

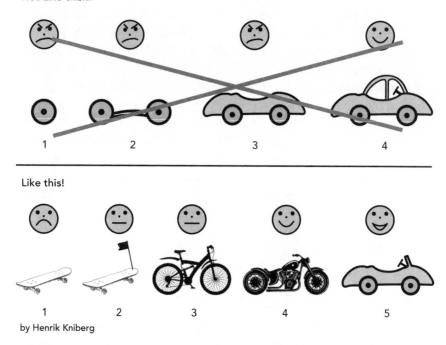

Like this!

by Henrik Kniberg

FIG. 3.1. Henrik Kniberg's Chart depicting a Minimal Viable Product.

scenario, not just any old car but a Maserati. It is not that the clients do not find the car useful. The problem is that no value is created along the way. Instead of providing value with, for example, a skateboard, then a scooter, then a bike, then a motorcycle, etc., the lawyer provides only the car. This often makes the end product not worth the costs because it either overreaches the goal (maybe the client only needs to go a few blocks, making a car superfluous) or underreaches its value-add potential—in the top picture, the client only gets the car, whereas in the bottom picture, the client gets the car in addition to the motorcycle, bicycle, scooter, and skateboard.

Clients are frustrated with their lawyers for not providing value along the way and for giving them the Maserati or the Rolls Royce job when all they needed was the scooter, the quick and dirty view.[3] Moreover, clients want lawyers to give executable advice; clients want to know how to ride the scooter or drive the car.

"A firm will send seven pages of advice but is it something I can act on and do something with? Because I can read the law as well. I want an executive summary and a recommendation—so my business clients only have to read the first paragraph. The issues are attached on the back. Presenting legal advice in a way that helps me and the business make a decision rather than legal advice I have to decipher and figure out what to do." —Senior corporate counsel, multinational insurance company headquartered in Australia[4]

"They need to think like legal counsel—dealing directly with the business unit. Think about how I'm providing the service and do what an in-house might normally do. If we ask you one question, we don't need seven answers for five times the price. And we need it packaged up and in a language so the business unit person can understand the advice and put it in practice vs. needing an intermediary to translate." —CEO, a specialist real estate investment management company in Australia[5]

In other words, clients want their lawyers to help, but to help differently. Learning how to provide the scooter and the bike (and directions on how to drive them) is a skill that lawyers need to learn.

From Attorney-at-Law to Law Counselor: The Return of the Consigliere

In-house business clients are asking their in-house lawyers to help manage change, learn new skills, and partner to solve problems. In turn, in-house counsel are asking their law firm lawyers the same thing. They need lawyers that are experts not only in their practice but also in their industry and specific business. They need lawyers that approach their problems from an industry and business focal point.

"Strategic (not just legal) advice is considered the highest value output of the legal department . . . It is this kind of advice that directly adds value to the company's projects and overall strategic goals. For this kind of highly valued work, understanding the business is a critical success factor." —Max Hübner, Executive Director Legal Management & Operations (formerly Director Corporate Legal and Tax, PGGM N.V.)[6]

Some lawyers and law firms are making real efforts to meet this need. For example, Holland & Knight has reorganized by industry sector to establish cross-sectional client teams where partners open up their client relationships to a real collaborative endeavor. But most of the lawyers I have come across believe they are meeting this need already—when they are not—at least not according to the clients with whom I have spoken. When I interview clients, I hear the same complaints about law firm lawyers from all over the world—from those at the big, elite firms to those at the midtier and midsize firms. Client are sick and tired of advice that does not take into account their industry and their particular business, brand, and culture. Clients are tired of advice that has no *there* there. They want advice that is executable and that provides options (in layman's language) and then a point of view on those options. Instead, it seems as though law firm lawyers continue to provide answers like the scarecrow in the Wizard of Oz. When Dorothy asks him which way to go, all the scarecrow can do is criss-cross his arms and point in opposite directions, without providing any answer or direction at all.

> *"It's all about preventative lawyering. Reconceptualize your knowledge so that you can apply it in a way that is preventative rather than traditional (where you) wait for the problem to arise and then advise—often that advice is not executable."* —Head of legal, large international airline[7]

And it's not just help with their "legal" problems that clients are looking for. In-house clients also want help in managing their department better. They want their law firm lawyers to figure out a way to utilize technology to provide solutions for their business (not just legal) problems to help manage the inefficiencies and bureaucracies that in-house counsel are experiencing. They want their lawyers to help them deal with the needs and demands of their internal business clients.[8]

In-house counsels are facing immense demands from business clients who prioritize everything as a high and want everything right away—not to mention the endless repetitive requests and questions by the business about contracts and marketing language and NDAs, for example. They need help suppressing demands from their business clients.

> *"We need more self-service for non-legal users . . . The time saved can be used to deliver more value-added services in the field of ever-increasing regulatory matters."* —Max Hübner, Executive Director Legal Management & Operations (formerly Director Corporate Legal and Tax, PGGM N.V.)[9]

Indeed, law firms are winning awards for doing just that type of work: for providing neither *legal* advice nor *legal* services in the traditional sense, but instead law-related services to help legal departments suppress demand from their business clients and manage their departments as a business. For example, HSF won a *Financial Times* award in 2017 for helping Telstra lower internal legal department costs associated with meetings, overhead, and inefficient processes.[10] Gilbert and Tobin won a *Financial Times* award in 2017 for hosting a hackathon in conjunction with its client Westpac Banking Corporation and LegalVision in which teams hacked on challenges to help free up lawyers from time-consuming, inefficient tasks. One such example is an app created by Gilbert & Tobin that provides corporate legal teams with tips and draft clauses so that they can service their business clients' contracting needs faster.[11]

Clients want you to get to know them and their department and to help them run their business or their department.[12] And you know what else? They want open-ended problem solving. They would love it if their lawyers had conversations just to explore what is not working and then come to them with a point of view of what might help them.

> *"I think what works really well is when the firm takes a lot of opportunity not just to get to know maybe the GC but to get to know multiple levels throughout the organization because that really pays dividends . . . I would love to hear from law firms and I would love for someone from a law firm to come to me and say 'We have a point of view on the kinds of technologies that are gonna make your legal services better in the next five years. Would you like to talk to us about them? Would you like for us to present to you on them and take a look at some of your internal processes and look out how you could maybe tweak those to deliver better services for your clients and help your business?' I would love to have those conversations—and I'm rarely asked that. In fact, I'm never asked that."*—VP and associate GC, American multinational enterprise information technology company[13]

And they want all of this now—all of the time. They want their attorneys to be their eyes and ears looking out for them in the back alleys and into the future. They want them to provide law consulting services like the Big 4 will (and does) as part and parcel of legal advice or other professional services they provide. And they want law firms to, if not deliver, at least quarterback what Steven Walker, former vice president and associate general counsel of Hewlett-Packard Enterprises, calls "end-to-end solutions," which are solutions that provide "the optimal combinations of people, process, tools and technology, and hybrid inside/outside sourcing models, to meet their client's business and legal challenges."[14] This is the future for legal services for legal departments. Although it is unclear whether the law firms will be the ones to play the role of quarterback to create the new in-house legal departments of the future, it is clear that GCs today are asking for help in envisioning and shaping it.

> *"The question is: if I am going to invest in you for the next two to three years' worth of fees, how can you invest back in me? What is your tech strategy? How can you help me unbundle? What are doing in the legal management space? . . . How can law firms help GCs manage the consumption of legal services? Firms can come with a POV for GCs and say look, we are here to look around the corner for you. We know you can't always look around the corner for yourselves, but we can help you on that journey. Here is our POV on the technology you need and the type of investments you might like to consider making and here are the independent experts we can bring to you . . . To me, that is the opportunity for law firms. To come with that point of view and that expertise makes them stickier, stickier, and stickier rather than less relevant."*
> —VP and associate GC, American multinational enterprise information technology company[15]

And this requires a more consistent and intense relationship as opposed to the sporadic relationship that often occurs between lawyers and clients (i.e., client and lawyer interact when client needs legal advice, and then when that is over, the interaction lulls).[16] This requires the attorneys-at-law to serve as counselors-at-law, like consiglieres (ethical ones of course).

Overview of the Lawyer Skills Delta

So what is today's lawyer—and more importantly, tomorrow's lawyer—to do? What does helping together and differently mean in terms of skills? What skills do lawyers need to transform the way they work with clients to solve problems and meet their new needs and desires?

Based on my research and work in LawWithoutWalls over the past eight years, I believe there are three levels of skills that are needed

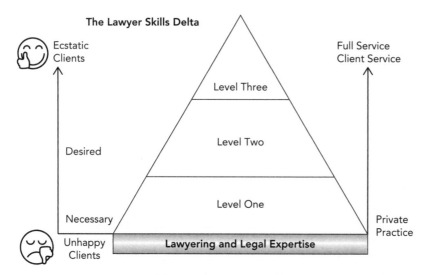

FIG. 3.2. The Lawyer Skills Delta outlining the three new levels of skills needed for lawyers to provide full-service client service.

or desired of lawyers today that go above and beyond the base skills required of all lawyers (i.e., legal expertise and lawyering skills). Think of these three new areas of skills as the building blocks that can bridge the gap between private practice and full-service client service. These three areas can be mapped onto a pyramid shape that ascends vertically from required skills, which are relatively easy to procure, to desired skills—those skills that may be more difficult to procure but have the potential to add real value and differentiate lawyers. This pyramid, not coincidentally, also ranges from dissatisfied to satisfied clients along the same vertical axis.

At the base of the pyramid is lawyering and legal expertise—the base is not even part of the three levels. As these are the basic fodder of law schools and junior associate training programs, I won't spend much time on them here except to point out that you would be surprised how many lawyers master the base and consider themselves equipped for the job into the next several decades. The base of the Lawyer Skills Delta, however, is not even the real beginning of what will be required in years to come.[17]

Level 1: The C.O.S.T Skills (Sunk Costs)

The first level of the Lawyer Skills Delta (beyond the most basic abilities in the base) are what I call C.O.S.T skills, an acronym for *c*oncrete, *o*rganizational, *s*ervice-oriented, *t*echnology-related skills. These skills are concrete in that they can be taught and then honed with practice. They are related to the organization in which the lawyer works (the law firm or legal department) and for which the lawyer works (the client's company). They are service-oriented, meaning that they also involve the use of project management and other skills that provide professional services (not just legal services). And in today's workforce, they necessarily involve the use of some technology.

I also call them C.O.S.T skills because they are sunk cost skills. Honing these skills is the cost of doing business as a lawyer or, better put, the cost of providing legal services as a business professional. And for the most part, the value these skills deliver for clients (and the revenue they return for lawyers) isn't measureable. These skills are at the bottom third of the pyramid because they are less than what is desired. They are considered necessary in today's legal marketplace. Without them, clients will not be satisfied and lawyers will not be able to compete.

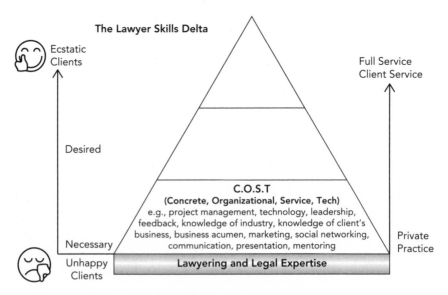

FIG. 3.3. The Lawyer Skills Delta detailing Level 1 of the new skills needed for lawyers to provide full-service client service.

To be adept at lawyering today, at a minimum, lawyers must excel at skills such as managing projects, communicating, making presentations, mentoring, and giving feedback. Many of these skills have not been emphasized as important to lawyering—indeed, the opposite has often been true. But as my client and GC interviews make clear, lawyers today must be business-focused and business-minded, readily able to harness technology and social media to their and their clients' advantage. They must be leaders that are experts in their industry (not just specialized area of practice) and in their clients' organization.

And they must be service-oriented. Clients want lawyers to approach legal services like business services. They want lawyers who communicate the way a businessperson communicates—with positioning and branding and target audience in mind.

> *"So, what we need to do is make sure that the lawyers are participating fully as leaders . . . getting to the space where they are business leaders who happen to be lawyers, can bring that experience and expertise, and are also participating in the business calls being made."* —Siobhán Moriarty, GC of Diageo[18]

Clients want lawyers to deliver advice in the right tone and at the right length. They want the whole package—in other words, they need information much more succinctly than in the past. They want lawyers to at least know the concept and intention behind the acronym TL;DR (*too long; didn't read*). They want answers despite the fact that they transgress into the business domain and potentially create risk.

> *"External lawyers differentiate themselves when willing to go the extra step in terms of decision-support, industry-vertical knowledge and helping the GC understand how to balance the risks of options against the benefits. Typically, a suitably-considered, good response with a fast turnaround is more valuable than a detailed analysis requiring a longer lead time . . . [and that] avoids transgression into the business domain and is consistent with the firm's risk posture and insurance arrangements."* —Steven Walker, former VP and regional GC, Hewlett-Packard Enterprise[19]

And finally, clients want lawyers who know how to give feedback and advice—and not just about the legal issues.

"What we have seen is more and more a need for lawyers to migrate from the classic role of just giving legal advice and yes-no answers and more and more becoming project managers. Our demands have changed for lawyers. We need them to be a part of the team . . . the world is more complex with more areas overlapping and lawyers can see these overlaps that most people in business units can't. So the lawyer's role has naturally grown into the project management role. And we ask them to change to assume the role of speaking their mind and assuming the project management role versus only providing narrow legal advice. It's about transitioning people from legal experts to being project managers and business partners. This is the main change (beyond tech) that we are asking of lawyers." —GC, large media and telecommunications company in Australia[20]

These are the skills that every lawyer can and must master no matter what future job we envision (whether it is one of the eight new jobs predicted by Richard Susskind[21] or something not yet even imagined). Yet this is just the beginning of what is needed. This is only the first level of skills needed now and in the future.[22]

Level 2: Collaboration and Creative Problem-Solving Skills (the "Soft Skills" That Are So Hard)

What clients desire next is lawyers who can collaborate, who are creative problem solvers and problem finders, and who can identify opportunities. Let me unpack that.

As demonstrated by researchers such as Heidi Gardner and law firm executives such as Henry N. Nassau, the #1 call to lawyers is for collaboration.[23] Nassau calls it the "superpower" to "optimizing value to lead in the future."[24] Gardner agrees but points out that what is meant by this call to collaborate is not cross-selling. If you are working on an M&A deal, cross-selling is saying to your client, 'Hey I have a partner who does great litigation work. I can do an e-intro for you, and maybe you can think about using him for your next bit of litigation.' Collaboration is 'Hey my partner is an expert in deal making—he works in our real estate area and might be able to help us think through this problem from a slightly different angle. Want me to set up lunch for us so that we can brainstorm together?'

Clients are asking for collaboration not only between partners at the same firm but also with other professionals at the law firm—as well as professionals outside the firm and maybe even outside the legal field altogether. Today clients expect their outside law firms to be a source of knowledge benchmarking and insights so that they can look smart with their business clients and prevent risks.

"We are considering what additional skill sets and competencies are needed to operate in a VUCA world, some of which may well come internally, but if not, how do we partner with externals like our panel law firms who can bring that insight—not just from the oil and gas industry, but also in terms of trends happening in other industries that could eventually find their way to the oil and gas industry." —Donny Ching, legal director, Royal Dutch Shell.[25]

Lawyers can only deliver these insights if they collaborate not only with other partners but also with the marketing and business development professionals at the law firm whose job is to have their fingers on the pulse of the sector and who can help "market" or position the information to in-house clients.

Clients are also asking their firms to collaborate with lawyers from other law firms and with legal start-ups and other types of service providers because they want help in identifying not only risks but also opportunities; their business clients want them to "horizon scan." What is coming down the pike in terms of regulatory change? What can we do now to prevent future risk of transgressions?

"We have an obsession with horizon scanning, meaning figuring out what is riding toward you over the horizon like a regulatory change or a new case. Can we plan and not be caught? And can we do so in a way that we are not getting 11 PDFs in our inbox each month from each of our panel firms. We are drowning under the volume of email." —Lead counsel, large global bank headquartered in the United Kingdom[26]

Research has shown that the best problem solvers are the best problem finders.[27] The best problem finders are collaborative, inquisitive, open to failure, and inclusive. Clients need their lawyers to be problem finders and to work in multicultural, multidisciplinary teams—to move, in other words, from the role of service provider to partner, partnering with their clients to find the right problems and solutions.

To partner with business clients, lawyers need to harness multiple skills (e.g., public relations, communication, marketing, business acumen, and lobbying). And when they do, when they add nontraditional expertise and advice, they add value.

> *"The challenges we have are multifaceted. The legal issues are a manifestation of a problem but the way you solve it is not the law. Sometimes it's the relationship, sometimes it is with lobbying or public relations and communications. It is with a variety of skills that are not inherently legal in nature. It requires sometimes acting with others in industry or coalitions. You have to understand the business and that a lot of legal issues cannot be solved by changing the law or with a legal solution but through changing the business model. You can't start with a legal discussion. You have to have a vision and a combination of skill sets that come from a number of disciplines."* —GC, global music streaming service[28]

> *"These are the value adds. The things that they can provide us that are not the traditional model of advice or documentation . . . a transition to thinking away from tech to the softer side, to developing that broader set of soft skills . . . Some law firms are running [training] programs . . . and offer some spots for us to come along. That's been interesting inviting us to piggyback on their efforts. But what we keep saying to our panel firms is let's do something together—let's develop together— bring in an external provider and work with them to together develop a training program and give us an opportunity to work together on learning opportunities."* —Head of knowledge and development, Compliance and Secretariat, a Big Four Australian bank and financial service provider[29]

The operative words in the quote above are "that's been interesting." Although many Americans might not interpret those words the way they are intended, I learned the hard way that when a person from Britain or Australia says that something is "interesting," it means "there is no bleeping way *that* is interesting." Here, the point is, GCs want to collaborate with their law firm lawyers—as in together—not just have them bring them a solution, or even more often, a new problem.

This may seem obvious, yet it is exactly the opposite of how lawyers are trained to work with clients. As discussed in detail in the next chapter, lawyers are not taught to collaborate like this. They are taught to problem solve for sure. But collaboration for a lawyer often means that I deliver my part and you deliver yours . . . and then we'll put them together.

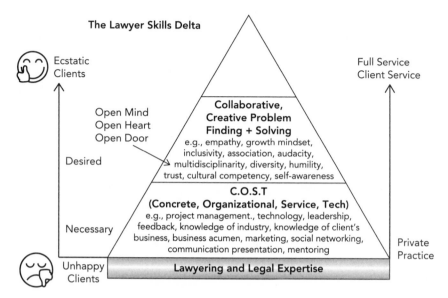

FIG. 3.4. The Lawyer Skills Delta detailing Level 2 of the new skills needed for lawyers to provide full-service client service.[32]

GCs and chief exec clients alike want lawyers who are creative problem solvers, problem finders, and opportunity finders who understand their clients' needs and create solutions with empathy and ingenuity. They want lawyers who are cross-competent leaders with wide networks and have the ability to team across countries, cultures, and disciplines. They want lawyers who have a growth mindset and will put their egos aside and work with people of different levels of experience and expertise. And they want lawyers who not only have passion and perseverance but also take risks and embrace failure. They want someone who has accepted the idea that she/he doesn't know everything and will ask for help from a wide and diverse set of inputs—in other words, someone with self-awareness and a dash of humility who doesn't always think she/he is the smartest and best in the room.

To sum up this block in the Lawyer Skills Delta, clients want lawyers who can play by the Three Rules of Engagement for innovation (described in detail in Part II), rules designed for lawyers so that they can become collaborative, creative problem finders and solvers. They want lawyers who collaborate with an Open Mind, Open Heart, and Open Door. They want lawyers who own those misnamed soft skills that are oh so hard. The good news is that research predicts that those professionals who can do all of this will thrive in 2030 when robots and AI will have taken on more tasks and jobs from all professionals including lawyers.[30] The GC of a global music streaming service explained it this way:

> *"A level of professional creativity in terms of helping you devise innovative approaches to deal with legal problems has always been seen a part of the legal profession. That's not a new trend. Lawyers are creative in finding the right answers to the right problems. Competence in this type of creativity in advice is a commodity. It is a prerequisite. But most successful lawyers are not necessarily the ones with the right IQ and substantive expertise. They are the ones that combine those skills with soft skills . . . It takes a lot of dedication and commitment and empathy and ability to listen."*[31]

Level 3: Innovation (The Newest Four-Letter Word)

I'm sure you saw this coming in a book on innovation, right? Whether they say so indirectly or directly, what clients are really asking for is what one client interviewee called the newest four-letter swear word: *innovation*.[33] They want lawyers who approach collaboration and creative problem solving like innovators do. But innovation does not have to be some bewildering magic trick. In fact, the key ingredients to innovation are right there in the middle part of the Lawyer Skills Delta.

The word *innovation* may conjure up images of the scientist alone in his/her lab when along comes a Eureka moment. But these ahas are rare; instead, innovation is far more likely to come from collaborative, creative problem solving where one person's ideas impact another person's ideas that impact another person's ideas. Slowly, over time, the ideas change and migrate. And as Steven Johnson points out, it is that migration that delivers the "pearl of the oyster."[34]

Many clients ask for innovation indirectly; they may simply ask for what they call the "soft skills" that enable innovation and hope to catch lightning in a bottle. Others come right out and ask for innovation directly; for example, they request proof of innovation in their RFPs (requests for proposals). One CIO interviewee said that his firm was required to designate an innovation partner on the client's business

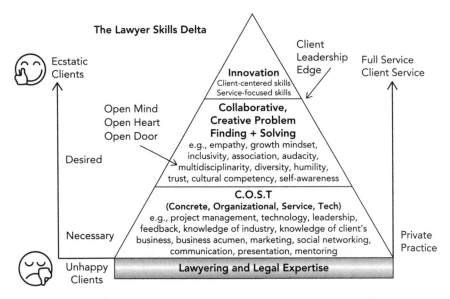

FIG. 3.5. The Lawyer Skills Delta detailing Level 3 of the new skills needed for lawyers to provide full-service client service.[42]

to stay on the panel. That is how much clients want their firms to innovate.

As a great *Harvard Business Review* article points out, we are at a point when capital costs are low, and when that is the case, people concentrate on finding new opportunities for growth versus simply improving upon that which is already profit-generating.[35] The C.O.S.T skills help with the latter. Collaboration and creative problem solving and innovation skills help with the former. But although the skills needed to be creative collaborative problem solvers and problem finders are a prerequisite to innovation, more is needed to actually innovate. And the GCs are demanding this next level from their law firms because innovating is what a true business partner does. I heard this time and time again from the client interviewees. When a law firm innovates with a client, that law firm is considered special.

"To me, it is essential that my law firm is helping me innovate because if they are not, there are other law firms I can go to . . . . When a firm innovates with me, this is something really special and makes me think very highly of what a great business partner the firm is." —GC, large media and telecommunications company in Australia[36]

When I asked one GC what it means to be *special*—does this mean you will hire this firm more?—he replied, "It's actually the other way around. If you don't want to be an innovation partner with me, then I'm going to be inclined *not* to give you business."[37]

When I asked this GC, whose law firm innovated with him and whose company was a recipient of an innovation award, whether he gave more business to the firm, he replied, "My gut feel is that it stayed the same but I would also say that it could have gone down but for it."[38]

Putting the two together? With innovation, a law firm is considered special. Without it, a law firm in this market is at risk of losing business. If a law firm doesn't innovate, the client will seek a law firm that does.

In part, this may be driven by the fact that in-house lawyers' internal business clients are asking for innovation and proof of innovation from them.

> *"I think innovation in how we deliver our legal services it's not even just an option it is a necessity for us now in my view . . . Unless we innovate how we do things, we will not keep up in my organization with the pace at which my organization wants to transform, and that is the thing I'm really trying to solve."* —Head of legal, a large international airline[39]

To reach the top of the pyramid, to scale to the top of the Lawyer Skills Delta, we need to create a culture of innovation between clients and lawyers to transform how they work together. This is what clients are asking of their lawyers: to create a new mindset and culture. They want the mindset, skill set, and behaviors of innovators because this results, consequentially, in a "service delivery transformation."[40]

> *"How do we create a mindset and culture of innovation? How can we be relentlessly curious in terms of understanding the new and what is happening and challenge the status quo? . . . I want to light a fire under my lawyers so that they see an urgent need to change the way we do things and to innovate. And it is not about tech or a particular innovation. It is really a mindset."* —Senior corporate counsel, multinational insurance company headquartered in Australia[41]

So clients are fired up about creating this transformation. Law firm lawyers, not so much. And there are three reasons why, and they are all wrapped up in what I call the Innovation Disconnect.

The Innovation Disconnect

If clients are asking for collaboration with lawyers and, specifically, for innovation with lawyers and, as discussed in the next chapter, they are rewarding lawyers for both, then why does innovation remain a four-letter word? The answer lies in part from an Innovation Disconnect that stems from three gaps:

1. The ask for innovation has been too vague;
2. There is a skills and behavior deficiency;
3. The leap from a culture of collegiality to one of collaboration has not been made.

These gaps in turn represent a huge opportunity for differentiation by the lawyers who fill them. Let's explore each of them in greater detail.

Gap 1: A Vague Ask for Innovation

> ## *"All the evolution we know of proceeds from the vague to the definite."*
>
> —Charles Sanders Peirce[43]

Let's face it: One of the reasons everyone is sick of the word *innovation* is because too many people are batting the term around without having a clear understanding of its meaning. Clients do not know exactly what they want when they ask for innovation. Yet they know when they are *not* getting what they want, and they know when they are getting what they want, sort of like the old definition of pornography: They know it when they see it but remain confused and vague in defining it.[44]

> *"I think the challenge right now is that GCs need to understand how to consume a new type of services and the law firms need to understand what that type of services is and how to sell it. So I don't necessarily see it as the law firm is to blame or the GC is to blame. I think there is a fundamental disconnect going on and the GC, as the buyer of legal services, should start driving that conversation. And the conversation should not just be: how can you trim your rack rates or how can you deliver innovation for me which is another classic but frankly not particularly constructive request. To me the question GCs should ask is: if I am going to invest in you for the next two to three years' worth of fees, how can you invest back in me? What's your technology*

roadmap—and your POV on technology strategy—how are you going to help me unbundle, co-source, multi-source—what are you doing in legal management legal services space, how can you prime for me with a whole number of other vendors delivering better value . . . to me? Those are the types of questions that are interesting."—VP and associate GC, American multinational enterprise information technology company[45]

Unfortunately, the right set of questions isn't being asked as often as it should be. GCs aren't asking the fire-lighting questions such as how can you help me manage my array of service providers, how can you help me predict my resources needs, and how can you help me quarterback my multiple legal service providers. Instead, they take the easy way out and simply ask their firms to *be more innovative*.

"It is easy for big corporates to say law firms 'you need to be more innovative.' They don't know as much as their law firms know what they are asking for."—Lead counsel, large global bank headquartered in the United Kingdom[46]

"We see a few but relatively few in house who push for change or for innovation or for different ways of doing things. Most of them have a tepid gentle push." —Former CEO, professional services firm located in the United States.[47]

As of right now, some (but not all) clients are asking law firms to demonstrate that they have been innovative in RFPs but not checking to see if what they claim is true. Furthermore, some clients are asking law firms to pledge that they will be innovative but not following up to see if what they promised was done. And clients and lawyers alike are claiming that they are innovative or that they are innovating—but are they?

One of my favorite quotes about innovation sums up the current state of the marketplace as it relates to innovation in law: "Innovation is like teenage sex; everyone talks about it, nobody really knows how to do it, everyone thinks everyone else is doing it, so everyone claims they are doing it."[48]

But if Charles Sanders Peirce is correct about evolution, the demands for innovation will, over time, proceed "from the vague to the definite." We have seen this trajectory happen before in the legal marketplace e.g., in GCs' call for diversity. The accredited original call for diversity happened in 1999 when former BellSouth general counsel Charles Morgan, in a white paper petition entitled "Diversity in the Workplace: A Statement of Principle," gathered the signatures of approximately 500 chief legal officers of major corporations to affirm their commitment to diversity in the legal profession and to promote diversity in law firms. That original call (like the current call for innovation) was vague. It didn't specify exactly what was meant by diversity or exactly how GCs would draw the line when it came to hiring law firms.

As the call for diversity went further in 2004 with then GC of Sara Lee, it attempted to translate the general principles of the original call to support diversity into a real action plan. It called for GCs to request diversity performance statistics and make hiring decisions based, at least in part, on those stats.[49] Companies signed on and responded by surveying their law firms to determine their stance on diversity principles and to gather diversity statistics. This led to companies setting diversity benchmarks and monitoring their law firms' progress in meeting the goals. They set quotas, at first very vague ones. For example, they might have said that we expect a certain percentage of all employees of the law firm to be female. This then lead to in-house lawyers setting more *exact* parameters for diversity. For example, they then said that they expect a certain percentage of all *partners* of the law firm to be female. Over time, the call for diversity matured. GCs began setting diversity benchmarks not only for law firms as a whole but also for internal teams working on their business at the firms. Today the requisite proof of a commitment to diversity isn't only in the concrete numbers or the faces around the table. Forward-thinking clients are looking for proof that the law firm provides meaningful opportunities for development to diverse lawyers, and they are looking at the law firm's flextime policies as a proxy for a firm's commitment to diversity. The thinking is that robust flextime policies enable a diverse workforce to work at a firm.[50] Almost 20 years later, clients are rewarding and punishing law firms based on their diversity efforts or lack thereof.[51]

True, not all clients are asking for innovation. In some cases, those that are asking for innovation are the early adopters; in other cases, they are being pushed to innovate and/or find more affordable solutions than law firms have traditionally provided. This relieves law firm lawyers from any sense of urgency. Regardless, the future likely holds more consistent calls for innovation by clients and more stringent benchmarking, evaluation, and measuring of innovation along the same trajectory as the call for diversity. And firms that do not measure up will not be hired.

"If the law firms don't do it, then new entrants will. And then the law firms will become less significant and less relevant. And the conversation will be less about demanding law firms to innovate and more

about the opportunity that law firms continue to miss out on and their ever-decreasing pie because they are not being proactive in helping us in areas that they had not traditionally helped us in past." —GC, large media and telecommunications company in Australia[52]

Who will lead this trajectory? Who will fill this gap and define what is meant by innovation—clients or legal service providers? If the former, will the clients forge together to create a more unified and influential voice? And if the latter, which types of legal service providers will set the pace (ALSPs? big law? PSFs?) And as questioned in the innovation trajectory chart in one of the reflection points of Chapter 2, will innovation come from outside law (via entrepreneurial alt-legal service providers or from within via intra-preneurs at firms)? The most innovation results will likely be co-created by lawyers and clients, sharing the risks and rewards, as they define, measure, and implement innovation.

Gap 2: Skills, Mindset, and Behaviors

"The truth won't set us free—until we develop the skills and the habit and the talent and the moral courage to use it."

—Margaret Heffernan[53]

As mentioned above, the focus is changing from what lawyers "do" to *how* they work—*how* they provide their service. In other words, the focus is on the C.O.S.T skills and collaborative, creative problem-solving skills in the Lawyer Skills Delta. In the past, what mattered is whether lawyers had the skills for private practice, the legal expertise, and that they provided high-quality work (the base of the Lawyer Skills Delta). Today what is desired is full-service client service that requires a whole set of compe-tencies that lawyers today often lack. The reality is that lawyers today are ill-equipped in all three levels of the Lawyer Skills Delta: Level 1: The C.O.S.T skills; Level 2: Collaborative, Creative Problem Finding and Solving; and Level 3: Innovation.

"My team is frustrated with law firms. They send us something and it seems so divorced. Over time, they are becoming less and less relevant." —GC, Australian division of a worldwide healthcare group based in the United Kingdom[54]

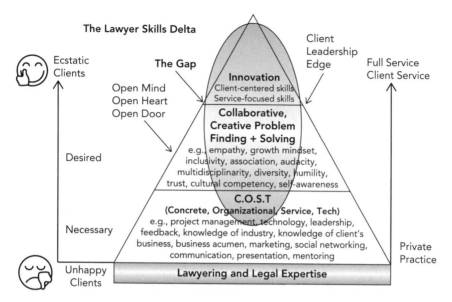

The Lawyer Skills Delta

Ecstatic Clients

The Gap

Client Leadership Edge

Full Service Client Service

Open Mind
Open Heart
Open Door

Innovation
Client-centered skills
Service-focused skills

Collaborative, Creative Problem Finding + Solving

Desired

e.g., empathy, growth mindset, inclusivity, association, audacity, multidisciplinarity, diversity, humility, trust, cultural competency, self-awareness

C.O.S.T
(Concrete, Organizational, Service, Tech)

Necessary

e.g., project management, technology, leadership, feedback, knowledge of industry, knowledge of client's business, business acumen, marketing, social networking, communication, presentation, mentoring

Private Practice

Unhappy Clients

Lawyering and Legal Expertise

FIG. 3.6. The Lawyer Skills Delta detailing the skills, mindset, and behavior gap.[55]

Starting with Level 1, C.O.S.T skills, there was a series of common complaints of deficiencies in these skills. Client interviewees often complained that the work product provided was unhelpful, un-actionable, and divorced from the clients' industry concerns and actual business needs. Clients have been complaining for years about the need for lawyers to up their skills about the industries within which the client works. And so there appears to have been some progress with respect to that competency. But one of the most repeated complaints by clients was a lack of understanding of business in general. Time and time again clients expressed dismay with a lack of business acumen and client service. They complained about the consistent lack of cost certainty and transparency and about projects that were not managed to meet deliverables on time. Clients want lawyers to learn how to communicate better and check in more often and provide and embrace feedback. It's a different level of client service than was required in the past, and lawyers are not providing it. Indeed, I had the opportunity to do some video interviews of a law firm's clients. These clients knew that they were being recorded and that the videos would be shown to the partners of the firm at their annual retreat. And they were forthcoming with these types of complaints with respect to skills gaps at the bottom of the pyramid. In addition to a lack of business acumen, there appears to be a lack of understanding of the clients' specific business. It is one of the reasons the client interviewees touted the benefits of secondments. They want their outside lawyers to work seamlessly with them, and that can only be done if they understand how their specific law department functions within their specific company business and culture.

"Some things I still find painful at times. No amount of feedback seems to address them. To be candid, stuff like over the top legal advice or un-commercial legal advice or lack of understanding of the issues as they relate to the business." —CEO, a specialist real estate investment management company in Australia[56]

"There are a couple of firms that we use that kind of see the advice of the legal adviser as a little bit removed and their job is to provide the technically correct legal advice in relation to the question that is asked whether or not that is particularly helpful and whether or not that is what is wanted. And it is almost like a high moral ground. We are here to tell you what the law is and you can go away and deal with it . . . we have other firms who are much more attuned to what it is the client (not me but our business areas) wants to achieve and find a way to do that and delivering advice that while still accurate takes into account where the client wants to go—and the law is very rarely black and white. There are lots of greys and it's how you work with greys to find the way through. The firms that don't do that well, do at times very much frustrate me—because they are not really delivering the service we need." —GC, government department of Australia[57]

Moving on to Level 2 of the Lawyer Skills Delta, client interviewees also made clear that their lawyers lacked the collaborative, creative problem finding and solving skills they needed. They want their lawyers to develop the skills that provide a collaborative mindset such as empathy, self-awareness, and humility because those skills are what turn a great lawyer into a great leader.

"I do think there is quite a number of things lawyers need to develop. Leadership starts with self, emotional intelligence and self-awareness. There is a huge difference between being a great lawyer versus a great leader. Do they actually lead people? Inspire, motivate, collaborate, and drive a team to high performance? There's a whole skill set required for lawyers around leadership and that requires a huge amount of investment." —Senior corporate counsel, multinational insurance company headquartered in Australia[58]

Clients want their law firm lawyers to invest more time in developing these skills, and they think they are ahead of their law firm lawyers in that respect.

> *"We are very keen on developing that broader set of soft skills. I don't know if we are kidding ourselves a little bit but I kinda get the sense that law firms are following us a bit not the other way around. They need human resources. People that think of their employees as an organism that needs nurturing."*—Head of knowledge and development, Compliance and Secretariat, a Big Four Australian bank and financial service provider[59]

And the #1 reason for the gap in skills and behaviors seems to boil down to one word: *investment.* The phrase "lack of investment" resonates with the clients—not only investment in mastering the skills in the Lawyer Skills Delta but also investment in more time spent problem finding (versus problem solving). As the senior legal counsel of a global management consulting and professional services company explained, the company wanted its lawyers to spend more time "getting to know them and understanding their paint points, what makes them tick."[60] They want more time talking and listening (and not being charged for that time).

> *"They want to have a one hour kickoff call but really just want to suck off info from you and they are sort of listening to you but also selling themselves and it's an hour and a half and then they bill you for it and you could have found it on my website and then asked five minutes of targeted questions and that would have showed your value."*—GC, global cybersecurity company based in the United States[61]

> *"What is important is: how do they then add value to make strategic decisions? We need more law firms to invest in the front add and provide a value add to go through the problem at an early stage and talk to us—and not charge us—and not jump to advice."*—Senior corporate counsel, multinational insurance company headquartered in Australia[62]

One GC told me about a law firm of theirs that keeps coming to him to tell him how the law firm is going to innovate *for* him—for his company. The firm even runs hackathons to solve his company's problems without inviting anyone from his company to join them. He was incredulous: "What I find hilarious, uh fascinating, is that they never asked us to do it . . . They *know* that I have been focusing efforts on creating an innovation forum. I find it *fascinating* that they think we would be excited about them trying to solve our problems without us in the room. It is really missing the mark with the best of intentions."[63] This story says it all. Today in their rush to solve the problems presented to them, lawyers often miss the mark, leaving clients unhappy and convinced that lawyers lack the ability to reach the top of the Lawyer Skills Delta: Innovation.

> *"I ask them to be innovative . . . but they are going on an old model. I find this with my team as well—they are getting frustrated with law firms. As time goes on, it's becoming less and less connected with what you need . . . Figure out what do I need? You could be providing training that I can't do because I'm too busy. You are selling me templates but I want to buy your judgement."*—GC, Australian division of a worldwide healthcare group based in the United Kingdom[64]

And it's a double bind: Clients are underserved, and lawyers are undervalued. Law firm lawyer interviews made the same complaints about other lawyers that the clients did.

> *"Lawyers are not very innovative, which is weird because the practice of law is a creative practice. Most don't appreciate the extent to which what they do is a really creative practice and that is a skill and talent that they do have. They see it as external to them and therefore are challenged by the concept. They ask: 'What does that mean to me? I'm not innovative. I'm not very creative. I just draft leases.' But I don't think that's true."*—Partner, midtier Australian law firm[65]

As a result, there is a misconception in the marketplace that lawyers cannot be creative, cannot be innovative, or cannot be team players. But in reality, they can. Furthermore, when tapped into in the right way, the value these lawyers add can be exponential.

Gap 3: A Culture of Collegiality Instead of Collaboration

"Your elbow is close, yet you can't bite it."[66]

—Russian Proverb

We have been discussing each gap as if it existed in a vacuum, but the truth is the three gaps are closely interrelated. For example, the vague ask for innovation contributes to the lack of investment by lawyers in honing the skills and behaviors, and the gap in skills and behaviors leads to a gap in a culture of collaboration within law firms and legal departments alike.[67] However, even if lawyers master the first block, the C.O.S.T skills, and learn the second block, how to problem solve creatively, in places and at times, there still might be a gap in the collaborative culture in the departments or firms in which they work.

This is due partly to the structure of the law firm, a group of separate fiefdoms under one house despite the one-firm gloss managing partners try to evoke. The client interviewees complained that law firms are essentially multiple practice area groups (each led by a lead partner) sharing an office and some profits without any real central leadership that has power to influence change in behavior. The relationship between the key partners and firm management is not unlike that between tenured faculty and the dean. The dean can suggest that faculty collaborate and put people in charge of committees to enact change in culture, but s/he doesn't have any real power to make faculty do things differently. And if faculty members don't want to change (and many of them don't) and they are in charge, change won't happen. The "elbow is so close, yet you can't bite it." The same Catch-22 occurs in law firms. The partners run the firm. And in the law partner world, power and the ability to influence is associated with revenue. Unfortunately, in large part, law firm management has not yet tied compensation to work that does not immediately generate revenue. Law firm partner interviewees made it clear that regardless of the collaboration mantra, the reality is that a revenue-based, eat-what-you-kill compensation structure is going to put up barriers. Furthermore, even partners who want to create change are limited in large part to the lawyers and staff in their own practice area, which in turns limits the potential for real change given that the people within the same practice area (because they are from the same practice area) tend to lack the requisite diversity and be like-minded and similarly situated. For this reason, some firms have attempted to restructure by industry segment to create more natural opportunities for collaboration across practice area. The success of such moves (if not supported by some type of incentive structure) is dependent on the willingness of partners to share clients out of the goodness of their hearts in the hope that doing so will yield benefits to both practice areas.

"We did this to ourselves. This structure of the law firm, is at the crux."
—GC, online legal technology company that helps clients create legal documents[68]

"The problem with law firms as a source of innovation is that most are not really a cohesive whole. They are a group of small business owners that share an office and do some profit sharing. Each partner has his/ her own business and own clients. Law firms don't have a lot of central strategic control over what their people are doing, especially their most successful people . . . Some firms are talking about innovation and putting people in charge of it. But does the head of innovation at a law firm have the ability to influence and convince the individual partners and senior associates to do anything differently?" —GC, American non-profit that designs public competitions for technological development[69]

"A great element in our firm is that revenue and revenue production on an individual basis still runs how people are remunerated, so there is a great deal of self-interest and fear, and fear breaks down collaboration. In its dumbest form, I'll collaborate with you if I can get something from you. It is not collaboration for collaboration's sake. I want a dollar number to come out of it . . . Our firm talks about it a lot. Nice words in a well-put together policy that doesn't translate into hard and fast rules on how to weight behaviors vs how much revenue you made." —Chief executive partner, top-tier Australian law firm[70]

"I think it has to do with a culture and a fear. The firm values the 'friendly be nice' culture above all else. That word 'culture' comes out all the time. We say we have this innovation focus. But when they say culture they mean something totally different. It harkens back to a thick wet blanket over the whole place. It's a culture of non-confrontation because you have to be nice. Nice is everything. If you draw criticism from anyone, then people want to put you through a fire squad. You can not perform or you can have paper files and commit all these sins that are against 'our culture,' but if you are nice? all of that is absolutely fine. And that really frustrates me and it is holding the firm back, the fear of conflict." —Partner, midtier Australian law firm[71]

And so what we end up with instead of a culture of collaboration is, at best, a culture dedicated to being nice, to being collegial. I often ask partners and other leaders of law firms to describe the culture of their firm in only three words. Besides proving to be a difficult request time and time again, one of the three words they choose is "collegial." This is true of lawyers at American firms, Australian firms, and firms in the United Kingdom.

"I chose the word collegial because people like working together and there is a good vibe and feel around the firm but they don't necessarily work through how they can use that vibe to sort of make it truly collaborative. I'd say we are friendly without being engaged for a purpose."
—Chief financial officer, top-tier Australian law firm[72]

But collegiality is not collaboration. Collegiality is not "good enough."[73] If the partners dominate the firm and its culture and they don't want to change, to move from collegiality to collaboration, the structure and incentives of the firm need to change.[74]

And this is the point clients make. Clients don't want "good enough"; they want what leading management consultant Subir Chowdhury calls "the difference."[75] What they care about is whether innovation and collaborative problem solving has infiltrated the culture of the firm in a way that is intrinsic and not just external, not just a few well-chosen words on the innovation page of a firm's website. Without this shift from collegiality to collaboration, law firms and lawyers within them cannot collaborate internally, and as a by product, they also cannot collaborate externally *with* clients in the way clients want them to and that adds the value that clients desire.

●...Reflection Point Consider the Lawyer Skills Delta above that is designed to show the skills that are necessary for 21st-century lawyering on a scale from "must have" (to have satisfied clients) to "great to have" (to have ecstatic clients). For lawyers, these skills appear to map alongside level of difficulty. In other words, the skills at the bottom of the pyramid are easier to master than those at the top. Does this resonate with you given what you know about lawyers? What types of skills are needed for collaboration and creative problem solving? And before you read Part II, take a stab at conjecturing: What do you think I mean by the Three Rules of Engagement: Open Mind, Open Heart, and Open Door?

●...Reflection Point How do you currently upskill your lawyers? Do those training programs hone the skills on the Lawyer Skills Delta? If so, which skills are being honed effectively and how? If not, which skills are not being honed effectively and why not? What type of training might work to hone those skills?

CHAPTER 4

Lawyers' Crutches: The Source of the Gap in Skills, Behavior, and Mindset

> *"I'm starting with the man in the mirror. I'm asking him to change his ways. And no message could have been any clearer. If you wanna make the world a better place. Take a look at yourself, and then make a change."*
>
> —Michael Jackson, "Man in the Mirror"[1]

We have reviewed three gaps that create an Innovation Disconnect—a disconnect between what legal clients are wanting and expecting and what the majority of today's lawyers can deliver. This chapter will go further and explore why this disconnect exists—why, given the plea by so many clients for change in the way lawyers service them, is there still a gap?

To answer this question, we can turn back to the Lawyer Skills Delta presented in the prior chapter because the source of this disconnect lies between the skills, behavior, and mindset that clients want and what they say lawyers are providing. Understanding this root cause requires some self-analysis and reflection. As Michael Jackson once sang, "I'm starting with the man in the mirror. I'm asking him to change his ways." Well, Michael Jackson had it right. The only way to make a change is to look in the mirror—and frankly, doing this, as well as embracing the content of this chapter, may be a bit difficult for lawyers. This is because the reflection portrayed by this chapter shows lawyers' every line and wrinkle in a magnified fashion.

This is where innovation can come to the rescue. The current mindset, skill set, and behaviors attributed to lawyers have a unique duality of being both the source of our success and the bane of our failures. Yet learning to innovate can shore up our weaknesses as we remember that this is a game we can't lose if only we step out on the court and play.

Self-Awareness, Self-Perception, and Self-Concepts

There are numerous articles and books on the importance of self-awareness, self-reflection, and self-examination as a key—even *the* key—to changing ourselves and, by extension, our industries.[2] These writings are directed at not only our personal lives but also our professional ones and, specifically, our ability to grow as business professionals and as managers and leaders. Classic *Harvard Business Review* articles on the topic date back to 1964.[3] For decades, companies and executive training programs (including Harvard Law School's Executive Education program on Leadership in Law Firms) have been giving personality tests to professionals for this reason. And there is research to support all of it. Research shows that a top criterion for successful leaders is high self-awareness.[4] This means that understanding not just our strengths but also our weaknesses will help us lead better and team better.[5] When we are aware of our deficiencies, we are more open to ideas and help from others because we understand that others might be better at some things than we are. Following this train of thought, we eventually seek people who are different from us to fill in what would be (without self-awareness) our blind spots. As discussed in Part III of this book, one of the reasons we have the individuals in LawWithoutWalls take personality tests and then map them out as a team to identify gaps is to gain these benefits.

Self-awareness, however, isn't easy to acquire. Studies show that generally, leaders' self-perception of their abilities is not accurate; people generally fail to recognize their weaknesses and tend to overrate their abilities.[6] This is sometimes referred to as the Dunning-Kruger Effect.[7] Worse yet, those who overrate their substantive abilities are also more likely to overrate their emotional intelligence and be reluctant to attempt to improve their EQ.[8] The title of a study demonstrating this says it all: "Emotionally Unskilled, Unaware, and Uninterested in Learning More: Reactions to Feedback about Deficits in Emotional Intelligence."[9] Self-awareness is essential to great leadership. Yet as Benjamin Franklin pointed out in 1750, like "steel" and "a diamond," "to know one's self," is "extremely hard."[10] And if you don't know yourself accurately, it is hard to change.

Another impediment to change (which is related to our faulty self-perception) is our self-concept. Paul J. Brouwer explained this in a *Harvard Business Review* article published in the 1960s:

"Each of us, whether we realize it or not, has a self-image. We see ourselves in some way—smart, slow, kindly, well-intentioned, lazy, misunderstood, meticulous, or shrewd; we all can pick adjectives that describe ourselves. This is the "I" behind the face in the mirror, the "I" that thinks, dreams, talks, feels, and believes, the "I" that no one knows fully."[11]

It would be difficult enough to attain self-awareness if we only had one self-concept. But we don't; we have multiple self-concepts that change based on the role we are playing.

Brouwer gives the following example: You may be someone who personally loves to travel. So when on a personal vacation, you attempt to learn about the history, culture, and customs of a location. Yet when you are on business trip, you might not ever leave the hotel that hosts the conference—even if you have time to do so. Brouwer explains that this is because your self-concept during that trip was as a businessperson versus a vacationing explorer. This self-concept works like a filter on what we see (or do not see), what we hear (or do not hear), and how we behave (or do not behave). Sometimes our different self-concepts are in conflict with each other internally, and sometimes they are in conflict externally, with how others see us.[12] According to Brouwer, the more integrated our self-concepts are and the more realistic they are, the more effective we are in both our professional and personal lives.[13]

It is important for us lawyers to understand what self-concept we have created that we rely on when we are acting as lawyers because this lawyer self-concept can lock us into preferences, tendencies, and practices that contribute to the skills and behavior gap even without our knowing it. We lawyers may have a knack for getting in our own way. But understanding this can make all the difference.

To help raise self-awareness among lawyer readers so that they can make the first step toward change—toward mastering the Three Rules of Engagement outlined in Part II of this book—this chapter attempts to identify the crutches that lawyers rely on that create the Innovation Disconnect and prevent lawyers from evolving higher up on the Lawyer Skills Delta. These self-obstructions can be divided into two, just like a pair of crutches: Under the *right* arm is the crutch that is related to what I call the lawyer's temperament, and under the *left* arm is the crutch attributable to what I call the lawyer's training.

Lawyers' Right-Arm Crutch: Our Temperament

"The big one for the profession is being open to change and being open to adapt. It is a mindset. It's not about technology or a new technique."

—GC, religious organization in Australia with almost 900,000 adherents[14]

According to interviewee after interviewee (like the GC quoted above), the lawyer's temperament can be the crux of the problem—the lawyer's disposition, nature, character, makeup, mind, spirit, and attitudes. Time and time again I heard comments such as: "Lawyers are not inherently innovative people by temperament."[15]

"Lawyers by upbringing, by tendencies, tend to be more traditionalist than others. They take longer to adapt to changes and embrace innovation. It is part of the mentality. Lawyers are risk averse and likely need to be to be good lawyers. Lawyers try to perform in the areas of their comfort zone but very few are into adopting and trying new things. As a whole, if you ask them to go to something completely unknown and new, it is just not in the lawyer's DNA. And the few that are good at it naturally stick out."—Deputy GC, global network and managed IT service provider that integrates communications products and services for multinational corporations from Germany[16]

Now, of course, there is no way to generalize about *all* lawyers accurately, and some types of lawyers (such as litigators and rainmakers) may have different temperaments. That said, research indicates that my law firm partner and client interviewees are not off the mark and that lawyers tend to be skeptical and less trusting, low on psychological resilience and introverted (despite being outwardly confident and powerful); they tend to be risk-averse "lightning rod salesmen" who are unable to see the forest for the trees.[17] Let's examine each of these alleged tendencies in turn.

Skeptical and Less Trusting

A typical lawyer's temperament does not just get in the way of collaborative, creative problem-solving and innovation skills. It derails them. If you are a lawyer, you might be thinking that's not possible. But by disagreeing with me before you finish reading the rest of this section, you are proving my point: lawyers are more skeptical and less trusting than other professionals. We say it ourselves:

> *"We are cynical, pessimistic, and skeptical."[18]*
>
> —Stephen Poor, *Chair Emeritus at Seyfarth Shaw*

Dr. Larry Richard, a former trial attorney and trained psychologist, has profiled thousands of lawyers over the past 30 years.[19] Relying on the Caliper assessment tool that uses approximately 10 traits to identify personality profiles, Dr. Richard's research indicates that lawyers are almost twice as skeptical as the general public[20] and have a very high inclination to doubt or question the motives of others.[21] True, his research is subjective and limited to lawyers in the United States, but it resonates with lawyers around the world. And it's supported by history and literature across the centuries.

Throughout time, lawyers have been doubting everyone's motives: the lawyers on the other side, the judges, the system, and their own clients. The lawyer's job is to uncover the truth, to sniff out lies and flubs. Similarly, people have been doubting lawyers—because their job is not only to uncover to the truth but also to cover it up—to protect the truth from coming out if need be. It doesn't matter whether you interpret Shakespeare's famous line "The first thing we do, let's kill all the lawyers"[22] as one signifying distrust of all lawyers, distrust of only the lawyers that protected the rich and not poor, or as a tribute to lawyers who prevent anarchy.[23] The quote itself demonstrates that skepticism of and lack of trust in lawyers has existed for centuries.

Lawyers live in a state of believing that someone is lying or is about to do something deceitful at any moment; it just isn't clear who. It is a very Hemmingway-esque way to look at the world (i.e, "[e]verybody behaves badly . . . [g]ive them the proper chance").[24] Lawyers are hired to defend people, many of whom have done some degree of wrong. If we are surrounded by a number of people who have behaved badly, no wonder we are skeptical. And as time goes on, as lawyers become leaders (managing partners and GCs), skepticism grows. In his book *Oxygen*, Andrew Miller couldn't have written a more apt statement of the human condition that applies to lawyers in miles when he wrote that at a certain age, "It's difficult to change the way you see the world. We take on a certain view when we are young, then spend the rest of our lives collecting the evidence."[25] Because that's what lawyers do. We learn early on that people are not to be trusted, and we spend the rest of our careers collecting the evidence. And collecting evidence? That's our job too.

Although skepticism and lack of trust can be useful traits when in an adversarial situation, they can detract from collaborating, especially at the initial stages of an innovation cycle when creative brainstorming in a safe environment is essential—and critique and lack of trust is not.

Low on Psychological Resilience and Introverted

In addition, according to Dr. Richard, lawyers have very low psychological resilience.[26] 90% of all lawyers score in the bottom 50% in resilience. This means that lawyers generally don't take criticism or rejection very well—and that is likely an understatement. Lawyers are not thick skinned. They are easily offended and defensive when they are criticized or rejected.[27] Many of the interviewees confirmed this attribute of lawyers. Part of the reason this might be so—especially of lawyers from elite law schools—is that they generally don't receive much negative feedback in college, law school, or practice. In college, many students never receive a grade lower than a B+. In law school, students are given one grade per class at the end of the semester and generally without any written feedback. It's one and done. You win or lose. And there is no explanation for why you get the grade you get, so it is easy to shrug it off as a one-off or a bogus test or a hard-grader. Feedback is not forthcoming in the law firm world either. So it is not surprising that lawyers are thin skinned.

"So many associates do not know how to meet adversity. Many of them come from old families, from great boarding schools, and even better

colleges and they've been getting A's and accolades their whole lives.
The first time someone doesn't answer the phone, they get disheart-
ened."—Partner, New York City–based law firm[28]

Combining this lack of resilience with a natural skepticism multiplies the inability of lawyers to "hear" or absorb the critical feedback essential to spur change because they don't believe it. On the other hand, even if they do hear it, they don't react in a way that helps them fix it. They react negatively because they don't believe it is true, but they may not show any reaction externally because, as will be explained below, lawyers are often introverted. Ironically, they don't want outward conflict despite the adversarial nature of legal work. And they get their strength behind closed doors (despite the fact that their job is to outwardly represent clients).

According to a study by Eva Wisnik, who has administered Myers-Briggs personality tests to more than 6,000 attorneys since 1990, more than 60% of lawyers are introverts.[29] This means that introverted lawyers get their energy in being alone as opposed to interacting with others. It also means that most lawyers are less sociable than others (i.e., they are less comfortable initiating new intimate relationships, preferring to rely on the existing relationships they have made over time). According to Dr. Larry Richard's research, lawyers have an average score of only 12.8% on sociability compared to 50% for the general public. Lawyers also have a strong sense of autonomy.[30] The combination of low sociability and a high sense of autonomy make it less likely that lawyers will seek or receive the feedback (that they might not hear anyway).[31] And when lawyers do work with others, it is often in silos. As Lee McIntyre, a research fellow at the Center for Philosophy and History of Science at Boston University, points out in his book *Respecting Truth: Willful Ignorance in the Internet Age*, "One real advantage of group reasoning is that you get critical feedback," McIntyre says. "If you're in a silo, you don't get critical feedback, you just get applause."[32]

This effect gets worse rather than better the higher a lawyer ascends the rungs of partnership. High-powered leaders (and thus high-powered lawyers) are less empathetic and less able to put themselves in other people's shoes and see others' perspectives.[33] As a law firm partner pointed out:

"Law firm partners don't have the mindset. To provide true client ser-
vice, you need a genuine sustained interest in the problems of others—
even if you don't like them. And most lawyers don't have that interest.

They are used to being the smartest person in the room and people just listening to them . . . Too many have their feet up on Madison Avenue and are convinced that they are quite bright, and they resent anyone that tries to make them feel otherwise. And the thing is, they are not that humble." —Partner, New York City–based law firm[34]

This makes sense in some ways. Law firm partners today have already been through—and won—multiple tournaments in law to get promoted from associate to senior associate to junior partner to partner. They are the cream of the crop and they know it, and they worked really hard to get there. And they want and believe that they deserve the power they wield.

This is why Daniel H. Pink recommends that people try to turn the dial down on feelings of power.[35] With your feet up on the desk and your hands behind your head, you can't see others' perspectives, you can't collaborate, you can't empathize with the consumer or target audience of a problem, and you definitely aren't open to changing yourself and your behavior. This leads to the final deleterious aspect of the lawyer's temperament.

Risk-Averse Lightning Rod Salesmen

Both client and law firm partner interviewees consistently made comments such as "lawyers are traditionally risk adverse and by definition, more cautious than other professionals."[36] The job of the lawyer (which is negative by nature) feeds risk aversion. Lawyers are hired to protect their clients from future risk or to limit the risk of a past action. They are often asked to determine whether a course of action can be taken legally (or to analyze whether the action taken was legally defensible). And in conducting that analysis, lawyers attempt to spot every single issue. And with the billable hour, the more issues they uncover, the more money they make.

"A law firm lawyer's value is not in solving the one *problem the client gives us. Instead it is taking the problem the client gives us and turning it into 50 problems and charging for* all *the problems. If a lawyer simply says yes, you can do this, that is a lost opportunity to make money."* —GC, online legal technology company that helps clients create legal documents[37]

To that end, lawyers have a tendency to be what Professor Robert Eli Rosen calls "lightning rod salesmen"[38]—seeing thunder and lightning everywhere. This is how law professors train the law school student's mind—to identify every issue, every flaw, every risk, every downside (and, of course, the counterarguments and more positive counterviews of those issues and risks and downsides). The problem in practice versus schooling is that there is a great deal of risk for not only the client but also the lawyer if the more positive viewpoint is wrong. So lawyers focus on the flaws and weaknesses, which has a tendency to scare clients, to freak them out when that is the opposite of what they need at the moment. When clients call on a Friday night with something urgent, they want their lawyer to have their back, to calm them down, to make them feel like she/he's "got this." One of my interviewees analogized the *ideal* role of the law firm partner to that of Mr. Wolf in the movie *Pulp Fiction*. In the movie, someone gets shot who isn't supposed to be shot, and the characters played by Samuel Jackson and John Travolta freak out because everything went wrong. They call the boss, and when the boss says, "I'm sending Mr. Wolf," they are immediately relieved. The boss calls Mr. Wolf. He explains that the location is 30 minutes away. Mr. Wolf assures the boss that all will be okay. He says, "I'll be there in ten." And he is. He shows up nine minutes and 37 seconds later. When Mr. Wolf arrives, he introduces himself as follows: "I'm Mr. Wolf. I solve problems."[39] I'm not suggesting that lawyers refrain from doing all the issue spotting. They should continue to look under every rock for every snake. But their job is not to serve back to the client the laundry list of *maybe* doomsdays that *might* happen. Their job is to instill in their clients that same sense of relief and confidence that Mr. Wolf instills and to *help* their client *solve* problems, not just identify them. To be clear, I'm not suggesting that the law firm partners solve the problem alone, which can lead to solutions that miss the mark (as discussed in the prior chapter). The lawyers' job is to collaborate to solve the problem together. Remember, wolves run in packs.

"One of the characteristics of lawyers of my vintage, 20 odd years in the profession is that you are taught to think a certain way. And rightly it is to look for the flaws in something. Where's the weakness? So it can be glass half empty—always the negative and what is the risk of parting from precedent?" —Partner, midtier Australian law firm[40]

"They are wonderful at issue spotting. What got them an A+ in law school makes the client feel terrible, just terrible. I tell them: that's not your job. Your job is to issue spot and keep the issues to yourselves. Your job is to offer just the solution. If you want to do this, then you need to do a, b, c. You are not supposed to show all your work here. Your job

is to be Mr. Wolf from Pulp Fiction *. . . You only get into the details and explain if the client asks you to—wants you to."* —Partner, New York City-based law firm[41]

Furthermore, lawyers (when they act as the lightning rod salesmen) are so busy selling umbrellas that they fail to see the rainbows—the opportunities.

"Some people have a tendency to default to seeing the risk, rather than identifying potential opportunities that can come out of some of the volatility that exists, and can actually help the business to grow." —Siobhan Moriarty, GC of Diageo[42]

The lawyer's temperament, therefore, is opposite of what is required to excel in the top two blocks of the Lawyer Skills Delta—the skills needed to innovate—to creatively, collaboratively problem find and solve. It is also opposite of some of the lower-level C.O.S.T skills such as giving feedback and mentoring. A worse crutch than the lawyer's temperament, however, is their training—which doesn't help lawyers hone most of the skills in the Lawyer Skills Delta for 21st-century lawyering.

Lawyers' Left Arm Crutch: Our Training

If we only had one crutch, the repercussions from the gap in the Lawyer Skills Delta might not be as great. However, we have a pair of crutches that work in tandem. The left arm crutch that pairs to the temperament crutch is our training. By training, I mean all of the education that aspiring and practicing lawyers receive, whether in law school or after graduation via executive education and continuing education offered by law and business schools or other professional organizations. Put simply, the way lawyers are trained in law school and retrained afterward helps create the skills and behavior gap.

For the most part, most practicing lawyers were not taught any of the skills in the Lawyer Skills Delta when they were trained to be lawyers. And although that is still largely true today, it simply is not sufficient. I'm not the first—or the last—to make this claim.[43] As Richard Susskind aptly points out, "We are schooling aspiring lawyers to become traditional one-to-one, solo, bespoke, face-to-face, consultative advisers who specialize in the black-letter law of individual jurisdictions and who charge by the hour"[44] instead of 21st-century lawyers. The few courses that exist at the few schools that are trying to teach some of the skills in the Lawyer Skills Delta prove the point of their overwhelming absence. For most law school students and practicing attorneys, the Lawyer Skills Delta is completely foreign to what they think about law school or even the concept of lawyering. It doesn't comport with their self-concept of what it means to be an attorney. If law schools taught the C.O.S.T and Collaborative, Creative Problem Finding and Solving Skills in conjunction with lawyering skills in a seamless way, our concept of lawyering might be primed more toward innovation and the type of relationship and service that clients desire. Perhaps the gaps wouldn't be as large. Instead, however, law school generally focuses its training at the very base of the skills pyramid, which leads to unhappy clients.

> *"Even though legal education continues to change and teamwork is now emphasized in programs like LawWithoutWalls, for the most part we are not training lawyers to be part of a team or to understand the needs and expectation or concerns of the other side, to be empathetic and creative and collaborative. The creation process is not something we teach in law school. The tradition in legal education is that you are building the hyper-smart, driven hero that will go and achieve big things by himself or work with a small team of juniors and paralegals."*
> —GC, global music streaming service[45]

Why does this continue to be such a struggle? In part, it might be because lawyers, for the most part, are graded individually and only on the finished product (the "final exam" or paper) and then it's done and never revisited. That's not how innovation, self awareness, or improvement happens. Moreover, lawyers are taught to follow precedent and what happened before which is also antithetical to creative brainstorming and innovating what could happen differently in the future.

> *"At its heart, the problem comes from the way we are trained as lawyers to literally follow the way things have been done previously. If you want to do something novel, it's uphill. You need to find a path that has been done before."* —Partner, midtier Australian law firm[46]

> *"I think lawyers can also experience some additional challenges associated because our learning and our training is all based on what happened before, precedent and how we used to do it. That said, I think that lawyers have headwinds when it comes to disrupting themselves, but they can definitely do it."* —VP and associate GC, American multinational enterprise information technology company[47]

They can definitely do it, disrupt themselves, but most unfortunately to do so, it is a matter of retraining rather than training—which is harder. Just as it is easier to learn a new language when we are younger, it is easier to learn these skills while we are in law school. Furthermore, it is almost as if we crush the creativity out of our future lawyers. They arrive the first semester of the first year so green and hopeful and confident in their ability to persuade and influence and advocate. And then, somehow, we, the professors, beat the hopefulness and confidence out of them.

> *"Lawyers are innately creative because generally lawyers like language, the humanities side of the profession. And if they like language and words that means they read a lot. So innately, lawyers have all the tools and really are experts in creativity. I think the problem is the way we train them, and the way we talk about what a lawyer's role is what curbs that creativity. We don't talk about lawyers being entrepreneurs or business people. And then after law school, we put them in law firms wearing suits—in offices, that are big and conservative and process driven—'Open the file; do the engagement letter.' 'Here's the environment. We will slot you in and expect you not to try to transform it. Just do your bit.'"*
> —Law firm partner interviewee, midtier Australian law firm[48]

The task of retraining is VUCA-like in nature. As you will recall from Chapter 1, VUCA problems are volatile, uncertain, complex, and ambiguous. The task of retraining is volatile because new core competency skills such as leadership, cultural competency, mentoring, business acumen, and project management were not honed even if they were studied. It is uncertain and complex because both in-house legal departments and firms may have up to five generations in the workforce, so legal departments and law firms are perplexed as to how to retrain for each of the generation's gaps. It is ambiguous because not everyone has been trained in all or some of these skills; instead, each generation (and person) has its own gap in the long list of skills needed to bridge the service gap.

Despite the efforts by law schools and executive education (or management learning) programs to teach these skills, the reality is that most of the C.O.S.T, Creative Collaborative Problem Finding/Solving, and Innovation skills are not easily taught in a typical classroom or course format like that provided in most law schools and executive education programs. In a classroom, learning is applied in theory versus practice; it cannot be tested or applied hands on. The kind of reskilling and upskilling of lawyers indicated by the Lawyer Skills Delta cannot be accomplished in a classroom or in a concentrated five-day course where participants are often like-minded and similarly situated, having little diversity in age, education, experience, or discipline, which is the exact opposite of what is needed for creative problem solving. It takes time and multicultural, multidisciplinary teaming, hands-on doing, and practice. As Aristotle said, "For the things we have to learn before we can do them, we learn by doing them."[49]

A Matter of Unlearning

> *"The first problem for all of us, men and women, is not to learn, but to unlearn."*
>
> —Gloria Steinem

Resistance to change, fear of failure, introversion, and a desire to avoid risk combined with being hired to serve as a specialized expert, all contribute to the skills gap. It leads to a mindset and behaviors that are exactly the opposite of what is required to collaboratively, creatively problem find and solve, let alone innovate—and it leads to the exact opposite of what clients are saying they want from their lawyers. To collaboratively, creatively problem solve, one needs to have empathy and humility, not outward confidence and bravado. One needs to have a diverse network of friends from varied backgrounds, not small silos, so that she/he can connect ideas and theories and receive input that varies. One needs to see challenges as opportunities, not as problems, and to try things even if they turn out being wrong. One needs to be a problem finder or what Tina Seelig calls a need-finder,[50] able to whittle a problem over and over to tighten in on the real source versus symptoms—problem and need finding are not the same as issue spotting. But to do that, lawyers need to not only adopt the innovator's mindset, skill set, and behavior but also need to unlearn some of their own.

The GC of the Australian division of a worldwide healthcare group based in the United Kingdom summed it up as follows: "Some things they have to unlearn to be innovative. Being confident, being a subject matter expert can get in the way of creativity. I like change. I want to change things all the time. I say, I don't want you to prepare for meetings. Sounds bizarre but if you are prepared, you are coming with your mind closed and not listening to what the problem is. You don't have to give the answer. Listen to what the problem is."[51]

So it isn't just a skills gap but a skills handicap because lawyers must unlearn some of the skills and behaviors that have made them most successful and that prevent them from honing what are sometimes referred to as "soft skills" but are so hard to master.

☁...Reflection Point What are all the reasons you think there is so much doubt about lawyers and innovation? What biases against lawyers are driving that doubt?

☁...Reflection Point What are some of the best training experiences you have had outside of law school or your law career (i.e., in high school, undergraduate college, extracurricular activities [e.g., sports, music, and hobbies])? What stands out about those experiences? What made them so effective and/or enjoyable? Make a list of what made them so. Now think about law school and any continuing learning or executive education training you have had during your legal career regarding the practice of law. Which ones were the best and why? Make a list of what made them effective. Now compare the two lists. How might you exapt some of the techniques and experiences you enjoyed in your external non-law training into how we train our future and current lawyers?

CHAPTER 5

The New Value Equation in Law: An A, B, C Primer

> *"Price is what you pay. Value is what you get."*
> —Warren Buffett

The New Value Equation in Law

Clients want lawyers to collaborate with them, and they want lawyers to innovate with them. Lawyers, however, are reluctant to attempt innovation for fear of failure of two kinds: failure to actually succeed in innovating and failure to get any real value out of attempting to innovate. Although it is true that many lawyers—especially those in big law—may not need to innovate now to continue to make money (or even increase revenue), this is far from a static equation. In the future, all of the law will have to innovate because of the coming New Value Equation in Law.

Before explaining what I mean by the new value equation, let's start by discussing how clients value innovation. Value generally equals benefit minus costs. Thus, one way to increase value is to provide the same benefit (same goods or services) at a reduced cost. Walmart is masterful at this; it buys in volume and pressures its suppliers to reduce costs. The other way to increase value is to give more benefit at a cost that doesn't increase at the same rate—something that more securely applies to the law. But this is tricky. When lawyers innovate with their clients, how do we measure the benefit? Perhaps in some situations, for example, with e-discovery or automated contracts, we can measure the benefit in terms of the number of hours saved and then equate those hours to dollars.

But even in that situation, there is not a true one-to-one calculation. Consider an example outside of law, such as the new digital billboards that have been proven to be more effective than static billboards. They track who drove by the sign and actually went to the client's store/restaurant advertised on the sign. That's measurable benefit, but it isn't proof that someone saw the billboard or that the billboard was the reason the person drove to the restaurant. Technology might improve this by tracking whether our eyes actually scanned the billboard, but even then, there are many soft factors that can't be measured. Perhaps the child in the car had to go to the bathroom, and the billboard had nothing to do with the stop at the restaurant. Perhaps the teenager in the car wanted to be able to boast to his friends that he ate at the great British wings disaster at the King's Head and had never even looked up from his phone as the car passed the billboard.

With innovation, can we really "subtract" cost from benefit to arrive at value? Value is what you get in exchange for what you give, but the value of a service like the one the law provides is often *perceived* value where the values assigned are subjective. Why does a consumer spend more money on, for example, 501 button fly jeans than another style when no one else can tell whether the person is wearing button fly (or zipper) jeans? How do you determine the ROI from a commercial? The same questions are arising in the law marketplace right now about innovation. Clients are saying that they value innovation, but that valuation is not linear. It affects who they are likely to hire, but in a roundabout way. As the GC of a large media and telecommunications company in Australia explained, "it won't be 'if you do this, you get that,' but you might be surprised by the benefit . . . [T]he financial benefit is likely to be further down the track."[1]

What I'm hearing from clients is that a willingness to innovate with the client puts you in the "special" category. It distinguishes you/your firm from the rest as being a better business partner, and it will help you get included in the panel or the RFP (i.e., meaning the gateway to the potential for more business). Going on an innovation journey with a client translates to more because it transforms the relationship between lawyer and client. The lawyer and client are in it together. Together they are feeling vulnerable and are taking risks, and they must trust each other. Essentially, innovating with a client is a new form of business development (that has a great deal of added value as discussed below).

"Innovation is part of the mix. If firms are demonstrating innovation in the way of supporting us in legal content or the way they are delivering legal services, we will recognize it and it will differentiate them and get them included in the mix." —Head of knowledge and development, Compliance and Secretariat, a Big Four Australian bank and financial service provider[2]

Furthermore, in the actual act of innovating, the law firm learns the company's DNA, internal processes, and communication preferences.

"I think it is inevitable. I think if someone is prepared to partner in that way you will be inside in the DNA of that company and you will know how we go about our internal processes and I also foresee a building block thing. Once you build the knowledge portal, at the end of the day, you can bolt on other modules . . . so you basically have the one stop shop." —Head of legal, large international airline[3]

And if that's not enough "value" for a firm to justify investing in innovating, there are also dollars and sense behind collaborating in the way that yields creative problem solving or an innovation. Heidi Gardner's research demonstrates that when lawyers collaborate, versus simply cross-sell (i.e., when two practice groups collaborate), annual revenue per client triples. A similar increase in profits accrue to individual lawyers that collaborate as well. These rainmakers? They don't just make it rain; they make it pour.

Gardner compares two nearly identical lawyers: Lawyer 1 and Lawyer 2. Lawyers 1 and 2 graduated from law school the same year, have been with the same firm for the same amount of time, and are in the same practice area. In one year, both of them billed almost the same number of hours. Lawyer 2's total revenue, however, was more than four times larger than revenue from Lawyer 1. The difference? Lawyer 2 had collaborated with a much broader network of partners. Lawyer 1 collaborated with six other partners (only three of which were outside his practice). Lawyer 2 collaborated with more than 30 other partners (20 of whom were from outside his practice).[4] Gardner's research demonstrates that the more a partner shares the work she/he originates with other partners and other practices, the larger the partner's book of business grows over time.[5]

Why is that? It is partly because, as will be discussed in Part II, collaboration yields better, more creative problem solving. Collaboration is a key ingredient to innovation. It is also partly because, as many client interviewees claim, the kind of collaboration that results in innovation changes focus and mindset.

"How do you measure innovation? You could force a quantitative analysis e.g., how many new ideas have translated into something or some system. But I don't know that we need to bid ourselves up that much. Just change in the service delivered or how delivered and the how will become apparent and become part of the experience and people will accept that the difference is driven by a change in focus and mindset. They will recognize that the change has happened and there is a driver of that change and the driver is thinking in a new way." —Head of knowledge and development, Compliance and Secretariat, a Big Four Australian bank and financial service provider[6]

And this is the real value equation in innovation. Some innovation may fail. I could tell you it is good that many successful entrepreneurs have failed. And failure is lauded in the start-up world. There is even a conference called FailCon that touts itself as a "one-day conference for technology entrepreneurs, investors, developers and designers to study their own and others' failures and prepare for success."[7]

So we can learn from failures as much as successes—the times the lightbulb turned on as well as all the other times it fizzled. But failure isn't a necessity. Research reported in the *Harvard Business Review* in 2014 found that successful entrepreneurs were just as likely not to have failed the first time as to have failed the first time. In other words, failure didn't make it more likely that the entrepreneur would succeed in his/her next venture.[8] Failure for failure's sake, especially for lawyers, is overrated. In truth, what matters are three things I call the ABCs of Innovation: *a*ttitude, *b*ehavior, and *c*ulture. They provide a primer for anyone ready to apply himself/herself to innovation: win, lose, or draw. And the best thing about this game is regardless of win, lose, or draw, you don't fail. Let me explain how that can be so.

A Is for Attitude

> *"If you cannot do great things, do small things in a great way."*
>
> —Napoleon Hill

Many people have bad attitudes about innovation in the law. Some don't think it's worth it; I can't tell you how many venture capitalists have said as much to me. Others don't think it's possible—at least not by lawyers. They make comments such as "Lawyers aren't going to change and neither are law firms, especially big law."[9] Others think it's not necessary. They prescribe to that horrible model *if it ain't broke, don't fix it.* For many lawyers, their business model isn't broken and if the pie is getting bigger—even if their piece isn't growing at the same rate as the rest of the pie—it's still growing. So why bother?

And still others think innovation is just too scary and too big to take on. They think innovation is about doing "great things" great, big things that are like TNT—explosive and immediately disruptive as in *boom, pow, bang!* They are wrong, and they are right. Innovation is like TNT, but it is not always explosive and disruptive. Instead, it can be TNT as in *T* for tiny, *N* for noticeable, and *T* for things that add lasting value. That's what James Batham, head of innovation and partner at Eversheds Sutherland, calls it and appropriately so. Clients want small, incremental changes that add lasting value. And as we have discussed, although clients do not know exactly what they are looking for when they call on their lawyers to innovate and they do not know exactly how to measure innovation or being innovative, most agree that the type of innovation they are looking for is this kind of TNT.

Innovation can simply be questioning why we are doing things the way we always have done them.

> *"Innovation is questioning the status quo and trying to improve upon the quality of the product you provide to your client."* —GC, iconic software and technology company from the United States[10]

> *"Don't beat yourself up over it. It doesn't need to be world class or patentable. If it is improving and sustaining? Fantastic. Give yourself a tick."* —Head of Knowledge and development, Compliance and Secretariat, a Big Four Australian bank and financial service provider[11]

Innovation doesn't have to be new or original; it just has to be practicable.

> *"It's not innovation unless it has a practical impact. It has to have something unique to it. It could be taking something that exists and applying it differently. I don't think it is innovation unless it is something people want. Creativity in action."* —GC, Australian division of a worldwide healthcare group based in the United Kingdom[12]

So what are some good examples of innovation—of a TNT? Examples include providing one of your clients an opportunity for training she/he might not have had otherwise, creating a new recruitment program that helps train future lawyers and provides free legal services to corporate client legal departments, and doing something that makes GCs lives easier when they are working with you.

> *"The law firm created a collaborative recruitment strategy for trainees that included a corporate legal intern arrangement in a rotation with the firm. It really boosted our standing among trainees and provided some service to us."* —GC, large financial services group based in Norway[13]

> *"We have an arrangement with one of our four firms that provides us with a $10,000 scholarship for one team member to go and do some amazing leadership course. It's almost like a gift. That's one of the value adds."* —Head of knowledge and development, Compliance and Secretariat, a Big Four Australian bank and financial service provider[14]

> *"I think the sweet spot for law firms is things that make in-house counsel's life easier—the website that has any kind of piece of information you would want about insurance or securities that you can log into or shared sites where we can keep every piece of case material (all referring to things the same way). That is pretty attractive: the ability to log into a place to see the status without having to pay for 15 minutes of the attorney time."* —Deputy GC, global insurance company based in the United States[15]

It's that easy. Send your client to one of Harvard Law School's Executive Education Programs or to LawWithoutWalls such as Eversheds, Pinsent Masons, Clyde & Co, Janders Dean, Linklaters, Holland & Knight, and White & Case have done. And get a check plus, or a tick as they say in Australia.

Innovation, TNT, can also be the story as opposed to a product or program. The tick can be the way in which you position/frame/market. Tim Brown provides the example of the microchip Intel created that sits inside the computer.[16] The innovation was tiny in physical size but TNT in the true sense of the word for impact because the computer would be useless without it. The tick, however, was the sticker on the outside that said "Intel inside." That is how Intel built its brand. Today Intel is not just what's inside the computer, and it's not exemplified just with a sticker. Today Intel is a serious competitor in the driverless car market, having purchased Mobileye, a device that helps the driverless cars "see" without a driver, for $15.3 billion dollars.[17] But the tick with kick? It came from a Tiny Noticeable Thing, a small sticker.

Innovation does not even have to be three dimensional to provide value. It can be a new service or a new user experience. As will be discussed in Part III, an integral component of human-centered design is understanding the user's experience with the product. You might ask how the user's experience with a *product* relates to the innovation in law market and by lawyers. What's the lawyer's product? As discussed in Chapter 2, today clients can buy legal products (e.g., automated contracts, legal project management software, and a prediction). But in most cases, the user is the client and the *product* is the lawyer or the firm. If that is the case, value can be provided by simply changing the client's experience with the lawyer or law firm. Think billing. One of the chief complaints about external law firms is the billing process—that it is not streamlined, easy, transparent, predictable, or on time. Just imagine the value add if that were changed.

Given the complaints outlined in the Lawyer Skills Delta (Chapter 3) about the lack of collaboration with clients, offering to have an off-the-clock meeting focused on problem or opportunity finding—offering to go on an innovation journey—with a client is a tick. Another tick is demonstrating a new attitude about creativity, collaboration, and innovation. The point is there are different types of innovations and different types of innovators—such as those discussed in Chapter 2. The type of innovation that gets a tick does not have to be that of an extrapreneur or entrepreneur but instead an intrapreneur—and an intrapreneur can be anyone who hones the skills of creative, collaborative problem solving and follows the Three Rules of Engagement outlined in Part II of this book. The new attitude yields riches in inches. In *The Man Without Qualities*, Robert Musil writes that it is easy "to think in miles when you've no idea what riches can be hidden in an inch."[18] Although this new attitude may be a movement in inches, it delivers riches. Furthermore, these riches lend a new attitude about leadership and what you value in leaders. The type of leader you aspire to be will shift just an inch from the traditional leadership traits you have been attempting to hone. That shift in attitude about creativity, collaboration, innovation, and leadership style? That's the *A* in the A, B, Cs of innovation. But those riches don't come easily because innovation isn't just about doing small things; it's about doing "small things in a great way." And that "great way" includes a new attitude and as Winston Churchill is sometimes credited for saying, "Attitude is a little thing that makes a big difference."[19] The big difference? That's in new behaviors. That's the *B*, in the A, B, Cs, to which the next section turns.

B Is for Behavior

"But of course we can't take any credit for our talents. It's how we use them that counts."

—Madeleine L'Engle, *A Wrinkle in Time*[20]

As mentioned (and is worth repeating), we are moving into an era where the focus is on how lawyers work versus what lawyers do. The paradox, however, is that lawyers still get paid for what they do and often for how long it takes. We have all heard the expression about lawyers—that they "eat what they kill." Ironically, this premise holds true in innovation as well—even if not in quite the same way. In innovation, the main thing you eat is time. And that's one of the reasons lawyers don't like/want to innovate. It takes time. And that time feels wasted if not undervalued because, as stated above, it is hard to measure. A. W. Tozer said that "When you kill time . . . it has no resurrection." In innovation, the opposite is true. In an innovation cycle, the time you kill is resurrected in new behaviors (brought on by new attitudes and new skills) that help bridge the gaps that currently exist within the Innovation Disconnect.

A key learning from my years of leading more than 190 multidisciplinary, global legal teams through innovation cycles is that in the process of learning how to innovate and actually attempting to do so, the skills and behaviors that are honed are those that clients demand, value, and want. Essentially, going on an innovation journey with a multidisciplinary team is a way to fill the very skills and training gaps we have been discussing. It's also a great form of business development, although many lawyers fail to see it that way.

First, those skills at the bottom of the pyramid that were identified as C.O.S.T skills are honed. Project management, technology, business acumen, social networking, communication, presentation, leadership, mentoring, feedback, and industry knowledge—all of these skills that cannot be taught in a typical classroom become second nature over the course of 16 weeks.

"Through LWOW, I experienced firsthand the new and evolving technologies on the market and more effective ways to communicate with my team and clients, gained a better understanding of the current challenges facing the legal market and generated ideas to help resolve some of the problems we face day to day in legal practice." —Mentor, senior associate, Eversheds

"I loved being involved in LWOW and felt privileged to be there. It gave me an opportunity to learn skills for the future. Dealing with the different nationalities, personalities and cultures in my team was a challenge and certainly developed my communication and interpersonal skills as well as mentoring skills. I will carry these back into my professional life." —Mentor, VP and legal counsel, Barclays

An innovation cycle also hones the skills in the middle of the pyramid, those skills that clients desire that are essential to collaboration and creative problem finding and solving, including a growth mindset, empathy, cultural competency, self-awareness, humility, and risk taking. As it turns out, these are the same qualities of successful and inclusive leaders: empathy, emotional intelligence, industry knowledge, open-mindedness, growth mindedness, communication skills, cultural competency, high risk tolerance, and humility, for example.[21] These skills are developed in the process of problem finding, problem refining, problem solving, identifying target audiences, problem analysis, business case development, prototyping, testing, solution refining, and retesting with people from different backgrounds and cultures in different locations. In the process of co-creating a real innovation—a practicable solution (including a prototype with branding and a commercial) that solves a real problem faced by clients, consumers, or lawyers in the law marketplace—lawyers uncover hidden talents and learn to better leverage the talents they've had (but perhaps forgotten that they have) all along.

There is one central problem that remains of course: authenticity. I recently took a course with IDEO called Leading for Creativity, and it struck me that the course should have been called Leading *with* Creativity. For it is only when we walk the walk and do as we do (not only what we say) that has an effect on others. Many of my law firm partner interviewees complained of a lack of authenticity, an innovation officer without any power, a management philosophy that is hammered at off-site meetings but has no follow-through or compensation/incentive structure. And they complain of too much tolerance, turning the blind eye, to the proliferation of bad habits. It's criticizeable but also understandable especially when the culprits are revenue generators for the firm.

"We talk about innovation, we talk the talk, but we don't walk the walk. So many people in the firm are very passive aggressive in their approach. They nod and say they prescribe to this vision, but they print out their emails in hard copy and hide them in file cabinets in their office because they really don't want to change. And, as a firm, we are really tolerant of it. What we need to do is shake those people up and get them on board. And too many of our partners are not on board and it depresses our younger staff. They think, this is a waste of my time and why are my leaders telling me something that is inconsistent with the message that we need to be innovative?" —Partner, midtier Australian law firm[22]

Individuals at firms are resisting learning the new skills that will lead to a new *a*ttitude and new *b*ehaviors. These new skills change how we utilize our talents to contribute. They enable lawyers to leverage their talents to better practice and service clients with an Open Mind, Open Heart, and Open Door as described in Part II; they enable lawyers to behave differently. They change how we interact with others, how we lawyer, how we treat clients, how we practice, and most important, how we build relationships. How lawyers leverage the skills from an innovation journey to build relationships internally and externally with clients and to become more client-centric, more creative, more collaborative is what counts—even if they don't want to innovate or quit (let alone change) their day jobs. This new "how" is an innovation itself, an innovation of the self.

C Is for a Culture of Collaboration

"A bonfire in a strong wind is not blown out, but
blazes even brighter."

—Dilgo Khyentse Rinpoche

As I have written about in prior articles, one of which was published in Harvard Law School's *The Practice*, every corporate client is seeking a culture of compliance.[23] That's a given. Yet clients are also seeking a culture of collaboration: internally across the organization, within the legal department, and with the law firms. And law firms are beginning to recognize that for this challenge, innovation is the solution.

> *"One of the biggest challenges any law firm has is to establish how culturally we are different than other firms. Innovation is a strategy to tie us together."*—Deputy chief executive partner, top-tier Australian law firm[24]

But how? How can innovation help in reaching that goal? It used to be that the way companies approached culture change, whether a culture of compliance or collaboration—or perhaps both—was to do it from the top down. The operation involved infiltrating the souls and minds of leadership down to the trenches. In some ways, companies used to look at culture change the same way they did hiring a new CEO. Turn in the old one and get a new one and voila! Culture change. That protocol has begun to shift to a culture change that takes place directionally from the bottom up—or even, as I suggested in my prior article, from the middle out.[25]

Recent research, however, has suggested an alternative approach, one that is in sync with the mission of this book, which is for lawyers to attempt an innovation cycle within a multidisciplinary global team. In a recent *Harvard Business Review* article, Jon R. Katzenbach, Ilona Steffen, and Caroline Kronley argue that the way to make "cultural change that sticks" is to work "with" and "within" the culture, focusing on small interventions designed to change a small set of behaviors.[26] They argue that this is how companies such as Apple, Four Seasons, Microsoft, and Southwest Airlines succeeded in changing their culture to attain a competitive edge. They claim that these "targeted and integrated cultural interventions designed around changing a few critical behaviors at a time" change culture. They "energize and engage your most talented people and enable them to collaborate more effectively and efficiently." And they spread the word. Chris White from Clyde & Co described that his strategy to get people to innovate at his firm was to light some bonfires. That analogy lit a bonfire in me. That's what this approach is about—starting bonfires with small groups of people to attract the attention of the others. That's exactly what I had been doing for the past eight years, lighting bonfires. When the LWOW journey ends, each person goes back and starts a new bonfire in his/her organization to spread and burn. Think about it. When you see a bonfire from far away, you are lured by the light, the laughter, and the embers floating in the sky. And that's the goal of a small intervention, of creating a multidisciplinary team and having them go through an innovation cycle. The goal is to lure the others to join over time to slowly create "cultural change that sticks." As the authors of *Rework* point out, culture cannot be installed in an instant big bang push; it takes time—like the aging of scotch, the good kind.[27] Culture is oxidated. Small teams working on vetted projects designed to deliver TNT to the firm and/or clients raise awareness. Over time, buy-in and momentum build like a slow-burning flame. It is true that given the lawyer's temperament, the lawyer's lack of training, and the structure of typical law firms, there is a "strong wind" going against lawyers' attempts to create culture change within firms. However, the bonfires that are lit by the small teams (that include staff and managers outside of law) charged with creating a TNT will stay lit and "blaze even brighter" because of it.

To be clear, I am not suggesting that innovation should be a strategy in and of itself. It should not. Here, I am suggesting using innovation as a tactic to learn a new way to approach problem solving and to create a culture of collaboration because it is by attempting to innovate—going through a 16-week innovation cycle, for example—that we learn how to collaborate the way clients desire. Also note that the goal is collaboration and not collegiality, as discussed in the Innovation Disconnect in Chapter 3. Being collegial is not the same as being collaborative, at least not in the sense clients want. They want a culture of co-creation, energy, and change. This type of culture, a culture that embraces change, is infused with energy and, importantly, meets clients' needs at the same time it motivates the future generations of lawyers—the millennials, who want it too—and enables them to find satisfaction in their careers.

Thus, creating a culture of collaboration lends both tangible and intangible value to an organization. As the managing partner of Vieira de Almeida (VDA) explained, after his firm won the *Financial Times* award in 2013 for continental Europe in part because they created an Innovation Forum designed to create not only innovations (80 projects and 20 ideas) but also culture change:[28]

"One is the value of innovation as far as business is concerned . . . it helps us keep clients, develop clients, find new clients. It has a business value. And then there's an intangible value . . . people sit together and talk innovation—and the simple thought that they are sitting and talking together, there's value just in that alone."[29]

My point here is like that of Mary Doria Russell in *Children of God* who wrote, "The sign of a good decision is the multiplicity of reasons for it."[30] This rings true here as well. There is a "multiplicity of reasons" for investing in an innovation cycle, the most important of which is that even if you fail, you don't fail. Even if at the end of an innovation journey your team has not created a project that is viable or feasible, it is still what we call in LawWithoutWalls a project of worth. The innovation cycle, regardless, results in the ABCs: *A* for a new attitude and understanding of what innovation is in the law market and that it is achievable, *B* for new behaviors the come from a combination of new skills and inherent talents, and *C* for a culture of collaboration that builds that sustained platform for co-creation with clients and others in your firm or department regardless of generation. The end result is a client leadership edge opportunity. Those firms that follow the ABCs will have stronger and more durable relationships with their clients and a competitive advantage.

◆...Reflection Point Consider the following question: What do calculus, steamboats, oxygen, and the evolution of man have in common?

Answer: For the correct answer, turn to the notes at the end of this book.[31]

- After reviewing the answer, ask yourself: Why does that matter? How does knowing that impact how you feel about innovation in law?
- Now consider Renren.com, originally called Xiaonei.com. It was a copycat version of Facebook. It was even designed to look exactly like Facebook in terms of color and layout and logo. Renren was an all-out imitation, but it has been wildly successful. Is it a tick? Why or why not?

◆...Reflection Point We have talked about innovation as TNT, *tiny noticeable things.* some innovation can be big and hairy and disruptive. These are the projects that do not just add incremental value; instead they create new offerings. Many experts have diagrammed innovation on a quadrant to identify goals and value. The goal according to design thinkers is to invest in four quadrants. A basic four-quadrant map is shown below.

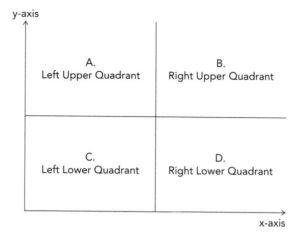

FIG. 5.1. A basic four-quadrant map to help diagram innovation goals and value add.

For the law market, however, investing in just one of the quadrants may make a difference in a low-risk way. But the quadrants vary by design thinker. Map out the four examples described below based on the quadrants and axes information provided. Then compare them. Which one best represents how your firm or department thinks of innovation? Which one does not resonate? Which one best represents how your biggest business client thinks of innovation?

- **Example 1:** A quadrant designed by Diego Rodriguez and Ryan Jacob[32] featured in Tim Brown's book.
  - **Y-axis:** From "Existing Offerings" at the bottom to "New Offerings" at the top
  - **X-axis:** From "Existing Users" on the left to "New Users" on the right
  - **A. Left Upper Quadrant:** "Extend Evolution"
  - **B. Right Upper Quadrant:** "Create Revolution"
  - **C. Left Lower Quadrant:** "Manage Incremental"
  - **D. Right Lower Quadrant:** "Adapt Evolution"
- **Example 2:** An innovation quadrant developed by Shirley Gregor, a professor of information systems (business informatics) at Australian National University, and Alan R. Hevner, a professor in Information Systems and Decision Sciences at the University of South Florida, called this the Knowledge Innovation Matrix (KIM). (Note: I especially like this because

it is first time I have seen anyone other than me use the word *exaptation* with regard to innovation in a business context.)[33]

- **Y-axis:** From low to high on "an Application Domain (Problem) Maturity Scale"
- **Y-axis:** From low on the left to high to the right
- **A. Left Upper Quadrant:** "Improvement: Develop new solutions for known problems"
- **B. Right Upper Quadrant:** "Exploitation: Apply known solution to known problems"
- **C. Left Lower Quadrant:** "Invention: Invent new solutions to new problems"
- **D. Right Lower Quadrant:** "Exaptation: Extend known solutions to new or different problems (Or adopt solutions from other fields)"
- **Example 3:** An "innovation management matrix" by Greg Satell, an author, a speaker, and an innovation adviser who frequently writes for the *Harvard Business Review.*[34]
  - **Y-axis:** Problem Definition: From "Not Well Defined" at the bottom to "Well Defined" at the top
  - **X-axis:** Domain Definition (as in "who has the talent/capability/ capacity"): From "Not Well Defined" on the left to "Well Defined" on the right.
  - **A. Left Upper Quadrant:** "Breakthrough Innovation"
  - **B. Right Upper Quadrant:** "Sustaining Innovation"
  - **C. Left Lower Quadrant:** "Basic Research"
  - **D. Right Lower Quadrant:** "Disruptive Innovation"
- **Example 4:** "The Four Quadrants of Innovation" developed by Hutch Carpenter, chief scientist at Revolution Credit, called Incremental Disruptive Innovations: Picking Your Spot.[35]
  - **Y-axis:** From "Manage Existing Market" on the low end to "Create New Market" on the high end
  - **X-axis:** From "Minimal Technology Change" on the left to "Radical Technology Change" to the right
  - **A. Left Upper Quadrant:** "Low risk, many competitors"
  - **B. Right Upper Quadrant:** "High risk, high reward"
  - **C. Left Lower Quadrant:** "Customer experience; cost savings"
  - **D. Right Lower Quadrant:** "High risk, defensive strategy"

The Three Rules of Engagement: Creating a Culture of Creativity, Collaboration, and Innovation

> *"It took me four years to paint like Raphael, but a lifetime to paint like a child."*
>
> —Pablo Picasso

Part II is designed to give lawyers specific approaches to face the current upheaval in the legal marketplace. It does so by focusing on the Three Rules of Engagement for creating a culture of creativity, collaboration, and innovation for lawyers: having an Open Mind, an Open Heart, and an Open Door.[1]

I call these the "rules" of engagement because lawyers are taught to think like lawyers with rules and strategy. In law school, we are taught to construct syllogisms or legal rubrics by connecting different rulings from different cases and putting them together under one analytical framework. I developed these rules the same way. I collected different theories from different types of research and put them together in one framework: Open Mind, Open Heart, and Open Door. These rules are important to learn even if—or especially if—you are a lawyer leader and you yourself do not want to innovate. There are two reasons for this.

First, you can't lead your team, department, or firm to innovate if you don't know what you are asking of your lawyers and are not exemplifying the mindset and behaviors of innovators. As Ralph Waldo Emerson stated, "What you do speaks so loudly" that others "cannot hear what you say." This may seem obvious, but I think it is worth repeating. I have been leading teams of lawyers for the past eight years in doing creative problem solving and developing innovations to law's problems. What I have learned is that in the legal field, it cannot just be about inspiring others to be creative—it cannot just be about leading *for* creativity. Instead it must be about leading *with* creativity. Some may believe it is sufficient to promote and support and even incentivize creativity and innovation in their firm. But as the director of knowledge and innovation delivery at an international law firm who is not a lawyer remarked, "It is not just being on a soapbox making the case for change [it is] working together . . . to implement change."[2]

At this point, I still have skeptical lawyers questioning why in the world they should be reading these silly rules of engagement let alone follow them. My response? Suspend your disbelief. Even if you don't *want* to innovate or you will never *attempt* to innovate or you don't want *hear about* innovation, you should follow these three rules. Why? Because (as repeated multiple times) the focus is changing from what lawyers do to how they do it. If you follow these three rules (professionally and/or personally), you will be better at listening, teaming, and creative problem solving. And the bonus? Your clients (and your loved ones) will like you more, and you will be a more inclusive leader. Unsurprisingly, the skills of inclusive leaders overlap with the skills of innovators.[3]

The best news about the Three Rules of Engagement is that in the mere act of following them, we adopt the feelings and behaviors that go with them and, in doing that, we may end up liking the rules, even if we didn't at first. Dr. Wiseman calls this the "As if Principle."[4] Common sense suggests that when we feel happy, we smile. There are myriads of examples and research that the counteropposite is true as well. If we smile *as if* we are happy, we eventually feel happy. So if we behave *as if* we want to follow the rules and *as if* we already have an Open Mind, Open Heart, and Open Door, eventually we feel as though we do and will enjoy it even if we set out with the opposite view. In fact, our views change in the process. When we are persuaded to do something we are convinced we don't/won't enjoy, psychology research shows that we often end up justifying our actions and convincing ourselves that what we are doing is not *that* bad and eventually it is even *okay*. So even if you are a skeptical lawyer at this moment, try out these three rules. You may end up convinced that following them isn't so bad after all.

This is not to say that learning and following the rules won't be difficult. The Pablo Picasso quote that opened this introduction is apropos to lawyers at this stage of our profession's development, where we struggle with the crutches of legal temperament and legal training described in Part I. Frameworks of and methods for innovation can be mastered—and that will be the focus of Part III of this book. But the mindset, skill set, and behaviors that are needed to innovate must be continuously honed. So this is the hardest part.

CHAPTER 6

Rule of Engagement 1: Open Mind

> *"A mind is like a parachute. It doesn't work if it is not open."*
>
> —Frank Zappa

Say "Yes, and . . ."

Most successful lawyers learned how to say no a long time ago. In law school, many of us were trained in the C-IRAC method for writing and organizing a legal discussion: you start with the conclusion; then you state the issue followed by the rule that leads to the conclusion; then you state your analysis, which is comprised of the facts as they apply to the rule and your reasoning; and then you repeat the conclusion. But if we're taught to start with the conclusion, how are we going to have an Open Mind? What do we do with things that are true but don't fit our conclusion if we are only looking for things that serve our conclusion? We say no to them.

Now we're grown-ups and we have grown-up jobs. We keep saying no. As lawyers, we still have to say no to our clients, but there is also a different kind of no we keep saying. Our bandwidth is limited, so to get things done, we must be selective about how we use our time. Learning to say no is actually in vogue now and continually makes lists that tout "the top 10 keys to productivity."[1] The problem with being good at saying no, however, is that we lose the benefits of saying yes.

My first "real" job after graduating from Dartmouth was in advertising. In 1991 I started working at Leo Burnett in Chicago. Before we were ever put in front of clients, we received a great deal of training on subjects such as our presentation style. We were forced to watch recordings of our presentations and critique them. At the time, I thought it was tough and scary, but today I thank Leo Burnett for getting me to stop saying *like* as much as my 16-year-old daughter does today and for teaching me the power of standing still—and pausing—when I present.

We also had the opportunity for some atypical training in improvisation. Leo Burnett paid for its employees to attend classes at Second City because it believed that learning how to improvise on stage would make us better listeners and communicators with our clients. It did. The backbone of improv, the one rule that *everyone* must follow to create a scene, is saying, "Yes, and . . ." The idea is that if you don't say "Yes, and . . ." during an improvised skit, you kill the scene. So if I say, for example, "I have this apple. Let's eat it together?" And you say, "No, I hate apples . . ." the scene dies, and I feel rejected (and the audience thinks you are a jerk). If you say, "Yes, I would like to join you as you eat your apple *and* I eat my orange . . ." we are not stuck. And I am not angry that you didn't eat my apple.

The reason "Yes, and . . ." works in real life (in addition to improv) is that saying, "Yes, and . . ." forces you to listen to what the other person is saying before you respond as opposed to simply interjecting what you want. Apparently, we spend most of our time forming our response when we are supposed to be listening, which is why we don't remember a great deal of what we hear.[2]

"Yes, and . . ." helps the listener tune in, and it helps the speaker feel as though she/he was heard—even if you disagree with his/her idea. Saying "Yes, and . . ." is not just about agreeing. It is about listening and building on what others have shared with you—not just waiting for your turn to talk.[3] As Daniel H. Pink explains in his book *To Sell Is Human*, we spend too much time listening *for* something and not enough time just listening and letting the scenario unfold like the actors do in improvisation.[4] Pink explains that doctors interrupt their patients in the first 18 seconds. Just as a doctor can't diagnose an illness in a patient if they don't listen to the patient, a lawyer can't solve the problem (or even understand what the problem is) if they don't listen to the client. I tell all of the lawyers that I teach at Harvard Law School's Executive Education Program and everyone who participates in LawWithoutWalls to erase the words *no* and *but* from their vocabulary and to start every sentence with "Yes, and . . ." I tell them—and I tell you now—that doing this one thing, saying "Yes, and . . ." will change the relationships in your life.

Saying "Yes, and . . ." is very hard to get used to. It feels funny coming out of your mouth because your body is screaming, "No *freaking* way!" But—or rather, *and* you should try it. If you don't believe me, try it on your children or your significant other. Consider the following real-life example that occurred between me and my 16-year-old daughter, Reading, when I had told her that she couldn't go out on a Friday night because my 17-year-old son, Jasper, needed to get up early the next morning to take his ACT test and I didn't want her to wake him accidentally when she came home.

> "Mom, it's simply not fair that I can't go out tonight. I don't see why I have to stay in just because Jasper has his stupid ACT test tomorrow."
>
> "*Yes*, I can see why you feel that isn't fair. After all, it's Jasper's ACT and not yours. *And* I have another reason you have to stay home, and that is because you didn't go to school today because you got a concussion last night at your soccer game."
>
> "But, Mom, I'm fine now. I just want to hang out at JoJos and watch a movie. That's not going to hurt my head, and I won't wake up Jasper when I get home. Seriously, this isn't fair."
>
> "*Yes*, I can understand that it seriously sucks to be in this position. If I were in your shoes, I would want to hang out with my friend too. *And* you know that when you have a concussion, you aren't supposed to watch any electronics. It's unfortunate, but it's what the doctors recommend so that you can heal quickly. If you are better by tomorrow night, I might let you stay out a little past your normal curfew. *And* this is a nice thing you can do for your brother. He will do the same for you next year when you have to take your ACT."

Try "Yes, and . . ." I promise it will change how people respond to you.

Putting "Yes, and . . ." into Practice

Now I understand that we can't go around literally saying "Yes, and . . ." all of the time; otherwise people will pick up on it and start to tune us out. But two ways come to mind as to how we can apply the "Yes, and . . ." mentality while in the service of the law.

To begin with, let's affirm that the law market is filled with hierarchies. There is a pecking order in the law, especially at law firms. These hierarchies, for whatever good they may do in terms of preserving the traditions of an organization, stop the flow of communication. They create preconceptions about who should speak and when—protocols that subconsciously dictate the value of any person's contributions.

The first strategy to apply "Yes, and . . ." at work is to avoid being the first person to speak at meetings. What would happen if we all came to a meeting embracing the idea that anyone can speak and that everyone who does speak should have the same amount of airtime (at least over the course of the project, if not doled out equally in every meeting)? According to research by Cass R. Sunstein and Reid Hastie, people generally follow the statements and actions of the person who speaks first in a meeting, and if that first speaker has power, people are more likely to silence themselves.[5] This is due to "cascade effects" and "reputational pressures," which can lead to groupthink—the opposite of the kind of thinking and collaboration we want for a group. When lawyer leaders (the people who are in power) speak first, they skew the rest of the meeting. I tell lawyers that if this is the *only* thing they get from my 90-minute session at Harvard on innovation, it will greatly change how meetings flow going forward: Just sit and wait and see who speaks first and listen to what she/he says.

In two different studies, joint researchers at Carnegie Mellon and MIT studied what makes teams smarter or more successful.[6] One of the three characteristics identified was that team members contributed equally to discussions over the course of the meeting day or project.[7] In other words, team discussions were not dominated by only a few[8] and, just as importantly, not the most senior few. This same elimination of hierarchy has been identified as one of the four principals that is key to the Toyota Production System, an immersion program that trains managers.[9] New managers work on the manufacturing line with production workers, breaking down the walls between manager and employee and between client and staff.[10] In the law firm context, given the hierarchies and incentive structures, lawyer leaders might have to be explicit about their intentions of equal airtime and require it. As one of the law firm partners I interviewed admitted, "Most of my best ideas are not my ideas. They come from the associates. But I have to force them to put their ideas on the table and make them speak at meetings . . . to ensure that others do not crowd out their voices."[11]

The second way of applying the "Yes, and . . ." mentality, in addition to not speaking first and giving equal airtime, is to consider that there is no ownership of ideas. This is hard for some people to accept. We've all had that boss who expects us to stay quiet unless we are asked a direct question. These are usually the bosses who only have us present something when she/he is scared that the his/her boss won't think it is a good idea or agree with it. But we also have likely had bosses who believe in "psychological safety," an atmosphere that creates confidence among team members that if they speak up, they will not be punished for their opinions or feel embarrassed or rejected as a result.[12]

What these good bosses buy into is the thinking behind crowd-sourcing and open sourcing. As Phyllis Dealy (an entrepreneur, advertising agency owner, and improv coach) often says, "Once you have an idea, it is the universe's idea . . . it's not yours. The moment it pops out of your mouth. It's out there for the world to gobble up." As discussed more in Chapter 8, Open Door, finding "the" idea is usually an additive process with others—a perfect usage of "Yes, and . . ." Steven Johnson puts it this way: "There are good ideas, and then there are good ideas that make it easier to have other good ideas."[13] "The" idea might not be the one you think is best. This can be hard for lawyers to accept because the nature of the law is to be self-protective and defensive. Yet what such closed-mindedness fails to realize is what Mary Kay Ash is quoted as saying: "A mediocre idea that generates enthusiasm will go further than a great idea that inspires no one."[14] This is why my closest friend from college, Jon Callaghan, founder of True Ventures, won't sign NDAs. If an entrepreneur asks for an NDA before pitching an idea, it is an immediate red flag. Clearly, this entrepreneur hasn't bounced his idea off enough people to get to "the" idea.

Exercise a Growth Mindset

Working the "Yes, and . . ." attitude through a nonhierarchical and equal brainstorming session is central to the process of innovation because it feeds what researcher Carol Dweck calls a "growth mindset." In her work, Dweck contrasts the growth mindset with a fixed mindset in the following way: People with growth mindsets believe that capability and intelligence can be grown by trying (and failing) and trying some more. People with fixed mindsets, on the other hand, believe they are born good at some things (and bad at others), so they are either smart or not, creative or not.[15]

It probably won't surprise you what research shows about lawyers. As discussed in Part I, we are more likely to be skeptical[16] and are more likely to have fixed mindsets,[17] which makes us risk averse and resistant to change.[18] Individuals with fixed mindsets seek out the things they are good at so that they succeed; this becomes a self-perpetuating cycle. According to Marcie Borgal Shunk, people with a fixed mindset view their past successes as proof of their brilliance and therefore are resistant to advice to help them improve and are apt to place blame for failures on others.[19] Thus lawyers might not keep up with the changing competitive marketplace described in Part I of this book; there the point was made that as the world has become a more complex place, its problems are not going to be solved by law alone. In fact, lawyering skills are just the base of what the legal professionals of today and tomorrow need. As described in the Lawyer Skills Delta (Chapter 3), they need to know project management, constructive teaming, and ways to build a business case, among many other skill sets necessary to contribute the way clients want. Finally, people with fixed mindsets may miss opportunities to grow and improve because they stick with what they are good at. If a lawyer with a fixed mindset doesn't think she/he is good at something and as a corollary doesn't believe she/he will ever learn, it isn't surprising that the lawyer doesn't take challenges that risk failure. Thus, as Shunk points out, efforts for cross-selling and collaboration among practice groups will often fail at law firms.

People with growth mindsets, on the other hand, believe that they can cultivate new skills and capabilities—that they can become smarter and more creative. Having a growth mindset is another way of describing having an Open Mind. A recent study about open-minded people shows that they are better able to change their perspectives and to demonstrate growth. They are flexible and do not have their minds totally made up. People with an open mindset are better able to suspend disbelief (i.e, live with cognitive dissonance, a theory developed by Leon Festinger in the 1950s). Cognitive dissonance is the ability to believe two apparently conflicting thoughts at the same time, and a recent study shows that open-minded people are better able to see two perspectives at one time.[20] Researchers showed participants two different squares. They put a red square in front of one of the participant's eyes and a green square in front of the other eye. They also had the participants take a personality test. Those participants who scored as being more open-minded were able to see both squares at one time, as opposed to those participants who had to alternate between the red and green boxes and were shown to be more closed-minded.

The good news is that the growth mindset, and by extension an open mind, can be honed.[21] At least Satya Nadella, CEO of Microsoft, is betting on it, as he has instituted a growth mindset company-wide initiative to do just that.[22] And Brad Smith, president and CLO, has jumped on board with the legal department. As part of that initiative, through my consul-tancy company MOVELΔW, I help the learning and development folks at Microsoft run an experiential learning program with teams made up of professionals from its corporate, executive, and legal affairs departments designed, in part, to teach lawyers to collaborate with a growth mindset. The program is modeled after LawWithoutWalls and the 3-4-5 Method of Innovation for Lawyers described in Part III. Mark Swatzell, a leader in learning and development at Microsoft, wrote an article about the pro-gram, describing it as the "perfect mix of guided and supported safety with real life stress and challenge, and builds skills in scoping, innovation, research, cross-group teaming, problem solving, storytelling, and presen-tation. Not just teaching concepts, but forcing you to use them in a real world environment."[23]

Make Yourself Lucky

> *"Chance favors the prepared mind."*
>
> —Louise Pasteur

The good news is we are not lucky by accident. If we can train ourselves to adopt a growth mindset—to open our minds—we can also make ourselves lucky. Many people chalk "luck" up to chance, to accident, in other words. "Lucky accidents" are given the credit for some of the best inventions of our day, such as penicillin.[24] Yet Alexander Fleming wasn't "lucky" to dis-cover penicillin. He had spent his life studying cures for diseases. He was studying influenza and went on vacation for two weeks; when he returned, a mold had formed on a staphylococcus culture plate. He then realized that the mold that had formed prevented the growth of staphylococcus. After that, he did many more tests to finally develop penicillin. In other words, Flemming spent his life and career investigating antibacterial sub-stances to cure disease, and after *all* that work, penicillin is considered a lucky accident?

A similar claim is often made about Post-its.[25] Like penicillin, Post-its weren't discovered by accident. A man by the name of Spencer Silver, an engineer at 3M, was working on adhesives when he discovered a glue that didn't stick. Almost everyone thought the invention was worthless except one man: Arthur Fry. Fry, also an engineer at 3M in the paper products division, attended Silver's presentation. Later when he was singing in the church choir, he became frustrated that the little pieces of paper he had put in the book to mark his places kept falling out—and that was when he had an aha moment. He reached down for the umpteenth time to pick up that little scrap of paper and thought to himself 'Yes! A glue that doesn't stick!' It wasn't luck. And it wasn't Eureka.[26]

Arthur had kept an open mind after attending Silver's presentation; by going to the presentation in the first place, he did what we all should do: he "stocked" it. He stocked his mind just as the headmaster Mr. O'Halloran urges in Frank McCourt's memoir *Angela's Ashes*: "You might be poor, your shoes might be broken, but your mind is a palace . . . Stock your minds and you can move through the world. Resplendent."[27]

When you have an open mind, you can stock it full of ideas and information and retain all of the various pieces to put them together later, like Alexander Fleming and Arthur Fry did. By keeping an open (and stocked) mind, you prepare your mind for chance, increasing the likelihood of connecting the dots when it matters most.

That lucky people aren't lucky by accident is something Dr. Richard Wiseman, a psychologist at the University of Hertfordshire in the United Kingdom and the author of *The Luck Factor*, has studies to prove. (The irony is not lost on me that a male doctor who sought to study luck was lucky to have been named a wise man.) Wiseman investigated why some people are luckier than others and whether it is possible to become lucky.[28] His research showed that lucky people are lucky, in part, because of their own attitudes and behavior. Lucky people follow their gut, expect positive outcomes, look at the bright side of failure, and maintain a good attitude when things go wrong. Compared to unlucky people, lucky people are more likely to see and take advantage of slim chances because unlucky people are too focused on looking for something specific. As an illustration of this, Wiseman describes unlucky people as people who go out with a specific purpose (to find their future spouse, for example). When they do that, they miss out on the chance that they might make a new friend or find a new business partner. Lucky people, on the other hand, make "lucky" decisions by keeping their options and vantage points open. Dr. Wiseman gave people a newspaper and asked them to look through it and tell him how many photographs it contained. The lucky people took only seconds, whereas the unlucky people took minutes to count the photographs. The reason? Dr. Wiseman had put a message on the second page of the newspaper that said in large bold letters more than two inches high: "Stop counting. There are

43 photographs in this newspaper." The unlucky people were so focused on counting the photographs that they didn't—or couldn't—see the words. Because they are so focused, they fail to see opportunities or to connect things in the way that both Fry and Fleming did.

Daniel Simons, co-author of *The Invisible Gorilla*,[29] is famous for his Monkey Business Illusion video on YouTube. He asks people to watch a video of a basketball game and count the number of times the ball is passed by one team. During the video, a gorilla walks into the middle of the game. Evidently, only about 50% of people see the gorilla. This can be attributed to what is called inattention blindness, an inability to notice something when you are not looking for it.[30] What does this mean for lawyers? First, highly skilled experts (like lawyers) may be more susceptible to inattention blindness than others.[31] This is because as we have become more expert at lawyering, we become better at it and better at predicting what will happen and deciding how to respond. With the development of expertise comes automation and expectation. We do things "automatically," failing to pay attention to them, and we notice what we expect and fail to notice that which we don't. Second, it is human nature to seek evidence for that which conforms to our expectations (also called confirmation bias). As lawyers, our job is to collect evidence. This leads to the third pitfall: We are more apt to notice what is relevant to us. This is likely why children who might otherwise sleep through a blaring siren, wake up from a deep sleep by just hearing their parent's voice. It's also why home smoke alarms have been created that use the parent's voice instead of a siren.[32] Children wake up because mom's voice telling them to wake up is relevant to them. A loud siren is not. So this relevancy-bent is true for everyone. Yet, it is riskier for lawyers because we are taught not simply to ignore but to discard that which is not relevant. Lastly, inattention blindness is tough to counteract because we have limited capacity.

To test that capacity, a few years after the first gorilla video, after too many people had heard of the gorilla, thereby rendering his study defunct, Simons created another video to see if people who knew that the test was about awareness would notice other peculiarities. Surprisingly, he came away with the same results. Knowing about the gorilla beforehand did help subjects see the gorilla—everyone did, in fact. However, knowing about the gorilla and the purpose of the test did not improve the subjects' ability to identify other unexpected events. Only 17% of those who had been tested with the old video noticed any of the other unexpected events in the new video. According to Simons, it doesn't matter what you are looking for—in the first case, the number of ball passes; in the second case, the gorilla and other possible changes—when you are looking for something specific, you miss the unexpected even when you are looking for the unexpected.[33]

So forget trying to expect the unexpected. That's not the answer. This is where some readers might be putting on the brakes because it sounds as though we can't be focused (or goal oriented) *and* open-minded (or lucky) at the same time. How do we square this with our need to focus in order to be successful?[34] The good news is that, as mentioned above, we can train our brains. We can train them to turn off. For example, we have trained our brains to unsee banner ads, one of the most popular advertising tools. This banner blindness, according to advertising research, occurs when a person is surfing the net for a specific purpose—to find something.[35] And we can train our brains to turn on. According to psychologists Chabris and Simons, we can do this simply by accepting (and remembering) that we all suffer from what they call the "illusion of attention"[36] (i.e., we believe we are seeing what is before us because we aren't aware of what we don't see).[37] That is, we can miss important details even when they are right in front of us. Staying conscious of this makes us less apt to presume that we are seeing all things or even things as they are. And according to Dr. Wiseman's studies, by practicing certain habits of lucky people (in mind-set and behavior), you can overcome the Monkey Business Illusions—and make yourself lucky (or luckier).[38]

Connect the Dots

> *"Chance favors the connected mind . . . [and those who can play Minecraft]."*
>
> —Steven Johnson, *Where Good Ideas Come From*[39]

It's not only preparedness that helps chance but also the ability to connect the varied stock we put in our brain in ways as yet unimaginable to us. In a twist on Pasteur's famous quote, Steven Johnson claims that successfully connecting seemingly unrelated issues, questions, problems, or ideas gets us to what he and the scientist Stuart Kauffman call "the adjacent possible."[40] Think about that term—it's not about reaching the possible, but what is *adjacent* to the possible. According to Johnson, the adjacent possible is "a kind of shadow future, hovering on the edges of the present state of things, a map of all the ways in which the present can reinvent itself."[41] This is a very apt description of how living with a growth mindset can help create the possibility for change. Yet the world is finite. The "adjacent possible" certainly does not equate to saying that *anything* is possible. In fact, only certain things are possible based on what has happened in the past, what is happening in the present, and what choices are made—what is adjacent, in other words. Johnson describes the process as a magically expanding house: "You begin in a room with four doors, each leading to a new room that you haven't visited yet. Those four rooms are the adjacent possible" opening up yet new rooms to explore.[42] My 12-year-old son would describe it like Minecraft, a computer game in which you make interconnected rooms, cities, or galaxies out of virtual blocks and doorways and paths.

But how do you get to the adjacent possible? Ironically, it's not that different from mastering Minecraft.[43] The answer is courage, curiosity, teamwork, and associating. According to research by Jeff Dyer, Hal Gregersen, and Clayton M. Christensen, associating is one of the five essential skills of disruptive innovators. (The other four are questioning, observing, networking, and experimenting.)[44] Association is the act of connecting things that might otherwise not be connected—even crazy things. Steve Jobs said famously, "Creativity is just connecting things."

Here's an example: In the early 2000s, the city of Glasgow hung blue lights on the streets to make them prettier. After the lights had been hung, crime decreased by approximately 9%. Although a causal connection couldn't be proven, Nara, Japan, decided to try it in its town—not to beautify the streets, but to see if crime would decrease. It did. Continuing to move along an associative track, the city of Yokohama thought that if blue lights could help reduce crime, it might help reduce that city's problem with track-jumping suicides, a real problem in modern-day Japan.[45] So the Keihin Electric Express Railway Co. changed the color of eight lights on the ends of platforms at Gumyōji Station (which had multiple suicides per year). The result? Suicide attempts went down to zero.

Even though the value of such associative thinking can be demonstrated in myriad ways, research shows that senior executives—especially at large companies—don't connect different things. According to Dyer et al., executives are great at analyzing, executing, implementing, and delivering results against defined goals.[46] They claim, in contrast to innovators, however, that senior execs don't know how to associate, which, as mentioned above, is one of the core attributes of innovators: They do not know how to connect the unexpected, such as a timer and a water bottle. As mentioned above, you can move from a fixed to a growth mindset, and you can learn to associate and think differently with practice.

⬛...Reflection Point Watch the following video about Vittel: www .youtube.com/watch?v=yyRgQJzlLus. Imagine how the team came up with the idea for putting a timer on a water bottle.

⬛...Reflection Point Ask each person on your team to take this quick test to assess what type of mindset she/he has: http://blog.mindsetworks .com/what-s-my-mindset. Discuss your results together.

⬛...Reflection Point Consider the following Taoist short story, "The Farmer's Luck," which has been told multiple times by multiple authors.[47] This rendition, my favorite, is by Jon J. Muth, author of *Zen Shorts*:[48]

"There was once an old farmer who had worked his crops for many years. One day, his horse ran away. Upon hearing the news, his neighbors came to visit. 'Such bad luck,' they said sympathetically. 'Maybe,' the farmer replied. The next morning the horse returned, bringing with it two other wild horses. 'Such good luck!' the neighbors exclaimed. 'Maybe,' replied the farmer. The following day, his son tried to ride one of the untamed horses, was thrown off, and broke his leg. Again, the neighbors came to offer their sympathy on his misfortune. 'Such bad luck,' they said. 'Maybe,' answered the farmer. The day after that, military officials came to the village to draft young men into the army to fight in a war. Seeing that the son's leg was broken, they passed him by. 'Such good luck!' cried the neighbors. 'Maybe,' said the farmer."

What is the main message about luck and mindset? Try to think of an example in your own life when you felt unlucky but, after a period of time, realized that you were lucky that things unfolded as they did. How does having an open mind change how you view what happens in your life? Is there such thing as luck?

CHAPTER 7

Rule of Engagement 2: Open Heart

> *"Now here is my secret. A very simple secret: it is only with the heart that one can see rightly; what is essential is invisible to the eye.*
>
> —Antoine de Saint-Excupery, *The Little Prince*[1]

Emotional Empathy

In Chapter 4 we discussed the lawyer's temperament and training: that collection of aptitudes and attitudes that hold true for a majority of lawyers in a majority of situations. One of the hardest things to tell a legal professional is about the value of empathy. And yet for the advantages it brings to teaming, innovation, sales, personal advancement, and company success, there are few traits on par with empathy.

Richard and Daniel Susskind believe that "the role and significance of empathy in the professions is often exaggerated" and that instead of teaching professional service providers how to be more empathetic, we should bifurcate the job.[2] It is almost as if they are suggesting that we should let the cold, unempathetic professional experts do their magic and the paraprofessionals who have a knack for empathy deliver the message. The problem with this solution is that to survive in the world in which the legal industry now operates—a world without walls, if I may—professional service providers must work in multidisciplinary teams. And if the other members of that team are cold, unempathetic professionals, bifurcation isn't a solution. It's a disaster.

In this chapter, we will look at empathy from a variety of angles, including its value for the entrepreneurial lawyer and teaming, its contagious quality, its contribution to cultural competency, and its necessity to providing valuable help.

The Entrepreneurial Lawyer, Teaming, and the Power of Emotion

Let's begin with the value of empathy for the entrepreneurial lawyer. As discussed further in Part III of this book, the only way to problem-solve creatively is to empathize with the target audience experiencing the problem. It is the core tenant of human-centered design. Think for a moment about the movie *Joy*. *Joy* was a story about a working-class, divorced mother with two children who developed the first self-wringing mop (with a removable head). It is only because Joy truly understood and empathized with women having to wring dirty mops by hand that she was able to create a mop as it should be. In *Joy*, the person who created the solution was the person who experienced the problem. The goal in innovation is to be able to experience the problem of the user or consumer to the same degree that she/he experiences it. Successful innovators, design thinkers, and creative problem solvers are empathetic. They put themselves in the shoes of the consumer.

Empathy is essential not only to solving problems but also to preventing them, especially when collaborating on multidisciplinary teams. Various studies, including those undertaken by MIT and Carnegie Mellon,[3] identify empathy as one of the top characteristics of smart, successful teams.[4] Teams are more effective when they are more socially sensitive to each other (i.e., when they can sense how others feel by reading verbal and nonverbal cues and relate to each other's differing vantage points and perspectives). The research shows that this ability to infer about other people's mental states, often called "theory of mind" (ToM) is also important for teams working virtually.[5] Those team members often need to be able to sense how others feel from nonvisual communications such as texts and email. Combining that with research conducted by Cass Sunstein demonstrates that teams fail when members misread or receive incorrect informational signals from each other. Therefore, we have our work cut out for us given that lawyers often work on global teams.[6] This means that lawyers must be good at both receiving and sending nonverbal messages (in person and virtually); otherwise, the team will not feel safe, and that can overshadow everything the team is trying to accomplish.

A recent study by Google demonstrated the importance of such "psychological safety" to a team's accomplishments (also discussed in the prior chapter).[7] Its Project Aristotle was named after the Greek philosopher who wrote extensively on the social aspect of human beings (i.e., how, as a species, we do well only in communal settings—in fact, we must live in groups to have society function at all). Rather than the common corporate practice known as "employee performance optimization," what this study of nearly 700 employees demonstrated was that when individuals share the personal, the messy, the emotional real-life events (versus sanitized tales from work life), team members bond, and that bond is more important to the team's success than expertise, ability, efficiency, or IQ. From the data-driven reaches of Silicon Valley comes the truth that emotional conversations matter most of all.

Before learning this, I had always believed that there were three fairly equal ways to motivate people: money, status/title, and love. This study proves that I was wrong; there is a hierarchy, and love/emotion is at the top. New research by Professor Amy Cuddy reveals a similar finding: that people make judgments and decisions about people they meet within seconds based first on a person's warmth.[8] Warmth was found to be more important than competence or imagined status. When someone is perceived as warm, they are also perceived as trustworthy. It is only when people trust us that they will share their true problems. This will likely come as no surprise to the rainmakers in the legal field who have been found to be less skeptical and more empathetic than other lawyers in Dr. Larry Richard's profiling study of more than 1,000 lawyers. In that same study, Richard demonstrates that empathy, along with ego drive and ego resilience, is one of the top three essential traits to being successful at sales (aka rainmaking) in the legal field.[9]

At this point, I may be getting a few head nods from the lawyers who are reading this. After all, they see the difference between the rainmakers and other lawyers. And although they may envy the rainmaking capability, developing the quality of empathy that helps drive this function makes them uncomfortable because of the lawyer temperament we have been discussing. The research on this temperament indicates that lawyers are not as sociable as other professionals and are uncomfortable with creating new, intimate relationships.[10] This does *not* mean that lawyers are antisocial or that they do not have intimate relationships in their life. Not at all. Instead they stick to the relationships that already exist—perhaps in part because their family or significant others helped them cultivate the relationships.[11] Combine this with the research indicating that lawyers are less inclined to enjoy the interactions that involve the heart than the mind,[12] and it makes sense that lawyers struggle in the area of empathy. No one likes being rescued less than lawyers (because really that's *our* job—to rescue others), but the research suggests that maybe, there are times we should let our guard down, get a little emotional, and let others on our team come to our emotional rescue.

When It Comes to Emotion: Beware, It's Contagious

Once the value of emotions in the legal workplace has been accepted, the next challenge is to sort out which emotions are of value because being clear on this matters. Besides helping us connect, emotion is infectious. Recent research by Sigal G. Barsade shows that moods are contagious not only among individuals but also at the group level, impacting group dynamics, cooperation, decision making, and performance. Barsade calls this "the ripple effect" and cautions group members to be aware that contagion is occurring even when the mood or emotion is not obvious or intense. Fortunately, his study found that positive moods were as contagious as negative moods, so the way out of the problem of teams that lack cohesion and innovation is the same way we got in, with real emotion but of the positive kind.

Emotions are caught two ways. One is that team members pick up on moods and emotions via nonverbal cues and behaviors.[13] This is different from a conscious use of empathy; here, people perceive the mood or emotions of another *subconsciously* and then copy them with their own facial expression, body language, and tone of voice.[14] The more empathetic people are, however, the more likely they are to mimic others.

The other way emotion is caught is by comparison and the power of conformity. People gauge the team members' mood. They then compare it to their own and almost automatically put themselves in the other members' position; they conform by catching the mood. Once one person does that, more people on the team do it in ripple effect. If a group is not diverse and therefore has a tendency to share similar moods or temperaments, the catchiness is multiplied.

As you might guess, positive moods had positive effects on team dynamics, improving cooperation, decreasing conflict, and increasing a team's perception of performance. The negative is also true, which has negative ramifications for anyone employed in a customer service job (which, let's face it, includes lawyers). The service provider can literally catch the negative mood of the unhappy customer, which then can lead the service provider to treat the client poorly, leaving the client even more dissatisfied. Even if the negative mood is resisted, the struggle in trying to overcome such a situation can lead to burnout.

What does this mean for lawyers? One downside: Lawyers are generally trying to help clients with their problems, and problems are often negative by their nature. Because their work immerses them in contentious struggle, lawyers are at risk for catching their clients' problems (i.e., the negativity associated with their problems). As we discussed earlier, the nature of legal work causes many practitioners to act as lightning rod salesmen, seeing thunder and lightning everywhere. They would do well then to check in with themselves periodically to make sure they are not creating an unnecessary wave of emotional paranoia.

The other downside is related to what Andrew M. Perlman, the dean of Suffolk Law School, pointed out in an article about the risk of conformity by subordinate lawyers.[15] Perlman makes the point that given the "laws" of conformity and the nature of hierarchy, subordinate lawyers will find it difficult to resist a superior's directive even if it is unethical. Similarly here, given the laws of conformity and the nature of hierarchy and the contagiousness of emotion, subordinate lawyers will find it difficult to resist a superior's emotional direction. As such, lawyer leaders have a great responsibility to lead with the emotion they want caught and copied, not the emotion they necessarily feel.

Does that sound easy? If so, consider the following social psychology experiments on conformity. In the 1950s, the social scientist Solomon Asch did a series of experiments to prove what is now called the Asch Paradigm that describes how someone's actions are influenced by a group. The television show *Candid Camera* attempted to exemplify this paradigm with the elevator experiment "Face the Rear,"[16] which was redone by the more recent program *Would You Fall for That?*[17] The two related experiments show the power of conformity when a person enters an elevator and everyone is purposefully facing the wrong way. The subject (the person who is not part of the "joke") enters the elevator and notices that everyone is facing the back of the elevator. Usually the unaware person makes some type of facial expression indicating that she/he thinks this is odd. Regardless, slowly but surely, the subject begins to turn so that she/he is also facing the back of the elevator. The power of social conformity hits home more intensely and amusingly when the experiment is varied so that instead of everyone facing the back of the elevator, at an agreed-upon cue, everyone starts dancing in the elevator. And yes, when the group starts dancing to a tune, the subjects join in as well.

This is the upside to the contagion of emotion. As lawyer leaders, this research means that we have power to lead not only with intelligence or effort but also with positive energy. Empirical evidence demonstrates that if leaders have a positive mood, it will be caught by employees and can improve work performance.[18] Furthermore, research shows that when members of a group share a common emotional state of being, they are better at tuning in with one another and that connection facilitates social interaction and group efficacy.[19] To that end, some companies have manipulated the catchiness of emotion to enhance productivity and change culture.

Cultural Competency: It's Like Making an Omelet—You Have to Break a Few Eggs

Empathy takes on another wrinkle when lawyers and legal teams are asked to connect and collaborate not only with individuals different from their own gender or race, but also country of origin and culture. Teaming across the cultural divides can provide challenging in even nonemotional situations. And yet cultural competency is likely the most important skill individuals need for successful lawyering in today's global world.

Just like technological competency doesn't come from reading about technology, cultural competency doesn't come from reading about how to get along with people exhibiting different cultural markers. Cultural competency comes from working with different people—and making mistakes. As I always tell my students, I become less culturally *incompetent* each year. I make many mistakes. I make assumptions that turn out to be wrong. I give advice to people that turns them off because of my tone, my word choice, or the rapidity of my speech. They may find it off-putting or "too American." Whatever the case, I only learn from my cultural mistakes if someone tells me or if I am emotionally empathetic enough to recognize the blunder when it occurs or shortly thereafter.

And sometimes I'm not. I remember my first lesson in cultural competency. It was the first year of LawWithoutWalls. At that time, six law schools were involved: four from the United States, one from the United Kingdom, and one from China. I had never worked with students who had been born and raised in China. We had our first meeting to go over the first three steps of the project the students would undertake. I suggested to the team members that they might conduct some interviews of lawyers and business professionals on their topic. I suggested that they might create their own survey. I also suggested some books and literature they might review. I made about 10 more suggestions, and I thought the meeting went great. I had given them many different resources and ways to approach their challenge and to learn more about the industry surrounding it.

The next week I got a call from the professor at the School of Transnational Law at Peking University. He asked me how I thought the meeting with the students had gone. I shared my enthusiasm until he interrupted to give me a very different and concerned take on the previous day's events. "I see," he began. "Well, what you don't understand is that to a Chinese student, a suggestion from a professor is not a suggestion. It is a requirement." His student had spent the last week trying desperately to finish all of the work I had "assigned." It was a learning experience for me (and for the student). In LawWithoutWalls, we always say that feedback is a gift that is hard to give but immensely valuable to the recipient. This professor gave me a great gift when he called me that day.

The cultural misunderstanding I just described was not just a misunderstanding of words, such as the difference between being "pissed" in America (i.e., angry) and "pissed" in Britain (i.e., drunk). It was a difference in vantage point. Groups of people of different nationalities view the world differently.[20] Our cultural map is the filter through which we see, hear, and feel the world. Culture greatly influences how we interpret what others say or do, and this applies not only to nationalities but also to the subcultures operating within one country at any given time. As the author Anaïs Nin once wrote, "We don't see things as they are; we see them as we are."[21] According to researchers such as Nancy J. Adler, this is because perception is "learned, culturally determined, constant, and, selective."[22] Adler's research identifies four sources of cultural misinterpretations—and evidently my blunder hit all four.[23]

1. **Subconscious Cultural Blinders.** These blinders occur when we make assumptions about someone's behavior based on how we behave in our own culture. Because so much interpretation of both speech and action occurs unconsciously, we may not have the awareness to question our assumptions. Without questioning those assumptions, we cannot address the chain of events that unintentionally leads from them.

2. **Lack of Cultural Self-Awareness.** Many people mistakenly believe that the hardest part about becoming more culturally competent is coming to understand others. Actually, the hardest part is understanding our own cultural characteristics and conditioning. By looking at ourselves through the lenses of others, we can become more self-aware—and refrain from using our results as an excuse to continue to behave a certain way.

3. **Projected Similarity.** Research shows that we assume that people foreign to us are more like us than they really are.[24] We view others in reference to ourselves, and as a result, we delude ourselves into thinking that we understand others and that they understand us. This can be exacerbated when everyone in a firm, an organization, or a department shares a similar type of job (e.g., lawyer).

4. **Parochialism.** Parochialism is at the core of projected similarity. We assume that there is only one way to be or to see the world: our way. In essence, we assume that the idiom "it is my way or the highway" is true. As Adler points out, "A rigid adherence to our own belief system is a form of parochialism."

Because lawyers are more skeptical and less willing to give others the benefit of the doubt, these four cultural competency landmines are particularly treacherous to navigate. The good news though is like the growth mindset, cultural competency can be honed. Unfortunately for lawyers who are resistant to risk and failure, the best way to learn and become more culturally competent is to fail at it—to break a few eggs. When we fail—and are made aware of it—we stop thinking that we know everything. We overcome what Christopher Chabris and Daniel Simons call the "illusion of confidence," which is essentially that the less competent we are at something, the more confident we might be that we are good at it.[25] If we study and practice something, however, we get better at the task and realize our real level of competence at it. As we stop overconfidently thinking that we know anything about another person's preferences as it relates to his/her culture, we can start to make progress. We can start seeing ourselves for the "very American" or "very male" person we seem to others. Most important, we stop talking. Instead, we learn to ask and to listen—not only to what is said but also to what is not said. As Kahlil Gibran is known for saying, "The reality of the other person lies not in what He reveals to you but in what He cannot reveal to you. Therefore, if you would understand Him, listen not to what He says but rather to what He does not say."[26]

Some Kind of Help Isn't Helpful

So far you may be feeling, 'Great! Empathy helps teaming. Lawyers like to help. I'm on board.' And, in fact, research has shown that one of the best ways team members can be helpful to their teams is by doing just that: being helpful.[27] For this reason, IDEO has made helpfulness a norm that spans all levels of its organization.[28] But being helpful (in the way it is especially needed in teaming) is not as easy as it seems, and it requires yet another kind of empathy and group awareness.

One of my best friends from college also went into advertising after college (at a different firm than Leo Burnett). She eventually had three children like me, and she project-managed her children like the advertising executive she had been trained to be. One of my fondest memories is her singing this song/poem by Shel Silverstein when she was cleaning up and her children were trying to "help."

> *Some kind of help is the kind of help*
> *that helping's all about.*
> *And some kind of help is the kind of help*
> *We all can do without.*[29]

I thought it was a brilliant (i.e., generationally competent) way to say, "Thank you, but no thank you." It pops into my mind periodically in my work when I experience people trained as lawyers trying to help and actually making things worse, yet having no self-awareness about it. We have all experienced this: the professor who changes your thesis as opposed to helping you tweak it and the overbearing investment adviser who starts every sentence with, "You should." We try to help. We think we are helping. Unfortunately, being effectively helpful in a unique situation doesn't necessarily come naturally, especially for lawyers. There are three reasons this is so.

1. Being Helpful Isn't the Same Thing as Fixing Things

There is this great video called "It's Not About the Nail" by Jason Headly. It opens with a woman sitting on a couch complaining to her boyfriend about the pounding pain in her forehead. We can't see all of the woman at first. We see part of her face and hear her, and we see her boyfriend's face trying desperately to hold his tongue as she describes the pain she is suffering in its different variations. Then she turns, and we see that she has a nail in her forehead. As soon as she is done explaining how she is feeling, the boyfriend points out that she has a nail in her head and suggests getting it out. Of course, she explodes and tells him that he *always* does that. He *always* rushes to fix things instead of really, *really* listening to her and trying to help her. "Can you just listen?" she begs. That is what she needs, she pleads. He says, "I'm just trying to point out that maybe the nail is causing this . . ." Then she gets even angrier. Finally, he acquiesces, and we watch him struggle (big time) to listen and to resist the urge to pull the nail out of her head as she describes in detail the pain she is feeling. It isn't until he stops trying to fix the problem and instead listens and says compassion-ately, "That sounds really hard," that she eventually thanks him for helping.

This video is a lesson about empathy and the importance of listening, as we discussed earlier. It is also a lesson about helping and how, sometimes, fixing is not helping. This may seem foreign to many who watch this video (and not just men, but yes, okay, men). Of course the nail in her head is what is causing her "sweaters to snag" as she complains about. But rushing to the solution of pulling the nail out could have many unforeseen conse-quences: she could bleed to death, the nail could be holding a tumor away from her prefrontal cortex, the blood could ruin the couch . . . These may sound far-fetched, but the point is that rushing to pull the nail out might cause another problem. Sometimes members of a team need to be helpful in a way that is needed at the time, as the right solution is worked toward.

For example, one of the four lessons identified as integral to Toyota's success with its total immersion training program is "Managers should coach, not fix." Steven Spear describes the journey of an upper-level man-ager (given the pseudonym of Bob Dallis) through Toyota's training pro-gram. According to Spear, through the training, Dallis learned that his job was not to improve operations. His job was to help the workers under-stand that improving operations was the workers' job and to help provide them with tools and opportunities to attempt to do so in a continuous learning loop.[30]

Unfortunately, lawyers are trained and paid to fix—to give answers. Therefore, they often listen only until they think they have the solution and then they jump to address the situation with their expertise. As suggested in Chapter 4, Lawyers' Crutches, sometimes empathic listening is needed so that we can understand the problem in its entirety. Sometimes team players are needed to go along while certain cultural issues are worked out. And sometimes asking more questions is more helpful than providing answers.

Being helpful isn't the same thing as offering to do the type of work you are good at in your specific area of competency or on a certain part of a project with your expertise. As we discussed earlier in the section on growth mindsets, lawyers tend to know what they do well and do that thing well over and over again. Thus, lawyers aren't naturally comfortable offering open-ended help. 'If the team needs a real estate expert's advice and that's my specialty, I'm all in. But if they need someone to count the widgets, why would I do that?' That attitude, however, is not the type of attitude that leads to helpfulness on teams.

A GC of a large media and telecommunications company in Australia described a great example of the type of attitude that is helpful on teams.[31] He had recently led an unsuccessful high-profile initiative to inspire innovative solutions to improve productivity and efficiency in the legal department. He was fed up, dejected, and at a crossroads. He was out to lunch with a partner from one of the law firms that had recently been awarded business because of its willingness to experiment with his company. The partner suggested that he talk to the firm's head of innovation and business development who had some experience in design thinking. She was a lawyer but no longer practicing. The GC thought it was worth a shot. He called her. She jumped at the opportunity and offered to explore and brainstorm with him. She met him soon after and asked questions—intentionally reserving any ideas for solutions. She asked him what was driving the efficiency and productivity issues. He explained that he didn't really know. Twice in the recent past he had hired external consultants to draft plans and processes to improve productivity, but the plans never panned out. She asked why. He thought for a minute and said that perhaps it was because there was no individual accountability and no support for the plan because it was driven from the outside in. So she asked how might she and her firm help co-develop a process that involves the department lawyers so that they have buy-in and that identifies what is driving the problems.

Together they developed the idea of hosting a couple of design thinking workshops to identify the pain points and ideate some solutions. She offered to lead these workshops. Her firm, although skeptical, agreed that she could lead them and agreed not to send a bunch of partners along that might stymie the workshops. The workshops included a mix of age and expertise of lawyers from the legal department. They conducted problem finding and idea inspiration exercises. Ultimately, the workshops led to great results, one of which was discovering that a big detriment to productivity was the number of hours spent in internal meetings. There was celebratory success in that alone—in identifying a source of the problem. The firm went on to help the GC and his department create a solution to the problem that ended up achieving a 55% decrease in the number of meeting hours, which translated to more than 30,000 work hours saved in one year. It also resulted in the corporation winning the "In-House Legal Team" *Financial Times* Innovative Lawyers Award for the year. And it was in large part because the firm offered to help its client in a way that was, well, *helpful*. True, the firm did many other things right (including spending time problem finding and fine-tuning, embracing failure, celebrating successes along the way, deep-diving into the culture and industry of the client's business, and collaborating in a multidisciplinary, nonhierarchical environment). But the first thing and likely the most important thing the firm did right was to offer to help in whatever way the client needed help. It offered to help on a completely internal issue with no expectation of a return on investment (as opposed to offering to help on issues that were related to the potential high billing work by the law firm). The firm asked how it could help and listened to the answers. Critically, it didn't rush to fix. It showed real empathy skills to understand the client's needs. And as a result, the firm provided the Shel Silverstein kind of help, "the kind of help that helping's all about."[32]

2. Followers Sometimes Help More Than Super Chickens

The second reason being helpful effectively doesn't necessarily come naturally for lawyers is because being helpful isn't about being the #1 producer, the superstar, or even the winner. This is a tough message for lawyers to hear—after all, our profession is adversarial by nature. We are taught from day one of graduate school that law is a competition, that our client comes first, and that winning is success. Moreover, we are taught to rely just on ourselves. Generally, we are graded individually and aren't assigned team projects—unless you consider co-writing a brief for a legal writing course as a 'team project' which might feature a conversation like this one: "Uh, you take the first part and I'll draft the second part and we'll turn it in as one paper." Repeatedly in law, each of us is graded separately and being better (aka a superstar) is rewarded.

Of course, there are some exceptions and more now since I started LawWithoutWalls. Indeed, I have witnessed an increase in project-based teaming in law schools by people who had been exposed to the LWOW model, including Georgetown Law's Iron Tech competition led by Tanina Rostain. This competition has students utilizing the technology from Neota Logic to develop apps to increase access to justice. Another example is the Legal Design Lab (developed by one of my first LWOW students, Margaret Hagan, and is very much like LWOW) designed to train law students and professionals in human-centered legal design through multidisciplinary teaming.[33] Even with these needed additions to the law school curriculum, by and large, law classes in the United States and the United Kingdom are focused on training individual lawyers to win alone, not teams of lawyers to succeed together. This is also true in law firms and even law departments, which reward lawyers chiefly or solely for their billable hour productivity. Again, there are exceptions, such as the experiential learning program I run for Microsoft via my consultancy MOVELΔW that is based on the 3-4-5 Method of Innovation for Lawyers (described in Part III). Another good example is Holland & Knight's recent initiative to team lawyers by industry sector groups (as opposed to only by practice area). To meet their goals, the lawyers are forced to share not only information but also their clients. The superstars aren't rewarded, and in fact, they are squelched by the new norms of behavior insisted upon by the managing partner. These initiatives should be applauded as a way to break down the walls that have been built in and across firms, departments, and law schools. It is these walls that have supported the hierarchical nature of law firms, legal departments, and law schools and the rewarding and valuing of superstars over teams. According to research, however, lauding superstars over team players may not lead to more productivity.

Margaret Heffernan has this great TED Talk entitled "Forget the Pecking Order at Work."[34] She talks about a study on productivity conducted by evolutionary biologists William M. Muir and Heng Wei Cheng.[35] Muir and Cheng, professors at Purdue University, study productivity by studying chickens in part because productivity in chickens is easy to asses: you simply count the eggs. (Ironically, they are based at Purdue University not Perdue Farms, the famous chicken processing company. And yes, that is a funny coincidence!) Muir and Cheng started with one flock of average productive chickens. They selected the most productive chickens (those that laid the most eggs) and put them in what they called the "super-flock" of chickens. They did this over six generations. They then compared the average flock to the super-flock. And guess what? The average flock was healthier than they were before (i.e., they were healthier without the superchickens), and they were *more productive* than the super-flock. Indeed, the super-flock had only three surviving chickens. The rest of the superchickens had been pecked to death. This study is one of many demonstrating that energy is wasted when there is a pecking order. When there is a star who is aggressively "eating" the largest share, it has a negative impact on all.[36] This is an especially tough lesson for lawyers to learn given that we are rewarded for being superchickens. We profit from the business we bring in, and the hours that we bill are counted just like eggs.

Being a superchicken is neither helpful on teams, nor is it the same thing as being a leader. Lawyers are not trained to be leaders in law school, and they are not they trained to be leaders (or rewarded for being leaders) in law firms.[37] Deborah Rhode makes this point in her book *Lawyers as Leaders*. She contends that the legal profession is filled with individuals who have the potential to be leaders, but because our training does not focus on some of the core essential attributes to be leaders, these could-be-lawyer-leaders are ill-equipped to lead. This is one of the reasons executive education programs such as Harvard Law School's Leadership in Law Firms and Accelerated Leadership Programs are so popular. Trained or not, lawyers must lead clients.[38] And lawyers are (or should be) held accountable for how they lead. In the wake of corporate malfeasance, scholars and judges alike have asked "where were the lawyers?"[39] Presumably, this was a rhetorical ethical question: lawyers influence clients, and therefore, had they influenced them in the "right way," the ethical transgressions may not have happened.

Although it is true that we need leaders on teams and we need leaders to create cultural change, leaders can't lead without followers. According to Derek Sivers in his TED Talk titled "How to Start a Movement," the first follower is more important than the leader because without the first follower, there is no movement—there is no cultural change.[40] A leader of none is not a leader. The first follower transforms the person (who starts a movement) into a leader and lowers the risk for the third, fourth, and fifth person who follows, thereby increasing the number of people who join. Sivers makes his point by showing a video of a man at an outdoor concert who stands up on the lawn and begins to do a weird dance as everyone else remains seated, looking at him as if he is foolish.[41] Eventually, the first follower stands up and begins to join him, which peaks interest and eventually turns the dance from foolishness to interesting. The second follower joins in and so on until the foolish folks are those few who refuse to get up and dance. The moral of the story is that to create culture change "that sticks" (as mentioned in Chapter 5), leaders can sometimes lead more effectively by following. As in partner dance, the leader initiates the movement, but it is the follower who actively harnesses the energy and creates the momentum.

3. Even Superstars Need Help So That They Don't Burn Out

For decades, corporate America has been following the superchicken model of recruiting top performers from competitors to help boost company revenues. Like partner dance, however, this model fails without the follower. Boris Groysberg, Ashish Nanda, and Nitin Nohria's research proves just that.[42] They tracked stars across all types of professional services (e.g., law, management consulting, public relations, advertising, and investment banking) for six years. They found that the top performers were more likely to burn out when they moved from one company to another. Although they shine at first, they quickly fade.

To determine why stars fade, why they were unable to maintain their success level, the trio of researchers completed another study of more than 1,000 top performers working at approximately 80 investments banks across the United States over an eight-year period. This research confirmed the earlier findings: stars do not stay in their new organizations for long despite the large salaries and incentives that enticed them to move in the first place. Even more surprising than their lack of longevity was the fact that the superstars' performance drops on average about 20% and does not rise back to prior levels even five years after their move. Furthermore, the performance of the group to which the star joined dips significantly and the company's valuation decreases.

The interesting part about this research, though, is why this occurs. And the why is that success doesn't come to us alone. Accomplished professionals tend to believe that they (individually) are the main contributors to their company's or team's success and that they may be indispensable. Neither is true, of course, and research shows it. For example, one study of the performance of more than 2,000 mutual fund managers over a six-year period found that 70% of the fund's performance was attributable to the manager's company and only 30% to the individual manager. It was the institution's resources, processes, leadership, internal networks, training, size, and culture that were predominant factors in success—and in failure, such as when a star moved from one institution to another that varied in these dimensions. In addition to the institution, the team is key to a star's success. Groysberg et al.'s research shows that stars moving from one service firm to another are more successful when they move with their teams. Research of chief legal officers at S&P Corporations (that I co-conducted with John Coates, Ashish Nanda, and David Wilkins) supports the theory that clients are moving away from hiring individual lawyers or law firms. Instead, the relevant unit of choice is teams and departments.[43] Perhaps this is why we are now seeing teams of lawyers moving laterally from firm to firm. The following is a commonplace headline: "Breaking: Freshfields loses entire Paris real estate team to Jones Day."[44]

This appears to be true for individuals in varied lines of work, from lawyers to creative artists. Musicians who perform in bands, for example, tend to outlive those who are predominantly solo acts.[45] Think Bruce Springsteen and the E Street Band or Keith Richards and the Rolling Stones versus Michael Jackson, Elvis Presley, or Amy Winehouse. Although a lifestyle rife with drug and alcohol abuse plays a role, research by a team at Liverpool John Moores University in the United Kingdom studied 1,500 rock stars from North America and Europe over a 50-year period and found that solo stars were twice as likely to die young than those who were a part of a band.[46] Why? Musicians in bands have greater peer support, which can help stars better manage the rough, lonely, and temptatious lifestyle options that come with fame.[47] Bruce Springsteen may have said it best during the E Street Band's induction to the Hall of Fame speech:

> *"We've enjoyed health, and we've suffered illness and aging and death together. We took care of one another when trouble knocked . . . And one thing is for certain: As I said before . . . I told a story with the E Street Band that was, and is, bigger than I ever could have told on my own."*[48]

So the stars in the constellations? It's not just that they don't burn out—they shine brighter. Someone better tell Justin Bieber. Even if he has the moves like Jagger, Bieber might want to consider joining a band.

⬤...Reflection Point Look at the following sentence and quickly count the number of Fs in the sentence.[49]

FINISHED FILES ARE THE RESULT OF YEARS OF SCIENTIFIC STUDY COMBINED WITH THE EXPERIENCE OF YEARS.

By Nancy J. Adler

FIG. 7.1 Nancy J. Adler's cultural competency test.

How many Fs did you count? Compared to native English speakers, non-native English speakers are more likely to spot all of the Fs. For the correct answer, turn to the Notes section of this book.[50]

Nancy Adler uses this example to demonstrate our cultural conditioning. She explains that the reason native English speakers miss some of the words is because they don't count words that are not essential to understanding a sentence (e.g., words such as *of*.)[51]

"We selectively see those words that are important according to our cultural conditioning (in this case, our linguistic conditioning). Once we see a phenomenon in a particular way, we usually continue to see it in that way. Once we stop seeing of's, we do not see them again (even when we look for them); we do not see things that do exist."[52]

This is akin to Daniel Simon's Monkey Business and inattention blindness discussed in the prior chapter, and it is especially critical for lawyers. We learn to gloss over things that don't matter (e.g., evidence that is not *material*). Similarly, native English speakers gloss over *of's* because *of's* don't matter. How many other things are we simply discounting as inconsequential because they don't matter to us?

⬤...Reflection Point Ask yourself: when you travel on a plane, do you prefer a window or an aisle seat? Now ask your team the same question (by show of hands).

You will likely not be surprised to find out that people have strong prefer-ences. You may, however, be surprised that many people prefer a type of seat different from what you prefer and that research shows that, the split between window and aisle seat lovers generally is about 50/50.[53] This is a classis case of "projected similarity" mentioned above.

Now consider that research also indicates that window and aisle seat lovers are different from each other. Those who prefer window seats like to be in control, prefer to "exist in their own bubble," and are more selfish and irritable.[54] If you are a window-seat-lover and this is disheartening (or funny), there is a positive. Those who prefer window seats like to "nest."[55] Those who prefer aisle seats are more reserved, sociable, considerate, and amenable—yet, they are also are more likely to rest and sleep on planes.[56] I have explained this information to lawyers. Some laugh and others disagree, and it doesn't matter. The point is not whether these are our true attributes but instead that we send messages by simple actions such as sitting in an aisle or window seat, and we make assumptions about others' preferences especially when they are different from our own. Imagine all of the other kinds of choices we are making that are sending messages and the assumptions we are making as a result.

💬...Reflection Point Consider the following true scenario.

Client hires law firm as a panel firm and over the course of two years builds a really strong relationship with the partners (who are servicing the client's account). They create some innovations together, and the client rewards the firm with more business. Law firm and client go on to win multiple awards for their collaboration. Six months later, client gets a call on the weekend from one of the law firm partners who says that the firm "had a conflict check that was rejected and we're trying to get to the bottom of it." Client then finds out that law firm was pitching for a big piece of business with a competitor despite the conflict of interest. Without waiting to see whether the law firm would continue to seek the competitive business or stick with client, client kicked the firm off the panel. Client "felt betrayed and that the firms' partners were shafting their own partners. It was a stab in the back to us (the client) and to their fellow partners (who had been working with us successfully for a while). It was pretty interesting and pretty sad." Worse yet, client was shocked that, "The firm was actually surprised when we turned around and said we aren't going to give you anything now. We are done. They were surprised? Really?"[57] The firm thought it was going to be able to provide sufficient assurances and firewalls so that the client would waive the conflict. They thought wrong.

What went wrong here and why? How would an "open heart" have helped?

Does it matter whether the conflict was a "direct and adverse" conflict of interest (the kind barred by professional responsibility rules in the United States) or, instead, what might be called a "business" conflict? In answering that question consider this:

* Research I co-conducted with John Coates, Ashish Nanda, and David Wilkins shows that relationships between law firms and clients are very sticky.[58] Although clients will put law firms in what we call "the penalty box" and reduce work, they do not often fire law firms outright. One of the dominant reasons for terminating law firms—in addition to unethical billing—was conflicts of interest. We found that chief legal officers (CLOs) took directly adverse *and* business conflicts very seriously. Why would that be? Why would a business conflict lead to termination?

* One CLO interviewee in our study explained that he fired a law firm because the law firm "took a position that it did not regard as being adverse for purposes of disqualifying the firm from representing either [it] or a new client. But on a matter of principle, [the client] decided that [the company] could not be represented by the law firm even in light of the firewalls that might be put up or other typically acceptable ways of dealing with conflicts."

💬...Reflection Point Mister Rogers once said, "Real strength has to do with helping others." What do you think he meant by that? When was the last time you had to use "real strength" to help a colleague at your firm or in your legal department? What kind of help did you give?

In LWOW, we say that feedback is a gift. We say this because it is a kind of help that is often hard to give. It is even harder to give when the feedback is up or out (i.e., to someone more senior or to someone outside the organization or team). When was the last time you gave feedback to someone who was more senior than you or was outside your team? Share stories among your team and discuss the norms of giving feedback and why/how feedback could be considered a gift but takes "real strength" to do naturally and empathetically.

CHAPTER 8

Rule of Engagement 3: Open Door

> **"If the doors of perception were [open], everything would appear to man as it is, infinite."**
>
> —William Blake, *The Marriage of Heaven and Hell*[1]

The third rule of engagement is exemplified by why one of the greatest bands of all times (in my opinion, of course), the Doors, are called the Doors. In Open Mind, we talked about the importance of being able to get to what Steven Johnson calls "the adjacent possible." In Open Door, we move from this adjacent possible to what we might call the *infinite* possible. The Doors named themselves after the title of Aldous Huxley's book *The Doors of Perception and Heaven and Hell*.[2] Huxley, in turn named, his book after a line from William Blake's poem "The Marriage of Heaven and Hell": "If the doors of perception were cleansed, everything would appear to man as it is, infinite." Blake uses the word *cleansed*, indicating that we need to keep the door as clear as glass, devoid of our own biases, blemishes, and ego. I have substituted the word *cleansed* with the word *open*. With the door wide open, you not only see the world as it truly is, you also touch, feel, perceive, and receive it so that you can reach what the world can be. Keeping the doors open creates a gateway to the infinite possible.

The Story of Stone Soup

> **"Bring what you've got. Put it in the pot."**
>
> —Heather Forest, *Stone Soup*[3]

The idea of the *infinite* possible may seem a bit lofty and far-fetched. But it isn't; it is as simple as the story of stone soup. There are several different versions of this tale. In the one I present, two hungry soldiers visit a village to beg for food. At first the townspeople try to shut out the soldiers: they are poor and don't have anything themselves—how can they give to strangers? The soldiers then gather in the center of the town and announce that they are going to make soup with a stone. The townspeople greet this proclamation with disbelief, but eventually they bring what little they have (half of an apple, the stems from some onions, a tomato) and throw it in the pot. Although their individual contributions were not enough to make a meal on their own, together they make the most rich and flavorful soup they ever tasted.

"Stone Soup" is a story not only about the whole being greater than the sum of its parts but also about keeping an open door to people of different cultures, experiences, ages, IQs, and expertise. It is a story about diversity, in other words. Here, the townspeople (eventually) opened their doors to the strangers and reaped the rewards. Just like really, really good soup, really, really good ideas come when people from different disciplines, with different expertise, and with different perspectives "bring what [they]'ve got and put it in the pot."

The lore wants to tell us the opposite. The lore is that really good ideas, discoveries, and inventions occur by scientists alone in a lab in a Eureka moment.[4] Neither of these assertions is true. Innovation is rarely accomplished solo, and it rarely happens as an aha. As we saw in numerous cases in the Open Mind chapter, only after preparation and association (and a healthy dose of trial and error) did the moment of brilliance come. It is only after our ideas and thoughts have mixed with others' ideas and thoughts that we reach the pinnacle. Jonah Lehrer in his article "How to Be Creative" explains that "We tend to assume that experts are the creative geniuses in their own fields. But big breakthroughs often depend on the naive daring of outsiders. For prompting creativity, few things are as important as time devoted to cross-pollination with fields outside our areas of expertise."[5]

Lehrer points to the success of the Broad Institute, a cooperative effort between Harvard and MIT.[6] The Broad Institute, launched in 2004, states that it was created because the traditional setup in biomedicine wherein scientists worked in individual labs within specific disciplines wasn't working. Instead, what was needed was a way to cross-pollinate between the sciences: biology, chemistry, mathematics, and more. Well, it worked. In 2017, the Broad Institute and MIT announced that they were moving forward with CRISPR, its gene-editing technology that might pave the way to modification of human embryos to eliminate genetic mutations that cause life-threatening diseases and that are inherited at birth.[7]

Dozens of studies support how diverse teams are better when it comes to innovation.[8] Empirical research shows that diversity positively impacts accuracy, flexibility, creativity, thoughtfulness, and information exchange.[9] Studies of college students show that group discussion and thinking is more complex among groups with racial diversity.[10] Similarly, studies of the effects of racial diversity on jury deliberations show that racially heterogeneous juries more thoroughly analyze a broader range of information and make more accurate determinations.[11] Importantly, this research shows that the enhanced problem-solving characteristics do not result because of the contribution of the minority members of the group. Instead, racial diversity itself transforms the way the majority thinks, communicates, and collaborates.[12]

Studies also show that diversity of all kinds enhances problem finding and complex problem solving.[13] Moreover, it's not just racial diversity that matters, but also cultural, gender, and even psychological and personality diversity.[14] The benefits resound even when there is diversity in intellectual ability. Intellectually diverse groups often outperform homogeneously smarter groups.[15] In his book *The Difference: How the Power of Diversity Creates Better Groups, Firms, Schools, and Societies*, Scott Page highlights that cognitive diversity improves problem solving and can be more important than actual ability.[16]

Imagine that: a group that is diverse performs better cognitively than does a group of the best and the brightest. The reason this is so is because the value the person adds to a team is more connected to the person's different perspective of and approach to the problem (in Page's terms "their toolbox") as opposed to the person's ability to solve the problem. It is the diversity of approach and opinion that spurs debate and the debate that stimulates the creativity, while the group's accuracy is increased with communication and sharing of information. Thus, as Steven Johnson points out, the individuals on the team actually get smarter because they are a part of the networked, diverse team.[17]

Even diversity in level of ambition is an element that can help teams come to better solutions. Half-jokingly I always ask my LawWithoutWalls teams why they should counterintuitively hope that they get a lazy person on their team. Answer: lazy people have a different set of values and perspectives and generally find a more efficient way to get the job done.[18] Thelonious Monk, a famous jazz musician, said it best: "The piano ain't got no wrong notes." Just like the piano, there are no wrong notes in diversity. We want diversity in race; we want diversity in level of intellect, in gender, even in ambition. When it comes teaming—the more diverse, the better.

Mirroring the Collaboration of Jazz

Thelonious Monk knew what he was talking about because he was steeped in music that was made possible by diversity. Interaction among diverse people of different cultures, socioeconomic backgrounds, expertise, and talents is credited as the reason the 1920s was such a prolific creative era and resulted in some of the most timeless, consummate art and literature in history. It's also how jazz was born. Jazz was born with an open door, the result of a comingling of people of different races and cultures, including French and Spanish colonists, African Americans, and immigrants from Europe in the late 19th century. Creating jazz music is, at its essence, collaborative and creative problem solving. Jazz players do not simply play a sequence of notes that are planned in advance. Instead, each player builds on the other players' melodic motifs. Building on the process discussed in the Open Heart chapter, jazz music is a co-creative additive process wherein one person takes a lead that the others follow, then switches when another person takes the lead. Even the leaders, however, are following in some respect as they can't just play whatever they want. They must say "Yes, and . . ." in the spirit of having an Open Mind. They must fit it in with and build on what was being played before to make it change and grow. Marc Gobe makes a similar connection between jazz and the creative process in the context of branding professionals and takes it one step further.[19] He recommends that branding professionals and consumers get together for a "brand jam" to brainstorm together so that companies develop and brand their products that are right for the market and stand the test of time.

Some of the most successful companies, such as Apple, Cisco, and Google, have adopted a jazz approach to develop innovative products and product improvements.[20] Steven Johnson describes Apple's development cycle as looking "more like a coffeehouse than an assembly line" where "design, manufacturing, engineering, sales—meet continuously through the product-development cycle, brainstorming, trading ideas and solutions, strategizing over the most pressing issues, and generally keeping the conversation open to a diverse group of perspectives."[21] Pfizer and Cisco have utilized this approach as well.[22] Essentially, what these companies know well is that notwithstanding the conflict that can develop with diversity,[23] diverse teams are more innovative, are more productive, and can provide a competitive advantage in the global marketplace.[24] A recent McKinsey report, Diversity Matters, examined 366 public companies across a range of industries and countries (including Canada, Latin America, the United Kingdom, and the United States) and found that companies that are more diverse across race, ethnicity, and gender are more likely to have financial returns above respective national industry medians.[25] McKinsey also found that companies with more diverse executive boards outperform other companies in earning and returns on equity.[26]

Diversity in the Legal Profession

This is at least partly why clients have been demanding diversity from their law firms for years. As we saw in Part I, the first calls for diversity came in 1999 and 2004. Then GC of Sara Lee, Rick Palmore, issued a "call to action" petitioning general counsels around the world to sign their names in commitment to advancing diversity in corporate legal departments and law firms.[27] This petition elicited rapid support. Within two months, over 70 GCs had signed the petition. Both the ACC (Association of Corporate Counsel) and MCCA (Minority Corporate Counsel Association) formally endorsed and supported it as well. One of the first companies to sign was Walmart, a leader in requiring their third-party vendors and professional service providers to commit to diversity.[28] Although the motivations for requiring diversity vary, many GCs have stated that a driving motivation is the benefit that comes when people from diverse backgrounds work together to develop creative solutions to problems.[29]

Consider for a moment the success story of VDA's *Financial Times* win in 2013 for most innovative law firm in continental Europe.[30] Two things made this firm different from other firms with regard to diversity. First, the founder himself, Vasco Vieira de Almeida, came from a diverse background. In addition to being a lawyer, he was a banker, a cabinet minister, an economic adviser, and, interestingly enough, a criminal—having been jailed two times. These diverse experiences, talents, and expertise enabled him to connect dots that others might not have done and to empathize in a way that is different from other lawyers. Second, likely because of his experience, Vasco added two positions to his law firm that at the time were not commonplace. He hired a financial director and an HR director. Likely both added value in strategic and important ways.

But this is the exception, not the rule. The world has caught on to the diversity secret . . . the legal profession, not so much. Despite calls for diversity having existed for two decades, according to research by Professor Deborah Rhode, Stanford Law School, the legal profession is one of the least diverse professions in the nation.[31] Despite the appearance of an increase in diversity among lawyers, recent statistics from the Bureau of Labor report that 88% of lawyers are white.[32] And the lack of diversity is even more prevalent when only law firms are considered; minorities are underrepresented in law schools, but even these figures, according to Rhode, do not explain the statistics in law firms. The numbers are even worse at the top. According to the leaders of Diversity Lab, the percentage of female equity partners has been at about 18% for the past 10 years and the percentage of minority equity partners appears to have dropped a few percentage points.[33] It appears as though the legal profession and especially law firms have a way to go.[34]

The Importance of Diverse Teams, Diverse Networks

Besides the need to work in diverse teams to be innovative, a key ingredient to being a successful innovator is having a diverse, larger network from which to learn. Martin Ruef studied Stanford business school graduates who had become entrepreneurs. He found that those with the most diverse social networks were the most innovative and successful.[35] The entrepreneurs with acquaintances outside their organization, family, and close friends were found to be three times more innovative than those with more uniform networks.[36] Rob Cross and Andrew Parker's research suggests the same.[37] Their research demonstrates, counterintuitively, that the power of diverse networks is not contingent on the strength of the ties. Strong ties are considered those with longevity, strong emotion, and reciprocity, whereas weak ties are less intimate and time-intensive. Yet it is these weak ties or alliances that can add more value because they are generally with people different—diverse—from us and our professions. In his article "The Strength of Weak Ties," Mark S. Granovetter makes this point.[38] He hypothesizes that weak interpersonal ties empower the wide dissemination of ideas and create connection between formally disconnected groups. This informal dotted line connection between people, organizations, and functions enables innovation.

According to Richard Ogle, the ideal situation is a combination of weak and strong ties.[39] A study of Broadway musicals suggests that the most successful casts were made up of a mix of people who had worked together before along with people who were totally new.[40] This is likely one of the reasons LawWithoutWalls has been so successful. One of the mottos of LWOW is that it is like the Eagles' Hotel California, "You can check out but you can never leave."[41] This line is often misunderstood,[42] yet makes so much sense in LWOW. The commitment level varies greatly role to role. You can stay involved in any way, small or big. We truly live by the concept of stone soup: bring what you got and put in the pot. Every year we have newbies who join our community and breathe new life into it in collaboration with the old-timers. And within the community, people build both strong and weak ties. Given how much LWOW offers and how much and how little investment it can entail, it is irresistible to leave.

Why an Open Door Is Difficult for Lawyers

Unfortunately, having a broad diverse network and weak ties (or a combination of the two) can prove difficult for lawyers for a couple of reasons.

First, lawyers are competitive and don't like to share. This may be in large part due to the compensation systems at many law firms, but it is also related to the lawyer's temperament discussed in Chapter 4. Heidi Gardner's research shows that when lawyers are working on the VUCA issues with their clients, they become even more risk-averse and more protective of their clients, thereby limiting access to other experts both within and outside the law firm who might be able to add value.[43]

Second, despite research that shows the value of weak ties (and a combination of both strong and weak ties), lawyers' professional rules and regulations (especially in the United States) favor the strong over the weak and disincentivize collaboration with other lawyers and even more so with professionals from other disciplines. For example, as I have written about extensively, protection from the attorney-client privilege and work product doctrine is put at risk when lawyers talk with third-party consultants—even when their advice is needed to help solve the problem.[44] For example, the U.S. Model Rules of Professional Conduct are written to specifically constrict interactions with people outside the legal profession.[45] Rule 5.4, called the "Professional Independence of a Lawyer," is written to ensure that lawyers' judgment is not even remotely impacted by outsiders.[46] It prohibits lawyers from forming partnerships related to the practice of law and sharing legal fees with nonlawyer professionals.[47] It prevents outside investment in ownership of law firms (something that is allowed in Australia and the United Kingdom).[48] It also prohibits weak alliances such as the formation of multidisciplinary partnerships in which both legal and nonlegal services are offered as a one-stop shop.[49] Essentially, these rules laud a closed environment and an exclusive one-to-one relationship between attorneys and their clients as opposed to collaborative problem solving on interdisciplinary and diverse teams. Instead of supporting the notion of stone soup, these rules imply that when lawyers collaborate with others (especially those without a law degree), there are too many cooks in the kitchen.

Although these rules may have been developed (in part) to protect clients, the public, and the integrity of the legal professionalism, they may also, as scholars such as Professor Bruce Green have suggested, be driven (in part) to protect the monopoly that U.S. lawyers have over the legal marketplace.[50] Regardless of motivation, they are inapposite to the research around the importance of diversity and multidisciplinary teaming. And they prevent lawyers in the United States from servicing clients the way they need to be serviced—with full-service client service as depicted in the Lawyer Skills Delta, Chapter 3. There is hope for lawyers, however, as countries such as the United Kingdom and Australia have opened up the legal marketplace to enable interdisciplinary collaboration in providing legal services.

Third, unlike the message of the movie *Field of Dreams*, just because we build it does not mean people will come. In other words, just because we open up the law market does not mean that the law market will suddenly become more collaborative. As is likely obvious by now, following the Three Rules of Engagement: Open Mind, Open Heart, and Open Door is not easy, especially for lawyers. The Open Door is particularly difficult for lawyers because (as discussed in Chapter 7, Open Heart) they are often uncomfortable with new, quick relationships, preferring to stick to what they know and whom they know, as well as to the intimate, solid, long-lasting relationships they have cultivated.[51] John Coates, Ashish Nanda, David Wilkins, and I conducted a study of more than 70 GCs of S&P 500 corporations to better understand corporate purchasing decisions. We found that relationships between in-house counsel and their lawyers are quite sticky. They are strong and long-lasting and require a great deal of time to cultivate.[52] Furthermore, as mentioned in Part I, Chapter 4, most lawyers, by nature, are introverts. Moreover, according to Susan Cain, a former practicing attorney and the author of *Quiet: The Power of Introverts in a World That Can't Stop Talking*, they are uncomfortable in groups.[53] Therefore, because lawyers are introverts, the door they must open is much heavier as it is antithetical to their nature. The door can be opened, however. Understanding that we are introverted (or extraverted) is the first step in attempting new behavior. According to Daniel H. Pink the ideal is, ironically, to be average—neither extremely introverted nor extroverted. This is why he urges readers in his book *To Sell Is Human* to "get in touch with [their] inner ambivert" by working on the skills of whichever they are not.[54] Indeed, having an Open Heart, Open Mind, and Open Door will help introverts and extroverts become ambiverts.

Third Places

> *"You will come to a place where the streets are not marked.*
>
> *Some windows are lighted, but mostly they're darked.*
> *A place you could sprain both your elbow and chin!*
> *Do you dare to stay out? Do you dare to go in?*
> *How much can you lose?*
> *How much can you win?"*
>
> —Dr. Seuss, *Oh, the Places You'll Go!*[55]

So far in Open Door we have talked about attitude and behavior. We haven't yet talked about place and space. Yet as Ray Oldenburg makes clear, the place and space in which we collaboratively problem solve can make a world of difference. A third place, according to Oldenburg, is an environment that is not the home and not the office wherein one can interact with people from different disciplines and walks of life.[56] These wonderlands flourish because they create open and eclectic environments where people from diverse backgrounds and cultures, of different ages, and with different experiences and talents can interact. Steven Johnson points out that Vienna, created in large part by Sigmund Freud, was a third place for physicians, philosophers, and scientists to share thoughts on psychoanalysis.[57] Similarly, in Paris during the 1920s, scientists, engineers, writers, artists, and workers interacted and cross-pollinated ideas.[58]

Companies have purposefully created third places for their employees for this reason. For example, Mattel's Project Platypus, a development process created by Ivy Ross, a senior VP, resulted in the successful Ello, an interactive toy for five- to 10-year-old girls that enables them to create and build.[59] Project Platypus consists of 12 members who work (or more aptly, play) for three months in a studio outside headquarters. Time is unstructured at the studio, and the members participate in exercises designed to inspire creative thinking and new collaborative behaviors not unlike the exercises we do at our LawWithoutWalls KickOff.

It is about not only the place but also the "space." This is why each LawWithoutWalls KickOff attempts to transport participants to another world with wall art, music, themes, and space in which to move and co-create. Tina Seelig emphasizes the importance of space in her book *inGenius: A Crash Course on Creativity*. The way the room is set up, the color of the walls, the view outside the windows, the music that is played—all of these things can impact creativity and collaboration.[60] For example, when creating the Broad Institute, mentioned above, the creators shaped space and place "to foster an atmosphere of creativity, risk-taking, and open sharing of data and research."[61] Even the layout of the building forces scientists and researchers to comingle.[62] In addition to that kind of space, space—as in time—is also essential. As will be discussed at greater length in the next part, creation takes not only hard work but also time. Initiatives such as 3M's "15 percent rule," Google's "20 percent time," and Hewlett-Packard Labs are designed to give employees the space (as in time) to work on projects outside of their assigned work projects. These off-time policies resulted in the creation of Post-its, Clear Bandages, painter's tape that doesn't bleed, Gmail, Google Earth, and Google News.

As proven by LawWithoutWalls and LWOW X, today's third place can even be virtual. LawWithoutWalls is our community's third place. The cross-pollination that gives rise to Projects of Worth occurs across geography, generation, expertise, and discipline, and it does so online in our weekly LWOW Live webinars and in the teams' virtual rooms, called "Qaun" rooms (discussed more in Part III). In fact, we have created three layers of third places: our general community LawWithoutWalls, our weekly LWOW Live webinars, and our virtual team rooms.

The point is that third places can be created almost anywhere. As long as the place is off site and the space enables and promotes interaction with people from diverse backgrounds—and as Dr. Seuss urges, as long as "you dare to go in"—you can "only win."

Keep an Open Door to Your Past

"You aren't just the age you are. You are all the ages you ever have been!"

—Kenneth Koch

The last piece to Open Door is having an open door to our past. Why? Because having fun and being playful (as we did naturally when we were young) are important to creativity.

Say "Silly" Not "Stupid"

Growing up with a sister who has Down syndrome and a mother who suffers from manic depression taught me a great deal about many things. And besides being different from other families—our family also had different rules. For example, we weren't allowed to say the word *crazy* or *stupid*. And whenever we did, whenever I said "that's so stupid" or "that's crazy," my mom would look at me sternly and say that we don't use that word in this family. I'd roll my eyes and ask, "What am I supposed to say then?" "You should say 'that's silly,'" she would reply almost indignantly—as if this was a normal response. And of course my teenage self would think inside my head "That's sooooo *stupid*—saying *silly* is so stupid!" Obviously, my mom felt the way she did because the words *stupid* and *crazy* were derogatory. It was the 1980s. The former word was used to describe people with mental retardation, the latter, mental illness. Looking back, I realize now that it was a brilliant rule and when combined with "Yes and . . ." it enables people to have the freedom to say the "stupidest," "craziest" of things because they know they won't get labeled as stupid or crazy—instead, just silly. Stupid ideas should not come to fruition, but silly ideas? Why not? As Albert Einstein is often quoted, "If at first, the idea is not absurd, then there is no hope for it." And just think of all the silly ideas that have made tons of money (e.g., pet rocks, the Slinky, Silly Bandz, Pokémon Go [well, I don't think that one has made millions, but you get the point]).[63] Think of the first pitch for Twitter. *What if we built a social utility network for people to communicate information to others that limited the letter characters to 140.* Now *that's* silly.[64]

Channel Your Seven-Year-Old Self

According to the famous cartoonist Hugh MacLeod, "Everyone is born creative; everyone is given a box of crayons in kindergarten. Then when you hit puberty they take the crayons away and replace them with dry, uninspiring books on algebra, history, etc. Being suddenly hit years later with the 'creative bug' is just a wee voice telling you, 'I'd like my crayons back, please.'"[65]

When you were seven years old and someone handed you some paper and crayons, you would start coloring. Today if someone handed you some paper and crayons, you might respond (at best) by asking, "What would you like me to color?" Or you might say, "Why are you giving me this?" At worst, you might wave your hand to signify that you didn't want paper and crayons at all. Same thing with LEGOs. If I told you right now that you had to play with one little LEGO figure and five LEGO blocks for the next hour and not talk to anyone but yourself, many of you would go bonkers. But when you were seven years old? The crayons and paper or the LEGOs (along with the solitude) might be a joy. Well, it turns out that if we imagine our seven-year-old self, we become more creative.[66] This is, in part, because fun triggers creativity. Indeed, research shows that people become more creative right after watching something funny.[67] And yet it's more than just about having fun. Keeping an open door to our past is representative of letting go of our inhibitions, tearing down the walls we put up and getting rid of the zippers we put on our lips (not to mention the behind-the-eyes eye-roll we have perfected so it doesn't show outwardly). Similarly, having a glass of wine can help creativity along with other relaxing activities such as taking a shower or going for a jog.[68] Essentially, keeping the door open to your past is one way to skip the glass of wine (but not the jog, of course). It is also a way for us to find our "flow," a concept first introduced by Mihaly Csikszentmihalyi.[69] Flow is that synergistic moment when we match our talents to the challenge at hand, so much so that we forget time and place. And at that moment, "we are all the ages we have ever been" and all the ages we will one day be—and it is at that moment that we know deep inside that we can reach the infinite possible.

☁...Reflection Point How much do you really know about the other people on your immediate team, in your practice area, in your department, or at your firm or company? How might they be similar to you? For example, they might have the same degree. How might they be different in nonobvious ways (i.e., in upbringing, outside interests, talents, networks)? And how might those differences add value? Importantly, how might you find out about those hidden differences?

☁...Reflection Point Imagine you shared a brain with five other people and the only way you could answer a question is by each person contributing only one word to each sentence. First, imagine the challenges that might pose for you. Second, imagine how differently you might respond to a question, what better answers you might give by combining your knowledge?

☁...Reflection Point As mentioned above, we were all born creative. When we were seven years old, we didn't hesitate to do the things we enjoyed with passion. Close your eyes. Imagine yourself at seven years old. Picture where you lived. Picture your room. Now picture your favorite toy or activity and see yourself playing with it or doing it. Try to capture the feeling. Then open your eyes. Try to bring your seven-year-old self to your next meeting.

PART III

The Innovation Possible: Putting Together the Theory, Practice, and Proof

> *"Though this be madness, yet there is method in't."*
>
> —William Shakespeare, Polonius in *Hamlet*[1]

During each of my interviews, I ask whether on a scale from 1–10 the interviewee agrees with the following statement: law firms must innovate or die.[2] Almost every interviewee responds with a seven or higher. Still, lawyers are sick of hearing it—especially big law partners. My research indicates that it is because of one (or more) of the following reasons: (1) their business model is not broken, (2) innovating doesn't come naturally to lawyers, and/or (3) lawyers don't know what we mean by innovation or *how* to innovate. Even if they are willing to adopt (or already have honed) the right skills and mindset, they are unsure how to actually innovate or lead their teams in an innovation cycle.

It is no wonder lawyers do not understand how to put all of the different theories and stages and behaviors together to "do" an innovation cycle from start to finish, especially given a lack of immediate financial urgency or the temperament to jump in with both feet. Furthermore, for an innovation framework to resonate, it must be catered to lawyers (i.e., designed to teach lawyers how to innovate in a way that overcomes the lawyer's temperament and training gap and that provides methods and tools to do it).[3]

Yes, although there is a "madness" to innovation, there is also "method in't." This part takes innovation from concept to action by putting together the theory (frameworks of innovation) with the practice (lawyers and a method of innovation for lawyers) and the proof (proof that lawyers can and do innovate with this method). To do so, this part introduces the Seven Essential Experiences that all lawyers must go through (and master) to achieve innovation and the 3-4-5 Method of Innovation for Lawyers, an innovation process designed specifically for lawyers who want to collaborate with clients to create innovative solutions to problems at the intersection of law and business. In the final chapter of this part, by mapping out the journey of one lawyer-led team that resulted in innovation from utilizing the Seven Essential Experiences and the 3-4-5 Method of Innovation for Lawyers, I provide proof that these experiences combined with this method work.

True, not every lawyer wants to learn to innovate or has the time to practice this method in its entirety. The beauty is that almost any project team can benefit from utilizing the basic structure of this method and adopting some of the Seven Essential Experiences. So this chapter is designed for all lawyers who want to better collaborate towards a more creative end-product whether that is an "innovation," or something more traditional like a three-year strategy, or a re-organization plan. This chapter provides the proof but as the old proverb, accredited to William Camden, claims, "the proof of a pudding is in the eating."

CHAPTER 9

The Theory:
The Seven Essential Experiences
for Creativity, Collaboration,
and Innovation

> *"We can't solve problems by using the same kind of thinking we used when we created them."*
>
> —Albert Einstein

It is not true that lawyers are not creative or that the practice of law is not a creative practice. It is. But as many law firm partner interviewees aptly point out, lawyers don't appreciate that the extent to what they do is creative and that creativity is a skill they have honed for years. And even if they do, they don't know how to apply that type of creativity to help them innovate. The challenge of applying creativity to our field is that lawyers are taught to use the same legal thinking in which they have engaged before, the same reasoning, the same processes, and the same opinions (precedents) to solve new problems. What we need is a new kind of thinking, a new theoretical framework, which is what this chapter is about. To that end, this chapter presents the Seven Essential Experiences that all lawyers must go through (and master) to achieve innovation.

Human-Centered Design Versus Design Thinking

Before we get to the Seven Essential Experiences, let's review another innovation framework that takes a human-centered approach. As many readers undoubtedly know, one of the latest buzzwords in innovation in the law is *design thinking*. It seems as though everyone who is talking about innovation in law is also talking about design thinking; sometimes you will hear people use the terms *design thinking* and *human-centered design* interchangeably. A useful way to compare and contrast the two is to say that design thinking is a method of human-centered design that was originally utilized by designers in the process of creating new products and was introduced later to the business world as a method of innovation.

Human-centered design (also sometimes referred to as user-centered design)[1] is an approach to innovation that is grounded in the needs and desires of the people who use the products and services that are being designed. Human-centered design focuses on two aspects related to the user:

1. The user interface (the interactions a person has with the product). For example, if the product is a Microsoft Surface Pro, the user interfaces with the size of the computer, the spacing of the keyboard, the way the keys push (and clickety-click), the shape, scope, and graphics of the screen, the way the keyboard connects to the screen, and the way applications open and relate to each other.
2. The user experience (the experience a person has during every interaction with the product). For example, the user experience of a smartphone includes the feelings and reactions related to the look and feel of the phone (i.e., the visual design), the marketing/advertising of the phone (i.e., the messaging by which a consumer finds out about the product), the branding of the phone (the message a consumer sends to others by having the smartphone), and the customer service related to purchasing, returning, and repairing the product.

Thus, inherent in any type of user-centered approach is research and analysis of the user and an iterative process of prototyping, reviewing, testing, reprototyping, rereviewing, and retesting with the user.[2] The ultimate purpose is to create a final product that is shaped *by* and *for* the user in both the user interface and the user experience.

Design thinking is a method of human-centered design that was transferred from the design world to the business world.[3] Thomas Lockwood's definition of design thinking is helpful here: "Design thinking is essentially a human-centered innovation process that emphasizes observation, collaboration, fast learning, visualization of ideas, rapid concept prototyping, and concurrent business analysis, which ultimately influences innovation and business strategy."[4] Since design thinking was introduced to the corporate world, it has been the subject of several well-known books and courses.[5] They vary in how they teach the method of design thinking. For example, Stanford d.school teaches design thinking as five overlapping, iterative phases: empathize, define, ideate, prototype, and test. IDEO teaches it as three overlapping, iterative spaces: inspiration, ideation, and implementation.[6] Heather Fraser exemplifies design thinking in business as three gears: (1) empathy and deep user understanding, (2) concept visualization, and (3) strategic business design (i.e., design of the business model).[7] Nonetheless, the essence of design thinking remains the same regardless of the number phases, steps, spaces, or nomenclature utilized.

Design Thinking and the Law Market

Design thinking, as a method of innovation, was slow to hit the law market. One of the reasons may have been because it was historically positioned as a way to create a new and better product and product experiences for the user—as opposed to a new and better service model that is not attached to a physical product. What has become clear, however, is that innovation required by clients is about not only products but also service. To meet this need, design thinking evolved to include what is called service design. Service design is intended not only to identify, connect, and optimize every contact point a client has with a particular service but also to help create new contact points.[8] As Tim Brown says, "Services are becoming more like experiences."[9] For those legal organizations that deliver a new product or a new type of service, creating a new type of experience is unavoidable. But even for those law firms that do not branch out in the types of services they offer, LawWithoutWalls and MOVELΔW demonstrate that design thinking methods can be used to help create service models in law that sync with the preferences of the client and enhance the client's experience.

Applying service design to the law market is somewhat complicated and challenging.[10] This is especially true at big law firms where client relationships are managed individually by partners instead of holistically by the firm. When service is managed by silos as opposed to being managed across an organization, it is even more difficult to ensure consistency and quality and to identify weaknesses and leverage learnings. Regardless of the hurdles, however, design thinking and service design are here to stay in the law market. Some of the best law schools (e.g., Harvard, Stanford, IE, and Oxford) offer innovation sessions or classes grounded in design thinking theory that are designed to teach the design thinking process. In addition, 35 law and business schools participate in LawWithoutWalls— which is an experiential learning program for lawyers (and aspiring lawyers) that is grounded in some of the principals of design thinking. The corporate law market, too, has caught the design thinking bug. Many of the GCs and heads of innovation that I interviewed mention that their departments, clients, or law firms have hired companies such as IDEO and Crazy Might Work to conduct design thinking workshops with their people. Furthermore, some of those big corporates along with some big corporate law firms have recently turned to MOVELΔW to help create and run short innovation workshops and longer innovation cycles for their legal department.

The Seven Essential Experiences for Creativity, Collaboration, and Innovation for Lawyers

Over the past eight years, I have put together my own way of teaching a human-centered design approach to innovation, like other thought leaders in the innovation space. Mine draws on my marketing and advertising background, where I was trained not only in business planning but also in professional services and to think not just of the numbers but also the delivery of the service. I was taught how to conduct consumer-focused research on both the end product and the user experience and to utilize that research to empathize with the end user and create solutions and new products that are viable, feasible, and desirable. And I worked on the development of new products with people from marketing, advertising, PR, events, legal, merchandising, product development, and sales. I have combined this with my legal training and research, along with my experience leading more than 190 lawyer-managed teams through a 16-week innovation cycle. Like most innovators or intrapreneurs, I am constantly tweaking my method, the 3-4-5 Method of Innovation for Lawyers, adding things that work and revising things that don't. Unlike most design thinkers, my focus is on teaching innovation to lawyers who are working with other types of professionals on multidisciplinary, multicultural, (and often) virtual teams.

For me, innovating (with lawyers) is a process that includes Seven Essential Experiences. These seven experiences are those that every highly successful innovation team must not only go through but also own—often repeatedly but not always in the same order. If you were to put the experiences in an ideal chronology, they would be as follows (even though they don't always occur in this order): (1) Nurturing (Self and the Team); (2) Falling in Love (with the Problem and the Target Audience); (3) Celebrating Important Moments (Births, Anniversaries, and Deaths); (4) Moving In (with a Narrower Problem and Target Audience); (5) Getting Engaged, Then Married (to a Problem and Solution); (6) Reflecting (Monitoring and Evaluating); and (7) Working Hard.

1. Nurturing: Self and the Team

At the core of most successful innovation journeys is a multidisciplinary team made up of very different types of individuals. Therefore an essential element throughout an innovation journey—and actually the very first stage of any journey—should be nurturing, focusing on the strengths and weaknesses of ourselves, the other individuals on the team, and the team as a whole. Every innovation cycle should start here, with nurturing and building trust, which is why in the 3-4-5 Method of Innovation we start with a KickOff that includes individual assessments, team personality mapping, individual and team goals setting, communication training, and teaming exercises. During the KickOff, we are first introduced to and practice the Three Rules of Engagement, including how to give constructive feedback, of course. Teaming and trusting do not necessarily come naturally to lawyers, so this step is even more important than it is in other types of industries.

To enhance this nurturing in LWOW, we provide teams with an anonymous hotline and a teaming coach. Regrettably, I didn't replicate this in MOVELΔW, as I thought the same types of teaming issues that occurred with and between students would not occur on teams comprised solely of professionals already in the workplace. I was wrong. In the MOVELΔW programs that I run, I have found that conflict can still arise when the teams do not spend enough time nurturing the teaming aspect of the team. No matter how old we are, we can "fight" and have conflict with team members, and that dissonance can derail progress regardless of how professional we are and how thick-skinned we are and how above all that we think we are. But airing these differences can help. Sometimes nurturing the self and nurturing the team can be in conflict because what is good for you individually and for your growth may not always coincide with what is good for the team and its growth and progress on its journey toward an innovation. Effective teaming is a balance between our own goals, our own cultures, and our own preferences and the needs of others and the objectives of the team.

2. Falling in Love (with the Problem and the Target Audience)

A core essential experience of innovation is what IDEO calls "Inspiration." I call it "Falling in Love." When we are falling in love in our personal lives, we are interested in every little detail (past, present, and future) of the other person. We ask all kinds of questions and attempt to connect with someone on multiple levels—from music, to food, to hobbies, to intellectual interests. We might even be fascinated with how our love interest brushes his/her teeth—seriously? That's wacky. And it is that crazy experience that we all need in innovation (multiple times). We need to fall in love with the problem. We need to fall in love with the people experiencing the problem.

Like the falling-in-love stage in our personal lives, in an innovation cycle, this is the time when we explore not only everything about the problem but also everything about the target audience: the user experiencing the problem or opportunity. It is at this stage that we create the consumer story from the point of view of the person who is experiencing the problem or has a need. The consumer/customer/target audience is the focal point. This is why Amazon's founder Jeff Bezos places one empty chair in each meeting. He does this to represent the customer.[11] When we are falling in love, all we see is the empty chair. We learn to empathize with the target audience (the group with whom we are falling in love) sitting in that chair and experiencing every facet of the problem.

Pretend for a moment that you were charged with solving the problems that a busy working mom has in making a salad as part of dinner for her three children. Your first reaction might be, seriously? How hard is it to make a salad? Then take a moment and think again. You are 43. You have three teenage children, two of whom are girls aged 14 and 15 who won't eat anything but salad because they are obsessed with their diet. Mom could just buy a salad from the same store she buys a grilled chicken for her son, but then it won't be "healthy," meaning it has more calories than a McDonald's hamburger and vanilla shake combined. Even if Mom can figure out a way to save time and have both the chicken and the lettuce delivered (bearing in mind that Instacart is not known for its ability to select produce), she must painstakingly wash each piece of lettuce to get rid of the dirt and grit. Then she has to pat the lettuce dry with a paper towel. And Mom must navigate between washing too little so that when her daughters begin to eat, she doesn't hear that little crunch when they bite down on a piece of grit that didn't get washed away or washing too much so that the lettuce tastes more like overcooked spinach than salad. Can you picture that? Then you understand what this part of the innovation experience is all about. It's about the problem. And it's about the mom experiencing the problem. Two different aspects of the problem that need to be experienced together and that were (thank goodness) fixed with prewashed and prebagged lettuce. (Now I just wish someone would fix the inevitable smell. Even when the date of expiration is five days away, bagged lettuce still has that awful smell.)

Ironically, the group of people that empathized with the working women with teenage children who developed bagged lettuce were not the lettuce growers. According to Professor Ranjay Gulati, this is because they were focusing on an "inside-out perspective"—on metrics related to sales and customer satisfaction—instead of what a pain it was for customers to prepare salad.[12] In a similar vein, in Bruce Turkel's book *All About Them*, Trukel warns us about the danger of seeing the world through our own personal understanding instead of attempting to see the world through our customer's point of view. He calls this "depending on one's own self-referencing criteria."[13] During this stage of design thinking, it is imperative that you consider the consumer's frame of reference, that you look at the problem from the consumer's point of view (not your self-referencing criteria) so that you can see what she/he sees and feel how she/he feels. It is about storytelling—but not yours. It's about telling the consumer's story in his/her voice through his/her lens. We have all of our teams create consumer stories in the 3-4-5 Method for this purpose.

This is especially tough for people in power. Daniel H. Pink cities studies showing that there is "an inverse relationship between power and perspective-taking."[14] Those in power are more likely to look at things from their own vantage point and less likely to adjust to that of others. Unfortunately, as mentioned in the section on Lawyers' Right-Arm Crutch: Our Temperament in Chapter 4, this means that empathizing—seeing things from a different vantage point—is especially tough for lawyers because lawyers are often the people in power in the room.

Of course, the goal is not just to empathize with the consumer, but to be inspired by him/her because when we are inspired, when we have passion for something, we are willing to put more work into it. Warren Buffett, Steve Jobs, and Mark Zuckerberg all have famous quotes about following your passion. And as in our personal lives, when we are in the falling-in-love stage, the best part is the passion. And passion is the only thing that gets us through the process of problem finding (which is hard and takes time). In a study of industrial design students, research concluded that creative results were more likely to be achieved by students who were problem-oriented (as opposed to solution-oriented.) [15] In other words, the more time a person spent understanding, defining, and framing the problem, the more creative the results were. This ability to frame and reframe is essential to the innovation process. We need to spend more time questioning to make sure we have identified the right problem in the right way for the right target group. In doing so, we are able to find a more effective solution more efficiently. As Albert Einstein once said, "If I had an hour to solve a problem and my life depended on the solution, I would spend the first 55 minutes determining the proper question to ask, for once I know the proper question, I could solve the problem in less than five minutes."[16]

People say that our job as lawyers is to solve our clients' problems, but that's not accurate. Our real job is to help our clients better understand their problems. As mentioned in Chapter 3 and as both Tina Seelig and Daniel H. Pink make clear, the best problem solvers are the best problem finders.[17] Consider this example by Pink. If someone says that she/he needs a new vacuum, a problem solver might suggest that the person go online and compare the different options and prices and order a vacuum online. A problem finder, on the other hand, might ask questions to determine *why* this person thinks she/he needs a new vacuum. I often ask lawyers to role play this scenario with me, and they struggle. I tell them to ask me "why?" after I tell them my vacuum cleaner is broken, and they laugh. They think: *What a silly question. Why would I ask you "why" you think your vacuum is broken when you have just told me it is and, frankly, it doesn't matter "why"?* Ah, but it does matter. In asking why, we might determine that the problem isn't that the vacuum needs replacing; instead, the problem may be that I just installed a new carpet and it is too thick for this type of vacuum. Or perhaps the carpet is made of such a material that no vacuum will work on it. If so, then what the person "needs" is a new carpet, not a new vacuum. In asking why, we bypass symptoms and find problems. Indeed, this is why we have all our teams practice the Five Whys (discussed in Chapter 11).

A similar example came from a group of my students. I co-teach a course at the University of Miami School of Law with Erika Pagano, called Innovation, Technology and the Law. For one of the group exercises, I have the students interview another group of students on a problem they have identified as related to law school. Then their job is to try to solve that other group's problem. The problem was identified as follows: too many undergraduates were using the law library, making it hard to find a quiet place to study. The team developed a solution that would track undergrads entering the library by utilizing a key card so that after a certain number had entered, no more could come in. When they presented the solution, the students who had complained about the problem originally were disappointed. The solution didn't solve the problem because the problem was not the amount of space the undergraduates took up; the problem was that they didn't follow the noise rules and thus made it hard to study. So what the students needed was not a way to prevent undergraduates from entering the law library and using it; instead, they needed a way to get the undergrads to comply with the rules about making noise. This group of students was eager to create a cool solution, and indeed their solution was pretty cool. But because they didn't spend more time interviewing their target audience (the group of students who had experienced the problem) and asking questions such as "why?" their solution missed the mark.

Furthermore, sometimes there is an opportunity to make something better that we don't see because we don't register the problem. What we have might work okay as it is. Consider bagged lettuce or bagless vacuums. We didn't *really* need either. But no one has likely ever changed a vacuum bag successfully without that gross "poof" of air and dirt that erupts from the bag when it is removed from the tube.[18] Tina Seelig calls this "need finding." She explains, "The key to need finding is identifying and filling gaps, that is, gaps in the way people use products, gaps in the services available, and gaps in the stories they tell when interviewed about their behavior."[19] Need finding is the exact opposite of one of the sayings I have already stated that I hate the most: if it ain't broke, don't fix it. One of the exercises I have created to help teams problem and need find is actually called just the opposite: "If it ain't Broke, Twist it and Fix it."[20]

The most important thing to remember at this stage is that what we are falling in love with is the problem or need—not the solution. So many times teams rush to solve a problem—rush to "move in" (the terminology we are using later in this chapter) before making sure they have fallen in love with the right problem. And it's important to celebrate the finding first because the finding is often the hardest part.

3. Celebrating Important Moments (Births, Anniversaries, and Deaths)

At this point, we have decided to zero in on one problem and one discrete audience. Now it's time to celebrate. That may sound crazy; we just started this journey, and now we are celebrating only that we have identified a problem (or perhaps the problem within a problem)? We are because problem finding for a discrete consumer/target audience is the most critical element and is often the most frustrating and debilitating to teams, causing conflict and disagreement. Just as you celebrate anniversaries with significant others, it is important to celebrate this transition. It is the thing that everyone forgets to do, and yet it is so easy . . . if only we would stop and take the time to do it.[21]

You will notice that the title in this experience also includes celebrating deaths. Just as people celebrate death with funerals or celebrate love with engagement parties, we need to take moments to celebrate our progress (or lack thereof) in the innovation cycle. This is because all team members likely must do what Stephen King is known for urging (via William Faulkner and he via Sir Arthur Thomas Quiller-Couch), and that is "kill their darlings"[22] at some point—to walk away from their exact interpretation of a problem or their previous framing of it. This "death" is progress. So this is a time to celebrate the deaths of those ideas and put aside any team conflict that might have arisen along the way. Whether we are moving forward with an idea or moving out to find a new idea we can love, we can celebrate that we took a risk, invested time and energy, and learned. Given that lawyers have a tendency to see risk under every rock, as mentioned in Part I, we don't always take the time to celebrate moments along the way to winning a case, solving a problem, or prevailing for our clients . . . because we might be wrong. As others have pointed out, the lawyer's job is to "pick things apart—to look for everything that can go wrong."[23] How can we celebrate until we know for sure we have won? Even when we are right about something, there is always the fear that something even worse is coming next and our job is to prevent it. Yet celebrating early on is important, especially for lawyers. Otherwise we risk burnout and team conflict. Actually, lawyers aren't the only ones who have trouble with celebration; it is a talent that many are losing:

> *"People of our time are losing the power of celebration. Instead of celebrating we seek to be amused or entertained. Celebration is an active state, an act of expressing reverence or appreciation. To be entertained is a passive state—it is to receive pleasure afforded by an amusing act or a spectacle . . . Celebration is a confrontation, Giving attention to the transcendent meaning of one's actions."*

—Abraham Joshua Heschel

4. Moving In (with a Narrower Problem and Target Audience)

The fourth essential experience in an innovation cycle is what IDEO calls "ideation." For me, this part of innovation is like moving in with someone. This is the phase in our personal lives wherein we lock in on person, perhaps with the hope of getting engaged. One discrete problem for one discrete target audience has been chosen, and now we start ideating possible solutions to that problem. Many different types of exercises can be used to generate problem-solving ideas, some of which are included in the companion handbook *The 3-4-5 Method of Innovation for Lawyers: A Handbook of Exercises and Best Practices.* Often, though, these exercises involve on-the-spot brainstorming, which can be uncomfortable for introverts (and therefore many lawyers). Therefore I recommend treating these exercises as tools you can use spontaneously during a team meeting not only as a way to spur creative thinking when you are stuck but also as scheduled exercises spaced out over a few days so that you are sure to discover that great thinking of the introverts (who need a few days to process).

As mentioned above, design thinking is an iterative, overlapping, and integrative process. The experiences are not attacked in order, progress is not incremental, and the enterprise requires a mix of left- and right-brain thinking. [24] This mix of processes can be difficult for lawyers because, as others such as Nicky Leijtens have experienced and pointed out, lawyers are results-driven, timekeepers, and methodical.[25] The back-and-forth between phases or steps and in types of thinking required can sometimes feel inefficient. Yet generating solutions demands nothing less.

During the move-in phase, we must focus on both divergent and convergent thinking. First divergent, then convergent, and then divergent and convergent again. Phil Charron provided a short description of both of these types of thinking in a blog in 2011.[26] He wrote, "Divergent thinking is taking a challenge and attempting to identify all of the possible drivers of that challenge, then listing all of the ways those drivers can be addressed. In practice, it's more than just brainstorming. Some analysis is needed so you don't put too many tools in your Swiss Army knife, but you shouldn't hamstring yourself with too many constraints, either." Convergent thinking, on the other hand, is what the crew on *Apollo 13* had to do to save the ship. They could only use what they had on board to solve the problem. Convergent thinking "is the practice of trying to solve a discrete challenge quickly and efficiently by selecting the optimal solution from a finite set."

Charron provides the following example to show the difference:

> Convergent thinking: I live four miles from work. My car gets 30 MPG. I want to use less fuel in my commute for financial and conservation reasons. Money is no object. Find the three best replacement vehicles for my car.

> Divergent thinking: I live four miles from work. My car gets 30 MPG. I want to use less fuel in my commute for financial and conservation reasons. Money is no object. What options do I have to reduce my fuel consumption?

Tim Brown defines the two types of thinking as follows: "During divergence, we are creating choices and during convergence we are making choices."[27]

Much like the time of engagement in our personal lives, during this phase, we test whether the solutions we come up with will work. We see what might be improved. Like couples moving in together to do a test run for marriage, we do a test run by creating a prototype and testing it on consumers and refining it and retesting it. Lawyers sometimes worry about this step. (Indeed, I see their faces cringe when I describe it). The word *prototype* conjures up three-dimensional images in their minds, and their skeptical side immediately thinks: *What in the world does this have to do with legal services?* But as design thinkers such as Tim Brown emphasize, a prototype can be "[a]nything tangible that lets us explore an idea, evaluate it, and push it forward."[28] It can be a static mock-up of a potential website or app that shows how a user would interface with the potential product.

Let me bring this to life as it relates to lawyers and the law market. The winning Project of Worth for LWOW X 2017 was Cybird, a game that teaches children how to recognize, report, and prevent cyberbullying. The Cybird team members didn't create the game in its entirety; rather, they mapped out the game flow and illustrated key components of the user experience using short animations to prototype the game and get feedback from our community.

A prototype can also be a skit or video that brings a story to life. One of the teams in LawWithoutWalls 2017 was tasked with making the relationship between lawyers and marketers more effective and efficient. This team was sponsored by a global healthcare company (which is why we will hereafter refer to it as the Healthcare Team). In response, the Healthcare Team devised Creative License, an AI-based solution that gives marketers instant feedback on high-risk words and phrases as they type—like having a lawyer, a compliance officer, and a brand guardian working on the same task at the same time. During its final presentation, the team set the stage for its problem using a video-recorded, humorous skit employing actual marketers and lawyers giving real examples of their concerns. (The skit even involved a LWOW team member from the company who played the hero as an anthropomorphized "Creative License.") To show Creative License in action, the team used another video composed of a sequence of screenshots with voice-overs to demonstrate how the product would look, work, and feel in real time. To see how the team got to this point, read Chapter 11, "The Proof: The 3-4-5 Method of Innovation Brought to Life" that details this team's journey through the 5 Steps to a Project of Worth.

Prototyping, therefore, is simply a way to bring an idea to life, to give it dimension—but not necessarily three dimensions. We prototype and tweak the prototypes until we are sure (as sure as we can be) that we are ready to implement the solution. However, one part of this phase that seems to be given short shrift in the literature is that during this stage, we must analyze not only the feasibility (workability and profitability) but also the viability of the solution (business growth and sustainability) to which we want to get engaged. This is why we move in with someone we have fallen in love with—to determine whether we can actually "do" this: cohabitate, share finances, co-own a dog, etc. After all of this analysis, we might still determine that the solution isn't viable for the long term or isn't feasible (e.g., the problem doesn't have a large enough target audience to make it worth solving). And we break up (i.e., we have to go backward). We must nurture ourselves to heal and then eventually move on to fall in love again. This breaking up is problematic for lawyers because it is an exemplification of weakness and failure that opens them up to rejection and criticism. As mentioned in Chapter 4, lawyers, according to Dr. Larry Richard, are in the 30% percentile in resilience and 90% of lawyers score in the bottom 50% for their capacity to handle rejection and criticism.[29]

5. Getting Engaged, Then Married (to a Problem and Solution)

The fifth essential experience is comparable to getting engaged and then married. We have selected one solution to implement for one target audience. The hope is that this engagement will go smoothly and we will get married to it (i.e., implement it for years and years to come). The hope is that the solution is targeted, viable, and feasible and that it achieves its objectives (e.g., makes money, builds brand recognition, etc.). By now, of course, it should not be just a hope. We should have put some numbers together in the moving in phase because we cannot select one idea without doing the business analysis. But at this stage, we fully test the business case, including the financials, timing, costs, projected revenue, or savings over the next five years.

This is a tough part of the innovation process for lawyers because in our industry, we generally don't have to create business plans and we weren't taught how to do that in law school. After eight years of leading 10 to 30 teams per year in which at least 50% of the teams are lawyers, I can say that lawyers of all kinds from different countries, firms, and legal departments do not like putting time, costs, or task flow/order into a plan. I constantly get pushback: "Why do we have to build a business case? If so-and-so thinks it is a good idea, he will find the money for it. We already showed you the need for it, and we justified it with some numbers." And I reply, "Yes, and we need more—more specifics, more numbers, more time estimates, and an analysis on ROI."

Another part of this essential experience is positioning and selling the prototype internally. This type of branding/marketing can't wait until we bring the product to market. This is why in the 3-4-5 Method of Innovation we require every team to have a brand name, logo, and commercial (in addition to a business case) for its proposal—even if the team's idea is a new organizational structure within its legal department. This is one of the biggest learning outcomes for internal legal teams. Why do we care about marketing or branding the idea when we will hire a team of branding experts to position it to our customers? The answer is because how you position and sell an idea internally is *as* important as the idea itself. Spoken like a true advertising executive.

Yet another type of branding and marketing and positioning is involved if the product or service is brought to market. The branding and advertising campaign that is developed "externally" after you sell the idea internally should be thought of as an entirely new project, one that needs to be put through the design thinking process of inspiration, ideation, and implementation. This leads naturally to the discussion of the next essential experience, which continually overlaps with this one (as well as the others).

6. Reflecting (Monitoring and Evaluating)

Throughout the process, there needs to be constant tweaking, testing, and improving along the way that can only be done by monitoring and evaluating and getting feedback. Because it can be hard to take time for these activities and because it is hard for lawyers to be critiqued, we institute feedback into the 3-4-5 Method of Innovation along the way at various intervals and in various forms. For example, at our KickOff, we introduce and provide training on giving and receiving feedback and we hammer home the message that feedback is a gift. Over the course of the four-month cycle, we have required feedback and coaching sessions and a midterm written reflection progress report.

We also assign every team what we call "Shadow Teams." Shadow Teams are based loosely on the concept of red teams. I first learned about red teaming from Cass Sunstein and Reid Hastie's article "Making Dumb Groups Smarter."[30] The term *red team* comes from the practice during the Cold War of having U.S. officers try to "think red" (i.e., like a Soviet trying to figure out how he might defeat U.S. strategies). U.S. red teams utilized Soviet technology and theory to try to destroy its own U.S. Navy submarine forces. The thinking is that by learning how to defeat yourself from the enemy's vantage point, you can protect yourself better. If you are offended by the concept of red teams, it might make you feel better to know that the Soviets did the same thing, calling them blue teams.[31]

In LWOW, the purpose of Shadow Teams is to play the role of devil's advocate, to find weaknesses. This doesn't mean we stop saying "Yes, and… " It means we also listen to the people who are saying "No, but" and who are poking holes in our inspiration and ideations. We look to the Shadow Team to be our naysayers to assist us in evaluating and reflecting on our projects to develop them further. We call them Shadow Teams instead of red teams because as Martin Luther King is known for saying, "Everything we see is a shadow cast by that which we do not see." The Shadow Teams are there to uncover what the shadow casts. In this case, a shadow is similar to the Jungian definition, where it is what we project but do not yet own. We help this owning by matching Shadow Teams based on personality gaps within the teams. First, we map each team utilizing DiSC, a personal assessment test that essentially identifies people as dominant doers, persuasive influencers, steady cooperators, and conscientious planners.[32] (This builds a common language on the team that proves useful during feedback.) We then match Shadow Teams in a way that fills each other's gaps (i.e., that have some of the personality types that are missing on a person's own team).

This essential experience is also important later, after implementation. Once a product or service has been created or improved, it must be continually monitored and improved in order to stay relevant and to compete with other products and services on the market. This is also true of ourselves. We need to continue to reflect on our own behaviors and efforts to ensure that we are living up to our potential—which leads nicely to the last essential experience.

7. Working Hard

The last but not least essential experience to any type of human-centered design innovation process is hard work. People often refer to Mozart's music as magic because of a fake letter that was published in a music newspaper in 1815. In this letter, Mozart supposedly claimed that his masterpieces came to him in one swoop, as if in a dream, as if by magic. All he had to do was wake up and write them down. In his book *How to Fly a Horse*, Kevin Ashton explains that the reality as evidenced by letters from Mozart to his family is quite the opposite.[33] Success followed failures. Mozart suffered from bouts of writer's block. He studied other musicians to learn from them. He rewrote and revised his compositions. The reality is that Mozart's music was magical, but it was not magic. Mozart's work was work.

In a similar way, further innovation involves taking risks, sharing ideas that are half baked as opposed to perfectly fleshed out, and running with ideas that are good enough as opposed to perfect. As mentioned in Part I, this is what clients want from their lawyers: partners in co-collaboration that are willing to proceed with something despite risk and incomplete information—even though this is especially tough for lawyers to do.

Thomas Edison's famous quote "Genius is one percent inspiration and 99 percent perspiration" defines design thinking. Indeed, he is in some ways, the father of design thinking. Tim Brown has contended that the idea of design thinking was exemplified by Thomas Edison's approach to the creation of a lightbulb because he did so in a customer-centric, systems thinking way.[34] If Edison is the father of design thinking, Albert Einstein is the son. And that is why I quote him at the beginning of this section. He understood that "We can't solve problems by using the same kind of thinking we used when we created them." Much like design thinkers today, Einstein understood that we need a new kind of thinking— a human-centered perspective—to solve old problems. Einstein used the scientific method, which isn't all that different from the design thinking process. Design thinking also utilizes a scientific approach to discovery. Like the scientific method, it begins with a problem and includes iterative feedback mechanisms to model, test, and revise a solution.[35]

Although it is true that design thinking cannot be distilled entirely cleanly into a step-by-step process, I believe, like Tim Brown does, that we can distill it into a systematic and practicable approach.[36] And this in large part is what the 3-4-5 Method of Innovation does for the law market: It combines parts of a design thinking framework with other kinds of business, marketing, and creative process methods to form an applicable (if iterative and messy) approach that can be followed to transform the culture of your organization or department and the ways lawyers collaborate to solve problems. It can also help lawyers create innovations, new service models, and better service experiences for clients. And the work never stops. Lawyers have been changing the way they practice since the beginning of time, adopting new technologies and new ways of doing business. That has no end in sight and neither does the need to keep innovating and changing.

◢... Reflection Point Which of the two types of thinking, divergent and convergent, do you think are harder for lawyers and why? Why might both be hard for lawyers? Consider the following:

a. Divergent Thinking: When I run innovation sessions with groups of lawyers and I give directions to brainstorm about a certain topic and to write down their ideas without any critique or reformatting, I am constantly telling the lawyers to stop talking or discussing one person's comment or idea, to stop analyzing it. This isn't true when I give the same directions to a group that is not dominated by lawyers. Why might this be so? Why is divergent thinking, especially on-the-spot divergent thinking in teams, hard for lawyers? Consider rereading the section in Part I about the lawyer's temperament.

b. Convergent Thinking: When I run innovation sessions with groups of lawyers and give directions to converge on one idea, eight times out of 10 the lawyers are fairly fast at converging and often use some type of voting process to converge. Sometimes a few of them in the group will feel passionately about one idea or another and take the floor to convince the others that this is the best option. Yet still, the way they ultimately decide is by a vote. And I have never witnessed a group asking another group (in the session) to weigh in on the vote. When I give similar directions to a group that is not dominated by lawyers or that is only business professionals, it takes the groups much longer to converge. Often they never use any voting system to select the direction in which they want to go. Instead, they confer with each other and build on each others thoughts. Then, eventually, as if by metamorphosis, they land in a unified position. And sometimes they even confer with other groups to get feedback. Compared to other types of professionals, why might lawyers be more inclined to resort to voting or advocacy or a combination the two? What are the pros and cons of the different ways to converge?

⚫...Reflection Point Consider the following challenge given to the Law-WithoutWalls team that was sponsored by Pinsent Masons:

- Cogito Ergo Sum: How can cognitive technologies transform the way financial institutions deal with the impact of regulatory change on their lending documentation?
- Now consider the solution this team created:
  - Clear Loan: A training tool for consumer borrowers and an analytics tools for banks to help banks reduce consumer complaints against it. The tool educated the consumer and at the same time gathered standardized evidence of compliance with regulatory rules the bank could use to counter complaints by consumer borrowers that might be later raised during the lending process. Thus the tool was designed to help protect consumers in the lending process but also help the bank avoid adverse judgments from the ombudsman when disputes arose regarding the terms of the loan and compliance with rules.
  - With whom did the team have to empathize to create this solution? How many target audiences are there for the tool the team created? (Hint: There are at least three.)

⚫...Reflection Point As mentioned above, part of design thinking is understanding the user's journeys with your product or service. Often innovation teams will create a user journey that maps out the way users currently interact with the service, website, or product. They do this to better understand user behavior and identify ways to support and/or enhance the experience. The first step in mapping out a user journey often starts with creating the user/consumer story (i.e., identifying your user's goals, motivations, pain points, and overall character—much like discussed above in Essential Experience 2: Falling in Love (with the Problem and the Target Audience). The second step is mapping each interaction the user has with the product or service. If you are a lawyer at a law firm, how might you map out a "law firm service experience" of one of your clients? What points of contact does the client have with your firm that occurs before you start working on the matter, during the time you are working on the matter, and then after you finish working on the matter? When does the client interact with professionals who are not lawyers at the firm? How else might the client interact with your firm (e.g., website, social media, different office, lawyer event, product/tool/portal/database offered by the firm)? Each time the client interacts with the firm, what is the context for the client, how is she/he interacting with the firm (through what devices, with how many different people), what type of service, response, functionality is she/he expecting, and what is his/her emotional state each step of the way? (Is she/he happy, annoyed, frustrated, urgent, interested?). Try mapping this out and see what problems or opportunities you discover.

CHAPTER 10

The Practice:
The 3-4-5 Method of Innovation
for Lawyers

> *"Inspiration is for amateurs; the rest of us just show up and get to work. If you wait around for the clouds to part and a bolt of lightning to strike you in the brain, you are not going to make an awful lot of work. All the best ideas come out of the process; they come out of the work itself counts."*
>
> —Chuck Close

This quote encompasses my attitude toward the 3-4-5 Method of Innovation I have developed over the years. It's a process, and every piece contributes. Everything matters—every moment and every little detail. This is the execution of innovation as opposed to its vision. It's one thing to describe the Seven Essential Experiences necessary for innovation; it is quite another to map it out into a process with steps, an order (even if repetitive at times and not entirely linear at other times), and exercises so that other people can do it. And it is yet still another thing to do this in a way that resonates with lawyers and their mindset. As Alfred North

Whitehead is known for stating, "We think in generalities, but we live in details." Following is a detailed description of this method I created so that lawyers working on multidisciplinary, global teams can make sense of the process of innovation and lead their teams in using it. Following is a process that will help the best ideas unfold because they aren't simply "wait[ing] around for the clouds to part and a bolt of lighning to strike." (For step-by-step instructions and real-life best practices, read my companion handbook to this book, *The 3-4-5 Method of Innovation for Lawyers: A Handbook of Exercises and Best Practices.*)

The 3-4-5 Method of Innovation for Lawyers

The 3-4-5 Method of Innovation for Lawyers is called this because it is divided into three phases over four months with five iterative steps overlaid along the way. It is designed to help teams (with lawyers on them) to learn to innovate and to create a solution to a problem—but that is just the top of the pyramid of skills required in the 21st century. It is also designed as a journey to create culture change and build relationships and to fill in the skills and training gaps identified in Part I of this book (e.g., the C.O.S.T skills at the bottom of the pyramid and the creative and collaborative problem-solving and problem-finding skills in the middle [that may be best represented by the Three Rules of Engagement: Open Mind, Open Heart, and Open Door]).

More specifically, this method is designed to do the following:

1. Foster a climate and culture for innovation and collaboration across the entity's business.
2. Connect people in teams across different offices, departments, and practice areas.
3. Develop the skills of participants in the following areas: group teamwork, creative problem finding and solving, design to delivery, leadership, mentorship, collaboration, intrapreneurship, project management, presentation, branding/marketing, and IT.
4. Deepen entities' relationships with clients (internal or external) through team-based collaboration.
5. Find solutions for business problems and identify new opportunities through innovation.

Three Phases

"Ends and beginnings—there are no such things.
There are only middles."

—Robert Frost[1]

There are three key phases in the 3-4-5 Method of Innovation for Lawyers. In some ways, the three phases mark the beginning, the middle, and the end—KickOff being the beginning, Virtual Teaming being the middle, and ConPosium being the end. But as you will see, although it marks the beginning, before it is over, the KickOff is as much a "middle" as the middle. And the ConPosium, although appearing as the end, is not the end. It is a continuation of the middle. So despite the three phases being in sequential order, remember that they are all middles. Let me explain.

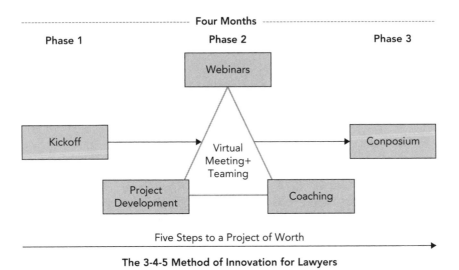

The 3-4-5 Method of Innovation for Lawyers

FIG. 10.1 A chart depicting the phases in the 3-4-5 Method of Innovation for Lawyers.

Phase 1: KickOff

"Existence Can be Rearranged, A Man Can Be Many Things."

—Tom Robbins, *Jitterbug Perfume*[2]

If you don't do anything recommended in this book aside from saying "Yes, and . . ." more often than suggested in Part II, definitely do this: provide a KickOff. It is the most essential ingredient to team success. I promise that if you host one—a real one—you will see a big change in teaming. This is because a good KickOff sets the tone and trajectory. When most lawyers (and law professors for that matter) are put on projects, they attend the first meeting of a committee where people discuss (or even read verbatim from) some email that was delivered with attachments about the goals of the committee. Generally, because the committee is too large (10+ people), the first decision is to divide into subcommittees. And being "sub" anything generally isn't good, especially for community building, teaming, and innovating.

So what is a real KickOff? A real KickOff is dedicated to nurturing the self and the team—the first essential experience of innovation described in the previous chapter. A real KickOff provides tools and sets protocols and expectations and, even more importantly, creates commitment. Every KickOff is designed to meet three goals:

1. Build an esprit de corps within and across teams;
2. Knit together engaged and committed teams of individuals;
3. Prepare participants for the personal and professional work ahead.

The length of the KickOff can be customized to the corporation's or department's needs but should be no less than three hours. In LawWithoutWalls, we come together for two days. In the experiential learning program I run for Microsoft via MOVELΔW, we come together for three days. At the very minimum, there should be a teaming exercise to meet Goals 1 and 2 above along with some kind of exercise that mimics what the teams will be asked to do over the course of the project and defines roles and expectations (Goals 2 and 3).

The teaming exercises can vary and be geared to the audience. But they need to be personal. They need to ensure that people bring their personalities and inner lives to light. Thus we give the teams big crates or big duffel bags full of tools—things to play with during our exercise (e.g., LEGOs, crayons, and spaghetti). And we play. We play with markers and crayons because it inspires us. We play music because it moves us. We play improvisation games because they change us. And we laugh hard.

One of the improv exercises we often "play" at the KickOff is called Mirroring. One person is designated the leader. The other(s) are the follower(s) (aka the mirrors). The leader(s) move and the follower(s) follow as if they are the reflection the leader would see in a mirror. We do this for about 30 seconds, then call out "Switch." We don't assign the next leader; someone just needs to take the reins naturally, and the rest follow. We do this a few times until eventually we say that we are not going to call out "Switch" again, and we tell the teams to switch roles organically—enabling one of the followers to take the lead or the leader to start to follow based on reading each other's body and facial cues.

So why do we do play games together like mirroring? We do it for the same reasons people sing in church, armies march in unison, dancers dance to the beat. We do it because (and this is proven by research) working in unison breaks down psychological walls, creates group cohesion,[3] and even has the added benefit of preventing free riding by team members. Seriously, two researchers from Stanford (Scott S. Wiltermuth and Chip Heath) tested this.[4] They put students in groups and asked them to walk around campus. Some groups were asked to walk around in unison in marching step as if they were in the army. Other groups were asked to learn a song and to walk around singing it together in time with the music. The rest of the groups were asked to walk around campus normally but as a group. When the groups returned, they were asked to play a board game. Those groups that had walked or sung in unison bonded more quickly and were more likely to help each other during the game (even when it involved personal sacrifice) compared to those groups that had not sung or walked in unison. For this same reason, we create a lip sync to a motivational bonding song such as "Ain't No Mountain High Enough" for every event. We have each person prerecord a tiny portion (in some silly manner that represents him/her), and then we weave it all together. We play it at the beginning of the KickOff as what we introduce as our "first collaborative effort." It is intentionally designed to display the entire community lip-syncing in unison—and in performing that act and in watching it together, we transform from individuals to a highly cooperative, socially integrated superorganism similar to a beehive. And if you think that's fantasmic, there's research to support it too! Selin Kesebir's research demonstrates that group identification drives humans to activate and display superorganismic features such as those displayed by beehives and ant colonies.[5]

In terms of substance, we always provide training on what the 3-4-5 Method of Innovation is and what the deliverables will be at the "end." We showcase examples of the method, either by having past teams present their journeys and their projects or by having the teams do an abbreviated (*very* abbreviated) innovation cycle themselves. For example, in years past, we have had the teams do a minihackathon over the course of the two days wherein the teams are tasked with solving a problem and creating a prototype over the course of 24 hours. They practice the Seven Essential Experiences and utilize the 5 Steps to a Project of Worth, thereby mimicking in shorthand the 16-week journey ahead. They find a problem, fine-tune a target audience and create a consumer story, create a solution, develop a pitch deck, and pitch the problem and solution to the entire audience in 10 minutes or less. We often have KickOff teams do this using an Ignite presentation format, which is a five-minute presentation with 20 slides and the slides advance automatically every 15 seconds. It is a challenging format that requires practice and discipline. Everyone learns how to say only the essentials in a language that everyone can understand. It is a useful technique to master. I'm convinced that this is how every lawyer should present any idea or solution to a client—with fewer than 20 slides (with very few words on them) and in five minutes or less—leaving the rest of the meeting for exploratory discussion and more detailed explanation of the parts the client cares about, as opposed to the parts the lawyer cares to explain.

Your KickOff will be even more effective if in addition to an exercise in teaming and in mimicking the project, you also include exercises designed to do the following:

1. Identify team members' work styles (e.g., through a personality test such as DiSC or Myers Briggs);
2. Teach problem finding and idea generation;
3. Provide communication and feedback skills training;
4. Identify and reinforce commitment to protocols, intentions, and goals.

If you have only three hours, that is not likely enough time for a real KickOff, but it is better than nothing. And no matter which exercises you select or how long your KickOff is, creating a culture of collaboration is the most important accomplishment. It is the secret sauce to meeting the three objectives above. How do we create this culture? How do we break down the walls and barriers and hierarchies, commit to the "now," and create a space of psychological safety? First, we teach the Three Rules of Engagement: Open Mind, Open Heart, Open Door (described in Part II). And we transform the space into a third place so that the Three Rules of Engagement are easy to follow. This enables collaboration and creativity and, just as importantly, rubbing elbows. We're all in it together.

As discussed in Chapter 4, in the Caliper Profile, lawyers score low on sociability; we'd rather enjoy existing relationships than create new ones.[6] The KickOff is designed literally to *kick off* those inhibitions. We remove tables, seating people in circles. We decorate the space to match a theme. We require casual dress code (no ties allowed); we use first names only and no titles. We do this to equalize (not de-statusfy) participants so that it is hard for people, even unintentionally, to use their power in status, title, or seniority to win a point through intimidation. David Rock, author of the article "SCARF: A Brain-Based Model for Collaborating with and Influencing Others," identifies status as one of the five domains of human social experience that can activate our brain and put us into threat mode. When someone challenges our status, it literally makes us feel as though we are being attacked by a burglar.[7] Instead we attempt to re-statusfy everyone: *You are now an LWOWer, part of the LWOW community, and we do not need to know your status in your other world.*

Then we celebrate our new existence. Talking about and embracing failure at KickOff is essential. But no one should feel as though s/he failed at the KickOff. At this stage, there needs to be much celebration, the metaphorical and actual ringing of bells, to create energy and excitement.

Finally, there is the planning. The good news is that lawyers are great at details. Although lawyers (by their own admission)[8] often overprocess (and overprocessing can be the death knell of innovation), this type of detailed thinking is essential for a successful KickOff. It is only by creating a planned-out KickOff designed to meet the three goals discussed above that we are able to create a culture of collaboration and rearrange existence. And that's how a KickOff should feel. KickOff participants should feel as though they have entered another world. And lawyers? They should feel as though they have entered into a new legal marketplace—a Law Without Walls.

Phase 2: Virtual Work

"Ring the bells that still can ring.
Forget your perfect offering
There is a crack in everything
That's how the light gets in."

—Leonard Cohen, *Anthem*[9]

Phase 2 is toughest because it is no longer about ringing our bells in celebration like it is at KickOff. It is about ringing the bells that "still can ring" even after things haven't gone so well. It is about finding gaps and cracks and letting the light shine in. Phase 2 is when the hard work gets done and many battles are *not* won. It is when the teams must adopt the Three Rules of Engagement to get through the iterativeness of the 5 Steps to a Project of Worth (explained later). It is also when the teams, in a virtual world, must live up to the intentions and protocols they set at KickOff. In the past eight years, I have noticed that at least 20% of teams experience a major teaming crisis that is founded on a lack of shared protocols, behaviors, norms, and expectations. This percentage is true across the board: in the programs I run with students in LWOW and the programs I run without students in MOVELΔW. In other words, in Phase 2, stuff gets real.

There are three core components of Phase 2: (1) real-time webinars, (2) virtual teaming, and (3) coaching.

1. *Real-Time Webinars:* Periodic, virtual, community webinars are essential for three reasons. First, they help keep alive the community bond that was formed at the KickOff despite the fact that members of the teams are all working from different locations. Second, they provide skills training that will help teams develop their Projects of Worth: sessions on branding and marketing, on building business plans, on storytelling, and on project management—all of which add value. Third, they inform participants about changes in the marketplace and entrepreneurism in law, which help bridge cultural divides and inform teams of the current and future landscape in which they are innovating.

2. *Virtual Teaming:* The second component, virtual teaming, is likely the most important life skill learned in any 16-week cycle under the 3-4-5

Method of Innovation. This is because the future of working is on global teams (if it isn't here already) and virtual teaming is *so* hard. It is hard enough to get the time zones right, let alone the technology, not to mention the even harder hurdle of cultural differences and preferences as they relate to virtual interaction (and interaction in general). But there is a right way and a wrong way to team virtually regardless of your age or culture or experience. The right way begins by establishing virtual connection norms as to what is acceptable—is it okay to be eating? Commuting? Hearing dogs barking in the background? The second is to require video most of the time (even better if you require it all the time). If you don't believe me and you prefer conference calls, watch the YouTube video "A Conference Call in Real Life." [10] It says it all. For me? When I am on a conference call with more than two people—especially when one group is on a squawk box and I'm connecting from my own line, I immediately chalk up the call to a colossal waste of time. And I make sure I have other things to do during the call. Just being honest! You would be amazed what a single working mother of three teenagers can get done when she's on mute. This is why requiring video is important—so that people are in the moment. Video greatly enhances connection, but even more than that, it enhances efficiency because everyone must pay attention. (It is almost impossible to text while videoconferencing—especially if you wear glasses. Beware of what can be seen in the reflection.) One of the things we stress at KickOff is the importance of creating virtual third places (as mentioned in Part II, Chapter 8, Rule of Engagement 3: Open Door). We call these virtual third places "*Quan* rooms." There is a scene in the movie *Jerry Maguire* when the character played by Cuba Gooding Jr. says to the character played by Tom Cruise: "You see some dudes might have the coin, but never the *quan*." Cruise asks, "What's the *quan*?" Gooding Jr. replies slowly with emphasis on each word "Love, [pause] respect, [pause] community [pause]. And the entire package?" he asks as he moves his hands to draw an imaginary circle, "that's the *quan*." For us, a *Quan* room is a virtual third place in which the team can co-create in real time utilizing video and other real-time collaboration tools and where they can find each other quickly when they have a brief question. It most definitely includes a chat option. During the protocols session at the KickOff, we stress the importance of developing the norms and parameters of this space so that it has the "*quan*" and not just the coin. Those teams that connect in this virtual *Quan* room at preestablished times and at the spur of the moment really gel as a team and are more efficient and effective. It doesn't matter which technological video vehicle is chosen (whether Skype, Google Hangouts, FaceTime, or Zoom) or which collaborative tools are included (Trello, Teams, Slack, or WhatsApp). What matters is that it is considered a third space, it is where the team meets consistently to collaborate, and it is where the norms of behavior—those norms that help us reach the *quan* and not just the coin—are followed.

3. *Coaching:* The third component is coaching and mentoring, an essential piece to teaming. The only way we can truly embrace the sixth essential experience of Reflecting, mentioned in the previous chapter, is to test our ideas on others. Therefore, over the course of this phase, teams meet virtually with their mentors and coaches (including external coaches who are experts in pitching and branding) to review their progress in the 5 Steps to a Project of Worth and to receive feedback to improve the viability, financial structure, and overall positioning and creativity of the project. This is part of the prototyping, testing, reassessing, and improving process. Also, teams meet with a teaming coach when conflict arises. Finally, teams meet with other teams. The experience of the Shadow Team described previously also falls under the heading of coaching—even if it feels more like hole poking.

Phase 3: The ConPosium

> ## *"Dieting is [not] the only game where you win when you lose."*
>
> —Karl Lagerfeld

The ConPosium is a community-wide event during which the teams present their solutions to a panel of multidisciplinary judges who assess and comment on the creativity, viability, and business case of the Project of Worth. They also assess the quality of the presentation. The ConPosium wraps three of the Seven Essential Experiences into one package: it's a community celebration, it's a form of reflection (monitoring and testing), and it's hard work.

First, the ConPosium is a community celebration. It is an event that reunites the community as one, despite the fact that, in some ways, the process has been a competition. We create the celebratory atmosphere in various ways: We include the audience with a live private Skype chat, a live public Twitter, and the ability to vote on the teams backed by plenty of music. In this way, it is a bit like *American Idol* meets dragon den . . . it feels like anything but a traditional conference or symposium. The ConPosium is called that because it is not a conference or a symposium. Instead, like the KickOff, it is a transport to an alternate world. It is big and bold and "all that." We celebrate our successes and our failures, and we reunite in person after all of the hard virtual work we have done together.

Of course, the ConPosium is not only about celebration; it also is a form of reflection (of monitoring and testing). Although it feels like the end, it is not. As part of the 5 Steps to a Project of Worth, the ConPosium is a time for receiving feedback, for testing our prototypes, and for analyzing our business cases. The ConPosium is an opportunity to present the problem, solution, and prototype (and commercial) in front of 200 people and receive critique from learned experts and from each other via the live Skype chat. At an LWOW ConPosium, the judging panel is usually comprised of a venture capitalist, a lawyer, a business professional, and an academic. At a MOVELΔW ConPosium, the panel of judges is often comprised of three senior people in the legal department reporting to the CLO or managing partner or chief executive of the entity. And frankly, as much as the ConPosium is about celebrating, it is also about accepting failure. Some of the projects aren't viable. But failure is part of the 3-4-5 Method, and some teams need this feedback more than others. In some cases, teams may have already heard similar feedback multiple times from their coaches, Shadow Teams, and mentors but pushed on regardless because of misplaced groupthink or because they were right. There are many stories about how entrepreneurs were told that their idea was stupid and they went forward and prevailed. If that happens at ConPosium and all of the coaches including me were wrong and one of the VC judges falls for the idea, that is fantastic. But if a team gets well-deserved critical feedback and it realizes that its project is not viable or feasible, that's okay too. We all can't win at ConPosium. We need to pick and choose which ideas we are going to go with, which harkens back to the convergent thinking discussed in the previous chapter. And you know what? There is still celebration. The project is still a

Project of Worth because of the substantive learnings and skills training of the team. And that leads to the final essential experience demonstrated at the ConPosium: hard work.

The ConPosium is hard work personified. Teams give a 20-minute dynamic presentation to more than 200 people that includes a commercial and an explanatory video, a branded prototype, a tag line, a business case, and a three-sentence elevator pitch. Even when the project is viable, feasible, and creative, putting together a 20-minute presentation with a prototype, memorizing it, and working through transitions with people from around the world (people you haven't seen for three months or never before) who don't share the same first language is hard work— almost as hard as creating the solution itself.

All teams present at ConPosium, even those that are harried and must go with half-baked ideas. The 3-4-5 Method is not designed only to create innovations but also to teach the 21st-century skills that are required and desired and where there is currently a skills gap in the Lawyer Skills Delta (displayed in Chapter 3). This part of the 3-4-5 Method of Innovation helps hone some of the Level 1 C.O.S.T skills: giving and receiving feedback, communicating, using social media, and making presentations. It is good training to learn how to put lipstick on a pig and present anything in front of 200 people. So even if the idea isn't viable, building the dynamic presentation, rehearsing the presentation, and then delivering the presentation with the team is valuable in itself. And even the worst ideas can sell if the person presents them well. VCs often say that they invest in the people more than the idea. I learned this from my closest friend from college, Jon Callaghan, co-founder of True Ventures, an early stage venture capital firm. He was at a meeting where he had to tell one of his favorite entrepreneurs that the entrepreneur had failed and that he was shutting down his start-up. The investment had cost millions. Still, as the entrepreneur left the room, Jon pulled him aside and said, "Let me know what you come up with next. I'll invest in any idea you pursue. I believe in you even if this latest idea of yours failed." Perhaps counterintuitively, the individuals who have come back to me (after reflection) to tell me how much they learned from LawWithoutWalls are often from the teams that had ideas that flopped or projects they couldn't complete because of the conflicts within the team. So in that way, as cheesy as it sounds everyone is a winner; "you win when you lose."

Four Months

> *"The most important thing is not to let yourself get impatient . . . Even if things are so tangled up you can't do anything, don't get desperate or blow a fuse and start yanking on one particular thread before it's ready to come undone. You have to figure it's going to be a long process and that you'll work on things slowly, one at a time. Do you think you can do that?"*

—Haruki Murakami, *Norwegian Wood*[11]

Unfortunately and fortunately, the 3-4-5 Method is "a long process." I say "unfortunately" because the business model of law firms is like Benjamin Franklin's famous quote "time is money." And an innovation cycle takes time, which makes this aspect one of the toughest challenges in teaching innovation to lawyers. I say "fortunately" because it is only through this long process that we learn to resist "yanking on one particular thread before its ready," that we learn to wait and "work on things slowly." Although it is true that you can learn a little bit about innovation in 90 minutes, you can't create an innovation in 90 minutes or learn the Three Rules of Engagement or hone the skills in the Lawyer Skills Delta. It takes even longer than an intensive week at an executive education program focused on teaching you design thinking. It takes the time that it takes (i.e., it takes the time to actually do it).

In my experience, teaching innovation takes at least four months (give or take a couple of weeks). Four months is long enough to digest the Three Rules of Engagement, to get to know the others on your team, to hone your art together, and to create something that is implementable and that you learn from (i.e., something that is a Project of Worth). And 4 months is short enough to feel as though you haven't wasted too much time if at the end of the cycle you don't have the right solution.

Can it be done in less? Yes, an innovation cycle can be done in 12–13 weeks, but it feels crammed and the intensity causes pressure to rise and creates teaming issues. If one of the major reasons of taking teams on an innovation journey is to create culture change and build relationships, then taking the *time that it takes* matters and makes a difference. I have repeatedly had heads of legal departments and firms ask me to do an innovation cycle in eight weeks or even less, but I won't do it. That is setting everyone up for failure. There is no quick trick to changing mindsets and behaviors despite recent articles touting the benefits of using "performance-enhancing" substances such as nootropics or microdosing LSD or even drinking bullet coffee.[12] These antidotes are not going to transform lawyers, not in the way an innovation cycle does.

The best way to meet the challenge of innovation is by a clear delineation of roles and responsibilities (as discussed in KickOff) *and* time commitments. Furthermore, there needs to be a timeline and project plan—something lawyers are often criticized for being bad at developing, let alone following. It is imperative to identify the resources and responsibilities of the team and create clarity around the roles and expected levels of engagement. This is not to say that some people will not end up playing multiple roles or giving more (or less) time than originally anticipated. However, what is true in our personal relationships is also true in our work relationships among teams: the expectations that aren't set are the expectations that aren't met.

Roles should be very well defined so that expectations are set and so that people do not become victims of what Cass Sunstein and Reid Hastie calls cascade effects: following groupthink based on what is thought or known by most.[13] According to Sunstein and Hastie, groups often focus on what is common knowledge—and thus don't even hear (let alone account for) key information of a minority number of people. Assigning roles enables people who have information that is different from what is common knowledge feel not only welcome but also *compelled* to share that information.

The way we divvy up roles in LawWithoutWalls and MOVELΔW is as follows: first we identify two or three people as the workers or "hackers," three or four people to serve as mentors, and one or two coaches or advisers for a total of approximately seven or eight team members. The hackers are responsible for project creation from start to finish. In LWOW, these are usually students. The mentors oversee and lead the development of the project from a substantive and process standpoint. (It is also good to

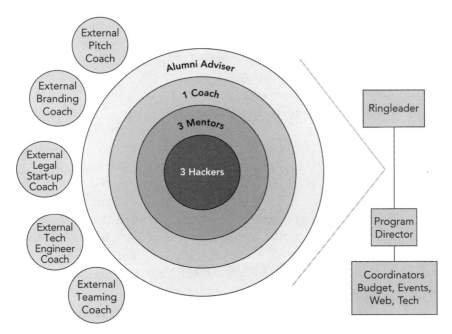

FIG. 10.2 A chart depicting the ideal team makeup and leadership roles to run a 16-week innovation cycle.

define the roles of the mentors because sometimes their advice can conflict. Generally, we identify two of the mentors to serve as the team leaders driving the project management and overseeing development much like a newly minted partner might over his/her associates; the third mentor serves as a topic expert providing mentoring on the topic.) The coaches help fine-tune the solutions and pitches. The team should have at least two coaches to serve as "pitch" coaches (at least one of whom should be external to the team). In both LWOW and MOVELΔW, we also include an alumnus (someone who was once a hacker) to serve as an adviser to the team leaders and learners. Teams are also provided access to a branding coach, a tech engineer coach, a legal start-up coach, and a teaming coach with whom they can meet with as needed during the 16 weeks.

Importantly, hierarchy need not define who fills the roles and the role label does not determine the level of influence/persuasion. In other words, a mentor does not necessarily need to be more senior than a hacker. And a coach can be just as influential as a hacker on any one team. Indeed, in the pilot program with Microsoft (the first year we ran an experiential learning program based on the 3-4-5 Method of Innovation), we tested whether this was true. Of the six teams, we had two where the mentors were more senior than the hackers, two where the hackers were more senior than the mentors, and two that were a mix. There was no difference in work effort or work product or the ability to team.

As depicted in the illustration above, in addition to the team members, other roles must be filled to run a successful four-month innovation cycle. First, at least two people must oversee all the groups on the cycle and be in leadership roles (e.g., a ringleader and program director). The ringleader leads the community in culture creation and engagement and gives tough love to every team as it journeys through the 5 Steps to a Project of Worth. This person provides critical feedback across the teams and serves as a consistent voice that all teams hear. For this to work, the ringleader must have the credibility and clout and prestige equal to that of the senior people within the entity going on the jouney and know what it's like to be a lawyer—something very hard to pull off if you haven't gone to law school or worked with lawyers in a serious way. Even better, the ringleader should have a law degree and experience in the law market. Furthermore, the ringleader should have solid experience in marketing, branding, presentation, entrepreneurship, and human-centered design. Second, there needs to be a program director, someone who oversees the progress deliverables of each team along the way and can help with the details from finding the right free animation tool to bringing the idea to life in the teaser video to perfecting the PowerPoint presentation in the moments before the ConPosium. The program director makes sure the trains run on time and that they get to the station. Finally, there needs to be one or two program coordinators who oversee details related to events, webinars, tech, and budget along with other operational and administrative tasks.

As shown above, over the course of the four months, in addition to meeting on their own, teams meet with the LWOW leadership team (a.k.a the ring-leader and program director) multiple times to present their progress on the 5 Steps to a Project of Worth and receive feedback. After meeting with us twice, about midway through the four months, teams meet with their Shadow Teams to practice pitching and giving and receiving feedback. After that, teams have a Five-Step Walk-Through meeting during which they do a walk-through of all five steps

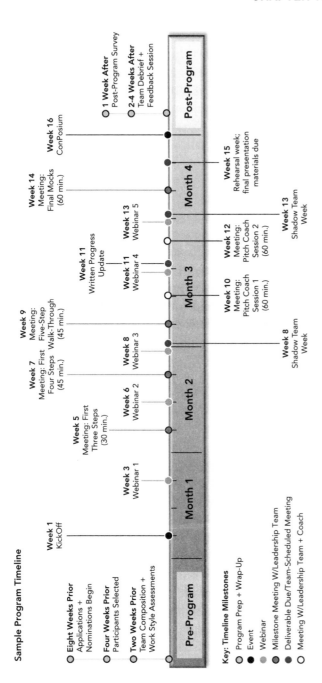

FIG. 10.3 A program timeline for a 16-week innovation cycle in the 3-4-5 Method of Innovation for Lawyers.

with the LWOW leadership team (incorporating the feedback from the Shadow Teams). In Weeks 10 and 12, teams pitch to the coaches. In LWOW, these coaches are external to the team (e.g., a start-up coach and a branding coach). In MOVELΔW, teams also pitch to the coach who is assigned to their team. The last two weeks are spent doing mock pitches and rehearsals and fine-tuning prototypes and the dynamic presentation for ConPosium.

During all the meetings, teams are provided multiple opportunities to "test" their problems and solutions and refine them. Indeed, almost every team must repeat a few steps or start over entirely as mentioned before—which is okay because the real purpose of these meetings is to leverage what is called the "Progress Principle." In a recent article in the *Harvard Business Review* called "The Power of Small Wins," written by Teresa Amabile and Steven J. Kramer, the authors write "Of all the things that can boost emotions, motivation, and perceptions during a workday, the single most important is making progress in meaningful work. And the more frequently people experience that sense of progress, the more likely they are to be creatively productive in the long run." Every team has at least ten opportunities (other than the KickOff and ConPosium) to get feedback and to experience progress and celebrate small wins.

As discussed above, in addition to the work during the four-month cycle, there is some pre- and posttime work to an innovation journey. The benefits of participation in an innovation journey are maximized with strategic planning and strong internal buy-in (e.g., support from the entity's leadership and internal PR around the program). The pre-time should be spent (1) setting goals, (2) identifying the participants and placing them on teams, and (3) selecting the challenges on which each team will hack.

The posttime is all about Reflecting (the sixth essential experience discussed in Chapter 9). Teams should be surveyed to provide real feed-back about what worked well and what could have been improved not only from a substantive standpoint but also from an individual standpoint. Therefore, in addition to the sixth essential experience, this posttime involves the first essential experience, which is about nurturing the team and the individual when they meet to debrief. It also involves the last (e.g., hard work) because giving and receiving feedback helps us grow even as it can be very difficult from both ends.

The 5 Steps to a Project of Worth

> *"Creation is . . . the consequence of acts that appear inconsequential by themselves but that when accumulated, change the world."*
>
> —Kevin Ashton, *How to Fly a Horse*[14]

The "5" in the 3-4-5 Method of Innovation stands for the 5 Steps each team must tackle to meet its objective: a viable, feasible solution to a defined problem for a discreet target audience along with a prototype, a commercial, and business case.

I created the 5 Steps after reading about a man named Tim Young who raised $10 million in one year by using just five "magic" slides in his fundraising deck.[15] This seemingly inconsequential act changed his world, and his advice resonated with me: "If you can't outline your business in just five slides, you should go back to the drawing board and simplify your messaging."[16] I took this to heart and created my own five-slide deck for bringing a Project of Worth to life. I did this for two reasons. First, I wanted to be able to explain to participating teams quickly and effectively how Projects of Worth were formed so that teams left the KickOff feeling as though they could do this—as opposed to feeling overwhelmed. It was too daunting to talk about it in terms of all of the meetings and all of the time they would need to invest. Lawyers want to know what they need to deliver, and the 5 Steps provides a hard deliverable that is not debilitating. Once they get into the 5 Steps, they realize how much they overlap and how hard they are. However, they leave with a tool that outlines the main end goals, and the steps to get there to help organize and motivate them. Second, I wanted the teams to have a format in which to pitch their Projects of Worth to others in five minutes or less for feedback and assessment. At ConPosium, we don't present the 5 Steps in a five-slide deck, but the content of the 5 Steps is essential to every presentation.

Step 1: Exploring and Investigating the Challenge, Background, and Big Picture

- Conduct primary and secondary investigatory research to answer the following quesions and more:
  - What is your overarching topic/challenge?

- What does the problem mean to you and your team?
- How do your interpretations vary given your varied cultures, expertise, and background?
- What context/history is important?
  - Where does this fit in the history of law and in the context of our world today?
  - How does what is happening now affect what might happen in the future?
  - How does this challenge fit into a larger context of education or business or your industry?
  - What does the past say?
  - Is this a global or local problem?
- Other things to consider: the regulatory environment, demographic trends, global impact, theory, and state of the market
- Step 1 begins at KickOff.

Step 2: Finding and Refining the Problem or Opportunity

- Consider:
  - What narrow problem/opportunity have you identified?
  - Have you separated the symptoms from the problem(s)?
  - What is the context/history behind the problem or opportunity? (i.e., go back to Step 1 about the narrow problem)
- Step 2 goes hand in hand with Step 3 and requires another look at Step 1.

Step 3: Defining, Understanding, and Empathizing with the Target Audience(s)

- Create the consumer story (or stories) and then go back and refine Step 2.
- Find the user story by answering the following questions:
  - What groups of people are most impacted by this problem?
  - What are the characteristics of those groups?
  - Which groups are most targetable for a solution?
  - What are the Five Whys for each group?
  - Which group are you going to target with your solution?
  - How large is this universe?
  - What other problems are the target audience experiencing?
  - What types of jobs/activities does the target audience do?
  - How do those within the target audience like to learn or absorb information?

Step 4: Solving the Problem; Ideating the Solution and Creating a Prototype

- Ask:
  - What form(s) or manifestation(s) will/can the solution take?
  - What will it "do"?
  - How many people will it target at what cost over what length of time?
  - What is your business case for the solution? Ask who, what, why, when, and, importantly, how. How will it come to fruition? How long will it take? How much will it cost in hours and dollars?
  - What is the solution's look, feel, formation, branding, marketing?
- Conduct a consumer journey and prototyping exercise to map out exactly how the user will interface with the solution and how the solution will work step by step.
- Stuck? Repeat Steps 3 and 2.
- Move on to Step 5 before you spend too much time on the solution.

Step 5: Planning, Assessment, and Testing; Build a Business Case and Pitch Your Idea

- Conduct a premortem exercise with your team. (ask what could go wrong, who stands in your way, and what the risks and weaknesses are.)
- Assess the strengths and opportunities.
- Build a business case and plan. (Put some numbers and ROI guestimates to your solution.)
- Consider marketing/branding/positioning (strategy, channels, and costs).
- Test your solution by building a prototype, creating an animation to bring the story to life, beta testing with the target audience, and pitching with as many people as possible (Shadow Teams, pitch coaches, ConPosium judges).
- Return to Steps 3 and 4 to reideate and refine the solution.

I will have much more to say about the 5 Steps to a Project of Worth in the next chapter. For now, I will simply point out that the hardest part about the 3-4-5 Method of Innovation is that we must repeat these steps. They are iterative. They are back and forth. Sometimes we take huge steps back and only baby steps forward. Sometimes progress feels chaotic before it feels integrative. There is no certainty that progress is made when moving from Step 1 to Step 2 or from Step 2 to Step 3 because what we find in Step 3 can send us back to Step 2. Furthermore, we often must go through more than one of the Seven Essential Experiences to move forward within a step. However messy it may appear, the results can often be sublime. And that is why this section opens with the quote by Kevin Ashton. The results are a "creation," a "consequence of acts that appear inconsequential by themselves," that "when accumulated" can "change the world." [17] The next chapter brings each of those acts, those steps to life and shows the iterative trajectory of the 3-4-5 Method by mapping out one sample innovation journey.

💬...Reflection Point Almost any project can be divided into the three phases of the 3-4-5 Method of Innovation for Lawyers.

- Take a moment to write down all of the benefits you think might be generated if you divided your next team project (any type of team project) into these three phases and held a KickOff (a community-wide meeting that was skills-focused), hosted team meetings with real-time video, and concluded with a closure meeting where solutions were shared and celebrated.
- Now make a list of all of the potential downsides.
- Compare the two lists.

💬...Reflection Point Consider the four-month program timeline (above) and the 5 Steps to a Project of Worth. How might you map out a similar process and utilize the 5 Steps the next time your team undertakes a project to ensure that the team is taking on the right problem for the right audience, not taking on too much, meeting the objectives of the key stakeholders, and doing so in the right amount of time with input from externals to get diverse viewpoints along the way?

CHAPTER 11

The Proof:
The 3-4-5 Method of Innovation
Brought to Life

> *"For those who believe, no*
> *proof is necessary.*
> *For those who don't believe, no*
> *proof is possible."*
> —Stuart Chase

The previous two chapters described the Seven Essential Experiences and the 3-4-5 Method of Innovation for Lawyers. This chapter is designed to show how they work together in a single Project of Worth campaign—from challenge to solution—utilizing one team's real experiences, obstacles, and eventual successes.

Since the inception of LWOW in 2011, we have prescribed to the notion that the team's goal is not to create an innovation, but what we call a Project of Worth. We call it that for two reasons. First, we call it that for the value it is designed to bring to others. In junior high, my "gifted" teacher, Mr. Shaw, required all of us eighth-graders to create Projects of Worth, some type of real project that helped real people, solved a real problem, and that contributed to society. We had to stretch ourselves. We had to add value. We had to uncover a problem and figure out a way to solve it. My project was dressing up as a clown and playing the piano at the local home for the aged every Thursday and then visiting all of the members on Saturday to learn about their families. I thought I was doing it to change the aged's lives. Instead, it changed mine in so many ways. This leads to the second reason we call the end products Projects of Worth, which is how it helps us grow as individuals. In my example, playing piano and dressing up as a clown changed the trajectory of my life because through that project, I discovered how much I liked to do the following: (1) sell an idea to unbelievers (the home's management, which thought I was a liability), (2) build community, and (3) make a difference to individuals through music. I had success in my endeavor, but even if I hadn't, it would still be a Project of Worth for Mr. Shaw and for LawWithoutWalls. This is why: even if the innovation we attempt to create fails, we have grown individually and learned collectively. And when starting again, we start from a place stronger than we were before personally and substantively. As Ursula K. Le Guin points out in *The Left Hand of Darkness*, although "It is good to have an end to journey towards; it is the journey that matters, in the end."[1] This is particularly true here, and the journey is the proof.

One Team's Journey through the 5 Steps to a Project of Worth

To bring to life how the Seven Essential Experiences work with the 5 Steps to a Project of Worth, we will follow the journey of one team. This team was sponsored by a global healthcare company (referred to as the Healthcare Team). The mentors and coaches included senior in-house lawyers from the healthcare company, an associate from a big law firm, a legal entrepreneur, and an academic. The hackers were three students: One JD/JM student (Peking University STL, China), one LLM student (EColehead, France), and one MLB[2] student (Bucerius, Germany).

The team's assigned challenge was as follows: Defying Death by Disclaimer: How Can In-House Lawyers Efficiently Manage the Legal Risks of Consumer Marketing in a Digital, Customer-Centric World?

The following material provides a review of the 3 Phases-4 Month-5 Step process, a generic description of the process each team goes through, and then describes how the Healthcare Team negotiated the phase or step and which of the Seven Essential Experiences they went through along the way.

Phase 1: Week 1; KickOff

At KickOff, the teams participate in a problem-finding exercise to identify a problem related to legal education. They then have 12–24 hours to solve the problem. To do so, they practice utilizing the 5 Steps and experience many of the Seven Essential Experiences in a short amount of time. Essentially, they participate in a minihackathon that culminates with short presentations to the entire community.

The KickOff Brought to Life

The entire Healthcare Team (except the external coaches) attended the KickOff at Harvard Law School in January 2017 and participated in teaming, idea generation exercises, personality mapping, setting of protocols, and a minihackathon. This team uncovered the problem that in law school, law students are not taught the specifics of drafting contracts. Therefore, as associates, their employing entities and colleagues must spend extra time and resources to provide them with substantive know-how on drafting terms, templates, and mechanics to fill the gap. To solve this problem, the team came up with the idea Contracto: a virtual platform that trains new law graduates and law interns on the terms and techniques of contract drafting through short on-demand videos, creative exercises to check knowledge base, and contract templates for reference.

Which of the Seven Essential Experiences Applied?

As described in the prior chapter, KickOff is hard work that includes a great deal of reflection and evaluation. It is also a time of nurturing of the self and the team. And it is above all else a time for celebrating the commitment of a community to a shared mission. Furthermore, through the course of the minihackathon, teams also get a taste of the falling in love, moving in, and getting engaged experiences. In the end then, to some degree, teams have experienced all seven of the Seven Essential Experiences over the course of the KickOff.

Phase 2: Weeks 2–4; Steps 1–3

During Phase 2, we go virtual. We meet weekly as a community in an online live webinar to build our skills and learn about the changing legal marketplace. This is the time we begin our teaming in earnest and start to dig into the 5 Steps to a Project of Worth. During Weeks 2–5, we focus primarily on the First three Steps as follows.

Step 1: Exploring and Investigating the Challenge, the Background, and Big Picture

> *"The only thing that makes life possible is permanent, intolerable uncertainty: not knowing what comes next."*
>
> —Ursula K. Le. Guin, *The Left Hand of Darkness*[3]

Step 1 is about exploring and investigating. During this stage, the team's job is to dig in and understand everything it possibly can about the challenge. Teams conduct primary research through interviews and surveys and secondary archival and bibliographical research to explore, for instance, the context of the challenge, its history and regulatory environment, the demographic trends and global impact affecting it, the current state of the market, and the technology. This step can be daunting because the topics are thorny and broad and outside the scope of knowledge that most lawyers have. For example, if the challenge is related to enhancing the safety of the cloud, the team members may be familiar with relevant laws and regulations but not necessarily the technology related to the cloud or how data security works.

There is a steep learning curve in this step. The good news is that this step is all about seeing the trees and not the forest—studying branches is something lawyers are good at. Eventually, however, teams need to refocus on the forest; this can prove difficult for lawyers who want to cover every aspect of a problem. It is simply not possible. Yet I have seen teams derailed by this need for thoroughness and have witnessed the tension that can occur when some members of the team are ready to move forward and others want to go back and redline some more documents. Perfection in innovation is not possible at the outset of a cycle; once a narrow problem or opportunity is identified, the work lies ahead and not behind.

Step 1 Brought to Life: During this step, the Healthcare Team asked and attempted to answer:

- What are the legal and regulatory risks surrounding consumer marketing of a global healthcare company?

- What are the marketplace consequences and government-imposed consequences in Australia about misleading or deceiving consumers and lack of disclosure and review?
- How is technology shaping the development (e.g., emotion, pace) and dissemination (e.g., platforms, channels) of marketing materials?
- What is the role of the legal department related to marketing materials?
- What is the relationship between the marketing and legal departments at the global healthcare company?
- How does the marketing department currently seek approval and review of materials?
- Are the professionals in the marketing department trained on the rules regarding misleading or deceiving consumers and disclosure?
- How much time is the legal department spending on reviewing marketing materials?
- What are the most common types of materials needing review? What are the most frequently asked questions? What are the most common mistakes that marketers make?

Which of the Seven Essential Experiences Applied? The main experience in Step 1 for this team was hard work—for which there is no substitute!

Step 2: Finding and Refining the Problem or Opportunity

"It is a scholar's task to find patterns in nature or cycles in history.

Initially, it's no different from finding portraits of animals and heroes in the stars.

The question is, have you discovered a preexisting truth?

Or have you imposed an arbitrary meaning on whatever it is you're considering?"

—Mary Doria Russell, *Children of God*[4]

As discussed earlier, the most successful problem solvers are the best problem finders. In this step, teams must whittle down the large challenge they have been given to a much smaller, narrower problem impacting a discrete audience. There might be a primary audience and a secondary audience or two equally targeted audiences. This audience will be further defined in Step 3—as such, there may be back-and-forth movement between Steps 2 and 3.

Because the goal in Step 2 is to identify the narrow problem, this also means there is some back-and-forth with Step 1 to determine the context or history behind the narrower problem or opportunity. This is again done by conducting interviews of the relevant group of people to uncover problems related to the topic. We suggest that team members practice the Five Whys, a tool used to uncover the root cause of the problem wherein you ask "Why?" five times. Essentially, after every answer from the interviewee, you respond by asking "Why?" and you do that five times. We also suggest that teams participate in an exercise I created called "I hate it when . . ." (an exercise in finding pain points and exaptation) and another that I created called "What I would love is . . ." along with others found in the companion handbook to this book, *The 3-4-5 Method of Innovation for Lawyers: A Handbook of Exercises and Best Practices.*

Step 2 often turns out to be the hardest of all of the steps. As mentioned in the prior chapter, we are often fooled into thinking that the symptom is the problem. For example, recently while conducting a problem-finding exercise with a group of GCs from a large private equity investment firm, the problem the group selected was that the internal businesspeople didn't read the GCs emails or contracts before forwarding them externally. However, after probing and conducting the Five Whys along with a problem finding exercise, the group uncovered that the real problem was lack of respect and understanding for the attorneys' work product. Evidently, time and again the attorneys would email the businesspeople (the internal clients) a contract with explanations and caveats—both of which were attorney work product and protected by privilege. The business professionals, however, would simply forward the entire email chain (including the attorney work product) to the outside vendor they were trying to get to sign the contract. Of course, this destroyed the attorney-client privilege but also the company's strategic advantage as sometimes the information in the email was provided to protect the client's margins. This simple action showed a profound lack of understanding of the value add that an attorney provides. Essentially, the originally identified problem was framed in a way to hide the real problem, resulting in an initial misdiagnosis.

These types of misdiagnoses happen all the time to teams as they journey toward a Project of Worth. Often, this misdiagnosis can stem from a lack of understanding of the group experiencing the problem and/or the group that is "causing" the problem. This is why Step 3 needs to be done in tandem with Step 2. Without that back and forth, a team might find patterns that strike their eye but do not yet reveal the truth, so they are led astray.

Step 2 Brought to Life: During this step, the Healthcare Team asked and attempted to answer the following questions:

- What are the shared tasks?
- How is the relationship characterized?
- What is the process for marketing content from idea to dissemination?
- Where are the individual and shared pain points?
- The team's key takeaways were as follows:
  - Interviews and surveys of the Australian legal team revealed that the legal department was frustrated with the marketing department. The marketing department was constantly asking redundant questions, requesting fast turnaround of review of materials, and providing copy that had grammatical and substantive errors that could have been remedied easily before material was sent to the legal department for review.
  - Feedback from the legal department to the marketing department about marketing materials frequently dealt with misleading information as well as factual mistakes.
  - As a result, the in-house lawyers had become exhausted from answering the same questions repeatedly from the people in the marketing department and by correcting the advertising copy that contained substantive, patent-protection, compliance, and regulatory errors.
  - The team identified that the marketing department didn't understand some of the simplest legal restrictions related to what could or couldn't be said, didn't give realistic turnaround times when requesting help, and didn't correct basic grammatical errors before sending copy on for legal review.

Which of the Seven Essential Experiences Applied? The main experience this team went through during Step 2—besides hard work—was falling love. They found patterns that helped them zero in on the problem with which they fell in love. And the way they did that was by entering Step 3 in tandem with Step 2 and empathizing with the lawyers in the legal department who worked with the marketers.

Step 3: Defining, Understanding, and Empathizing with the Target Audience(s)

> *"The ultimate truth is that history*
> *ought to consist only of the anecdotes of the*
> *little people who are caught up in it."*
>
> —Louis de Bernieres, *Corelli's Mandolin*[5]

Step 3 is all about finding a very narrow target audience and understanding everything about that target audience—all of the "anecdotes of the . . . people that are caught up in it." However, to understand those people, we often have to understand another audience as well. This can be conceptualized as the relationship between consumer and purchaser (or influencer and decision maker). For example, when I worked as an account executive to create advertising for Kellogg's Apple Jacks, we kept two target audiences in mind: the purchasers (the moms)[6] and the consumers/influencers (the children aged 6–11). Our research showed that moms felt guilty about buying sugary cereals for their children and the idea that there might be some apple in the cereals helped assuage that guilt. So creative, successful advertising for Kellogg's Apple Jacks worked for the moms because of the product's name. But how to reach children who wanted sugary cereals that tasted sweet and weren't necessarily healthy (with a name like that)? We needed to know a day in the life of a six-year old to an 11-year-old. What were they watching on TV? What were the latest video games they were playing? What did they wear? How did they dress and interact with their parents and older siblings? Why did they like the things they liked, and at what time of day and place did they like them? In this case, we learned that they didn't like Kellogg's Apple Jacks because they tasted like apple and that they didn't necessarily eat them for breakfast. This is, in part, why the commercials played on the fact that Kellog's Apple Jacks didn't taste like apple and displayed children eating them in the afternoon as a snack. The commercials from that time and that ad campaign were successful in helping Kellogg's Apple Jacks gain market share and can still be viewed on YouTube today.[7]

All of this investigation is intended to help the teams understand their target audience to a depth that is beyond what they think they need to know so that the solution they create is tight and relevant in every way: content, design, process, length, mood, brand, feel, and message. So in this step, we ask the teams to define the target audience from both sides (sometimes multiple sides) of the problem. This requires talking to people in the target audience group and getting real-life examples from them. And when I say real-life examples, I mean real-life examples, with times and dates and descriptions of the who, what, where, when, and how it happened—and, importantly, how it felt and why it happened/and or felt that way. We need context; we need to understand the consumer's experience with the product or service (or lack thereof) each step of the way and the pain points. We then ask the teams to create user stories for their target audience, a day in the life from the time they wake until the time they go to bed.

Step 3 Brought to Life: During this step, the Healthcare Team surveyed the legal department and conducted investigative interviews of lawyers within the legal department. The team's key takeaways were as follows:

- The legal department was frustrated by a high volume of content for review, a short window of time to review the material, and consistent challenges from marketers on the feedback given.
- Primary pain points when interacting with the marketing department included "I hated to constantly defend myself," "The volume of marketing review was overwhelming," "I couldn't manage my own time," and "I am constantly stressed."
- In sum, the frequent and fast turnaround of marketing materials left the legal team feeling as though these tasks took time away from their value-add business.

Which of the Seven Essential Experiences Applied? This team worked very hard to complete this step, and the participants had clearly fallen in love with the problem and the target audience. They were proud of their progress, applauding their work in achieving the first three steps so directly. As a team, they had congealed; everything was warm and fuzzy. So they were nurturing and celebrating. Having experienced four of the Seven Essential Experiences, they were ready to move in . . . but wait, not so fast. Things changed after their First Three Steps meeting.

Phase 2 (continued): Week 5; "First Three Steps" Milestone Meeting (with a Dash of Step 5)

At this point in the 3-4-5- Method of Innovation, after teams believe they have completed the first three steps, we have our first milestone meeting to assess progress. This occurs approximately one month after KickOff. At this point, teams should have a well-developed consumer story that illustrates the narrow problem they seek to address. At this point, the sixth essential experience comes into play: Reflecting (Monitoring and Evaluating). Essentially, this milestone meeting includes a part of Step 5. At this stage, we need to assess the strengths and weaknesses of the problem and target audience we have identified. This is why the First Three Steps meeting is described as having a dash of Step 5. Yes, there is a great deal more to do afterward when deep in Step 5 (such as refining the solution, putting together the business case, and testing the prototype on the intended audience). Yet even before we do that, we need to do some testing on the problem and the target audience with whom we have started to fall in love.

Furthermore, like Shakespeare's Hamlet, at this point, we often "must be cruel only to be kind." For this reason, these meetings (and I personally) have a reputation of being really tough. During an LWOW X KickOff a few years ago, I was visiting a team in its virtual "*Quan*" room as the participants worked on their project for the minihackathon. I gave some feedback, then said goodbye and shut off my video with plans to leave the room. As I was attempting to bop myself (virtually) out of this team's room into another team's room, there was a technological glitch and I couldn't leave. So I was "in" the room (without my video on but with the ability to see and hear the team members), but they didn't know I was there. (My name was still in the list of attendees on the left side of the screen, but because the team members were new to using this technology, I don't think they understood to look there to see who was in the room. They just assumed that the people in the room were those with their videos on). Well, as I was trying to fix the glitch, one of the students said something like "Michele is so sweet, right?" And one of the seasoned LWOW mentors piped in, "Ahh, don't jump to that conclusion. Just wait. She gets a lot meaner!" And that's true, sort of. I wouldn't say I get mean. I'd say I get honest and to the point. At KickOff, however, the teams have only seen my external-facing rah-rah motivating persona as opposed to my hard-nosed internal-facing examine-every-detail persona. Invariably I poke many holes in the work of most teams at their First Three Steps milestone meeting, and many (if not most) of them are told to repeat certain steps (e.g., their target audience is too broad or they have outlined a problem for a target audience that is too small to care about). Also, I advise many teams to start over entirely. One year we had a team that had completely misunderstood its challenge. The team was given the following prompt: "Alternative Courts on the Brain: Psychologically Based, But Are They Sound?" The mistake was *not* theirs—it was my mistake and the LWOW leadership team's mistake for not being culturally competent. Most if not all of the members were from outside the United States, and those from within the United States did not have a criminal law background. They didn't realize that in the United States, there were options such as as alternative courts (e.g., drug courts, juvenile courts, and veteran courts) that are designed to address the root cause of the arrest and to sidestep typical prison sentences to help combat recidivism; these courts were developed based on psychological research on how to motivate people to behave differently.[8] The team members didn't search that topic *at all* because they had interpreted the topic to be about judges and the psychology of judging—and understandably they were drowning in the broadness of it. The team (and LWOW) learned a great deal from this (i.e., we now pay more attention to how our topics are worded [vetting them to people from different countries beforehand] and we now have the role of topic expert on each team—someone who knows the parameters of the challenge and has some expertise in it). Regardless, each year we still have teams that need to start over after this meeting. And that's what this milestone meeting is for—catching problems and gaps before they create a chasm.

"First Three Steps" Milestone Meeting Brought to Life: The Healthcare Team had its First Three Steps milestone meeting with me and the associate director of LawWithoutWalls. The team members were engaged and energetic because they knew they had identified a real problem that was solvable, and they clearly had celebrated all of the work they had done to understand the problem and the people experiencing it. However, it was time for them to take a harder look at their identified problem and target audience because they hadn't considered the other target audience on the flip side. I asked the team to consider what might be missing from their problem statement. Whose point of view also should be considered before

creating a solution? More specifically, how might the story change if we looked at it from the marketing professionals' points of view?

The team members were a bit crushed that I was asking them to repeat Steps 2 and 3, but they took the feedback well. When you are in the thick of it and are part of the target audience (remember, many of the team members were part of the legal department at the Healthcare Team's company), what might seem obvious to others is anything but obvious to you.

Which of the Seven Essential Experiences Applied? This first milestone meeting can be a bit nerve-racking because it is the first time the team presents to people outside its internal team. It is a bubble-bursting moment to say the least, and you can actually hear the deflation of the energy in the team and its momentum when the members are asked to repeat steps or start over. It can cause a schism between the team and me for sure, and it can cause a schism internally for the team as those who had argued against the direction the team ultimately went won't feel as though they weren't listened to and those who got it wrong feel as though they have now been told so—no one likes that. So the most important essential experience in this step is the first: Nurturing Self and Team. We urge teams to save time immediately after these milestone meetings so that they can regroup—even unite against me if need be—in a celebration of a "death" of an idea or a concept (i.e., the third essential experience). And I don't mind being the scapegoat if it gets the team to tighten its work so that when the members repitch at their next milestone meeting, they have the ammunition and research needed to fight back and give justified reasons for their direction. In other words, I'm only able to poke holes when there isn't backing behind it. So this meeting also forces the team to go through the sixth essential experience (Reflecting).

Phase 2 (continued): Weeks 5 and 6; Repeat Steps 3 and 2 and Start Step 4

Repeated Step 3 Brought to Life: The team then went on to repeat Step 3. Surveys of the marketing department revealed a few primary pain points when interacting with the legal department: The marketing department believed that the creative process—including writing and grammar—was beyond the legal department's purview. The marketing department was annoyed because it thought legal was encroaching on its responsibilities.

Members of the marketing department were also frustrated by a perceived loss of creative control, a lengthy turnaround time for legal review, and a lack of clear, consistent guidelines on content choice. The marketing department felt judgment and annoyance from the lawyers, as if the lawyers believed marketing people were stupid. The marketers interpreted that to mean that the lawyers didn't think the marketing department should be a priority for them and that other legal work was more important.

Repeated Step 2 Brought to Life: Based on the findings from repeating Step 3, the Healthcare Team realized that the marketing and legal departments suffer from two sides of the same problem. The team's stress could be alleviated by a solution that addresses the pain points of both parties. The team members refined the problem as follows: Our client, the marketing department, needs to think about consumer law, digitalization, and the Australian regulatory marketplace. The marketing department needs a lawyer, a compliance officer, and a brand guardian all rolled into one who can provide high-quality feedback and guidance at an early stage, thereby allowing members of that department to consider legal risks early on. This would enhance alignment between legal resources and areas of risk so that conforming content could be approved quickly and nonconforming or high-risk content could be sent directly to the legal department for review. This would foster efficiency while still enabling friendly dialogue and collaboration between the two departments, which for the most part had been missing. But here was the question: What was the "this" that would do all of that?

Step 4: Solving the Problem; Ideating the Solution and Creating a Prototype

"The straight line, a respectable optical illusion which ruins many a man."

—Victor Hugo, *Les Misérables*

At this point, many teams will have done Steps 1, 2, and 3 multiple times. They may have been ideating a solution only to realize that they didn't have a real problem. This can occur when a team jumps from an ideation exercise to a cool idea and then tries to fit the solution into a target audience with the problem that their cool idea solves. Other times a team may have identified a problem but the solution they thought up already exists and/or the solution isn't viable or feasible or the solution only takes into account one side of the story. So, for example, had the Healthcare Team not investigated the frustrations of the marketing department (and its opinions of how the lawyers were currently handling its requests) whatever solution the team would have come up with would not have worked. The solution might have resonated with the lawyers, but it would not have resonated with marketers. What the team ended up creating was something that was nuanced for both the lawyer and the marketer. And importantly, it was positioned to the "user," which is the marketer; after all, a solution for the lawyers would only be useful if the "user" used it.

How did the team ideate its solution? Where did the team find its inspiration? Chip Heath and Dan Heath, authors of *Switch: How to Change Things When Change Is Hard,* write about the power of finding bright spots that can be replicated to solve the problem faced.[9] They cite work done by Jerry Sternin when he was working for Save the Children to help fight malnutrition in rural communities in Vietnam. Sternin's strategy was to search the Vietnamese communities for families that were producing healthier children despite the same disadvantages and lack of resources. The goal was to find out what the parents of the healthier children were doing differently. First, what he discovered was that the mothers of the healthier children were feeding them the same amount of food but in smaller portions more often during the day. Second, the mothers were adding brine shrimp from the rice paddies and the greens of sweet potatoes despite the fact that these foods were considered lower-class foods. Third, when serving the food, the mothers scraped the spoon on the bottom of the pot to make sure that anything that had settled to the bottom was served. By discovering what was working and replicating that, Sternin was able to find a solution to the problem. Similarly, in their book *Inside the Box*, Drew Boyd and Jacob Goldenberg show how we can find solutions by multiplying, dividing, adding, and subtracting what is working.[10] They make the point that sometimes we can find creative solutions by working "inside the box" with what we already have that is working, as opposed to working outside the box. Dr. Margaret Boden, a research professor in AI, psychology, philosophy, and computer science explains it this way: "Constraints, far from being opposed to creativity, make creativity possible."[11]

Another source of inspiration for ideating solutions comes from exercises that force us to do what the most successful entrepreneurs are good at doing—associating[12]—connecting two or more things together that might otherwise not be connected, as discussed in Chapter 6, Rule of Engagement 1: Open Mind. One fascinating derivation of association is called "exaptation."[13] Exaptation is when something is borrowed from one field and used to solve a problem in a totally unrelated field. Exaptation, like innovation, is a result of the cross-fertilization of different disciplines.[14] And exaptation is anything but a "straight line."

A recent example of exaptation helped save lives of U.S. Army members.[15] A group of special forces who were stationed in remote posts in Africa were getting sick from the only meat that was available to them, which was substandard. Soldiers would go to the markets, pick out the meat, buy it, cook it—and get really sick. The sergeant of the special forces knew he couldn't help the men after they had eaten the meat, but maybe he could help them before it got to that point. If the men could differentiate between good and bad meat, would that solve the problem? He called Jason Nauert, the head director of the Rocky Mountain Institute of Meat, a butchery school in Colorado Springs, to explore the idea. Nauert met the sergeant for a beer, and they brainstormed how to adapt the butchery school's classes to help meet the needs of soldiers who were in anything but the kind of controlled environment in which most chefs like to cook. Together they devised a plan not only to help the men differentiate between good and bad meat but also to teach them how to identify healthy animals before they butchered them, how to clean and butcher raw meat, how to store the meat to keep it from going bad, how to cook the meat to maximize nutrition and minimize bacteria, and even how to get the most out of the meat (e.g., use scraps to make sausage). This is a great example of both association and exaptation. The sergeant associated a butchery class with the army, and the director of a meat institute exapted a class made for chefs for the army situated in remote Africa.

Another example of an exaptation is the feeding of graphene, described as "an atomic-scale hexagonal lattice made up of carbon atoms," to spiders.[16] I'm not an expert in graphene, but it has some cool properties, including being one of the strongest materials known to humans and the basic structural element of graphite, for instance. In 1962, it was originally discovered in a microscope as a form of carbon. It made a comeback in 2004 when two scientists isolated the material that is the thickness of just one atom; the scientists were awarded a Nobel Prize in Physics in 2010 for their experiments with it.[17] Essentially, they extracted graphene from graphite as a two-dimensional material that is almost completely transparent, is a good conductor of heat, and can be used to produce touch screens and light panels. Well, now graphene is up for a trifecta with this exaptation. Scientists are feeding it to spiders, and as a result, spiders are making webs that are strong enough to hold the weight of a person. How did the scientists think of that? They associated the fact that insects have certain bio-minerals in their hard tissues that make the insects's jaws and teeth hard, with graphene's properties (hard as a diamond but stretchy). They thought why not see if a spider's silk properties could be reinforced artificially by the natural integration of graphene? And it worked. Now people are hypothesizing that we might have parachutes made of spider webs.

At KickOff, we have all of the teams participate in an Exaptation exercise I created to help them hack a solution to the problem they have identified during the minihackathon. For example, the Healthcare Team came up with and enhanced its solution, Contracto, by exapting some of the attributes of a Nespresso machine into the solution (e.g., the coffee's form [bite-sized pieces of information on demand] and many flavors [content customizable by user]).

Step 4 Brought to Life: At KickOff, the teams are introduced to many different types of idea generation exercises, including one that features exaptation (mentioned above) and another that focuses on bright spots (both of which are provided in the companion handbook). Most teams use both on their journey, and the source doesn't matter: It's the process and the solution that do. The Healthcare Team created Creative License, Write Away the Right Way, a user-friendly AI-based solution that measures risks and provides legal feedback in real time. It gives marketers instant feedback on high-risk words and phrases as they type. It's just what the marketers needed as it simulates a lawyer, a compliance officer, and a brand guardian all working on the same task at the same time. The tool gives marketers input from key stakeholders at an early stage, allowing them to consider legal risks and alignment between those areas of risk and legal resources. The tool frees marketers to concentrate on content, positioning, and strategy and enables the legal department to focus on compliance and risk (rather than spending time correcting preventable, frequent, and unnecessary errors). It included three scales related to whether the copy was likely to be signed off on (1) branding (a customer-centricity scale), (2) compliance (a risk of vocabulary scale), and (3) legal risk (the underlying risk of product scale).

How did they think of this? They exapted spell check and smart contracts and put them together with AI. The reason they were able to do this is because of the hard work they spent on understanding the target audience and redefining the problem. And the most positive result of the entire project—the part that truly makes this project a Project of Worth— is that in the process of investigating the problem, the legal team went and talked to the marketing team and *really listened*. They made friends and collaborated on the solution. And even if the solution never comes to life (although as of this writing, two different law firms have offered to bring it to life for them), there is value because of the deepened understanding of an internal client and a stronger relationship between two departments as a result.

Which of the Seven Essential Experiences Applied? Unfortunately, this team had to celebrate again but in a different way—it had to celebrate its losses. As mentioned above, the team had to back up and repeat Steps 2 and 3 before moving on to Step 4. So there was hard work and a celebration like the kind you would find at a funeral versus a wedding. There was also reflection and falling in love again, this time with the flip-side audience. This team nurtured itself and its relationship with the marketing department, which lead to the moving in with the narrower problem and double-sided target audience. Finally, albeit not in a "straight line," it got engaged to the problem and to one solution, Step 4. So all in all? All of the Seven Essential Experiences applied.

Phase 2 (continued): Weeks 7 and 8; "First Four Steps" Milestone Meeting and First Shadow Team Meeting (with Another Dash of Step 5)

At this point in the 3-4-5- Method of Innovation, after teams believe they have completed the first four steps, we have a meeting for them to pitch their revised Steps 2 and 3 and the solutions they have begun to create in their minds if not yet in 3D. This occurs just shy of two months after KickOff. At this point, teams should have a well-developed set of consumer stories that illustrates the narrow problem they seek to address for their target audience. And as with the First Three Steps milestone meeting, this meeting also incorporates a dash (or a couple of dashes) of Step 5. At this stage, we need to have started to assess the strengths and weaknesses of our solution. Indeed, at this stage teams likely have axed some solutions entirely for failing to pass the monitoring and reflection involved in Step 5. That said, at this stage, some teams come to the meeting with more than one solution option, wanting feedback based on the various pros/cons and the business case they have begun to develop for each. During this meeting, teams settle on a solution-course-of-action. At this meeting, we push teams to begin to prototype and to develop a consumer journey map that identifies all of the user interfaces. As discussed in the first chapter of this part, prototyping does not need to be the beta version of the end result. It merely needs to be some way to bring the solution to life—to show how it will work. It can be storyboards or mock-ups or a web page that isn't "live"—anything that can then be tested with the target audience to get feedback for the next step. After this meeting, the goal for the teams is to do a rough prototype to pitch to their Shadow Team the following week. In addition, the hope is that the teams will start working on a unique and creative way to bring the consumer story to life so that when their solution is pitched at ConPosium, the audience can empathize with the consumer experiencing the problem.

"First 4 Steps" Milestone Meeting Brought to Life: In this meeting, we urged the Creative License team to develop a prototype. How might their solution work from an end user experience A to B to C to D, and how might that experience differ if the user was the marketer or the lawyers? This team took the challenge head on and created a video composed of a sequence of screenshots with voice-overs to demonstrate how the product would look, work, and feel in real time. The team used this video to test its solution with its Shadow Team and then later with the LWOW leadership team, as part of Step 5.

Which of the Seven Essential Experiences Applied? There is definitely some celebration (Essential Experience 3) during this meeting as it is a feat to have gotten this far. There is also Essential Experience 5: Getting Engaged, Then Married to the solution and, of course, Essential Experience 6: Reflecting (Monitoring and Evaluating). Indeed, the latter is the focus for the Shadow Team meeting.

Phase 2 (continued): Weeks 8 and 9; Step 5 and the "Five-Step Walk-Through" Milestone Meeting

There are two weeks in this section, but really the remainder of the weeks are dedicated to Step 5. Essentially, we spend the first half of our cycle defining and solving the problem and the second half testing and refining the solution, which is not only the most time-intensive step but also, in some ways, *the* most important. As the Sigmund Freud quote below makes clear, Step 5 shatters our illusions and requires all teams to square their ideas with "some portion of reality."

Step 5: Planning, Assessment, and Testing; Build a Business Case and Pitch Your Idea

"We welcome illusions because they spare us emotional distress, and enable us instead to indulge in gratification. We must not then complain, then, if now and again they come into collision with some portion of reality and are shattered against it."

—Sigmund Freud, *Thoughts for the Time of War and Death*[18]

Specifically, we ask teams to first conduct a premortem exercise (i.e., imagine all the ways their idea might fail) to identify every possible thing that might go wrong.[19] Then we assess strengths and opportunities. Critical to this analysis, however, is building a timeline/action plan and a business case. It's interesting because as happily as lawyers do the first part is how unhappily they do the second. They are happy to talk all day about the cons and pros, but when it comes time to developing an action plan that identifies potential costs in terms of resources and time or lays out how long the solution might take to be implemented, they resist mightily. Yet it is only by creating that business plan that the team can really assess the strengths, weaknesses, opportunities, and threats. The two go hand in hand.

This step is not just about testing the substance, the feasibility, but also the viability with the target audience. To do that, the teams put the prototype they have developed in front of many people in different ways.

They create a 15-minute pitch along with a prototype supported by a five-slide deck. As mentioned above, a big part of Step 5 is assessment, and we include many opportunities for such assessment—feedback and reflection at the various milestone meetings, two external pitch coach sessions (one of which is with a branding coach), two Shadow Team meetings, a written progress update, a final mock meeting, and rehearsals before ConPosium, and the ConPosium itself. All of these "testing" sessions are part of Step 5, which is why in many ways it runs through all of the steps.

Step 5 can be difficult because sometimes a team will get engaged to a solution only to realize that it isn't going to happen. It is too expensive, too time-consuming. Sometimes the prototype isn't user friendly or technologically capable. And sometimes when a team gets to this point, it must start over again. Every year in every innovation cycle, at least one team gets to this point. It is why in the 3-4-5 Method of Innovation we have so many meetings with the LWOW leadership team and external pitch coaches. These meetings are designed to help teams identify weak links and shatter illusions before it is functionally too late.

Step 5 and Five-Step Walk-Through Milestone Meeting Brought to Life: The Healthcare Team tackled Step 5 head on and considered all angles. Team members estimated the initial costs of development, including front-end development and costs for salary, training, and marketing. They also estimated annual costs for ongoing development, use of APIs, and salary, training, and marketing. They projected that by year 2020, they would break even in the costs saved based on the level of investment. And unlike other teams, they did not stop there. They considered how they might monetize their idea outside their own company. They considered the size of the opportunity in the health insurance market (approximately $7.4 million). Then they went beyond that horizon and wondered how this idea might be monetized in tangential markets such as the Australian insurance market (approximately $49 million). In other words, Step 5 is not just about being "cruel only to be kind" or killing our darlings, but utilizing that killer instinct to our advantage, to look beyond ourselves for what we can slay. Furthermore, the 5 Steps Walk-Through milestone meeting is the first chance the team has to present all five steps in walk-through mode. It is not a formal pitch, but it still must be coordinated and practiced and teams are required to bring a deck with them to show their thought process visually. My job at this stage is to do a hard look at the business case and to urge the teams to begin to think about branding and positioning. How will this solution look and feel? What might it be called? What two-sentence description (tag line) might sum it up? How might it best be positioned to get buy-in at the team's specific company?

Which of the Seven Essential Experiences Applied? By now you get that every step includes the seventh Essential Experience of Working Hard. And most steps also include the sixth Essential Experience, Reflection. The fifth step is all about those two experiences combined, and it never ends. As explained earlier, even after implementation, you have to do Step 5. That's what brand managers do at every consumer product company: They plan, assess, and test . . . and repeat. So although at this point our Healthcare Team has completed its steps, it is just the beginning. Team members present at ConPosium to receive feedback (and to celebrate and work hard). They then need to ask themselves what they will do with the project to move it forward. And in the following weeks, they pitch over and over again to various external audiences and continue revising to eventually get to implementation. Regardless of the work remaining, this meeting is where the teams realize that they actually created a Project of Worth, and all of the team members have grown in the process of creating it. And so in the end, it feels a little bit like magic, even though everyone knows all the ins and outs of how it's done.

Phase 2 (continued): Weeks 10–13; Furthering Step 5 and Repeating Step 4

During this stage, to further Step 5, teams attend three different pitch meetings with various externals: (1) an external pitch coach, (2) an external branding coach, and (3) their Shadow Team. The team leaders (with the help of the other mentors and alumni advisors) write a progress update during this time. We have them do this so that they can reflect on and refine future solution development going forward as well as spend time reflecting on their past actions in an attempt to learn from the failures and successes in terms of the past project development process and of teaming as individuals and as a group. All of this is designed to ensure that teams repeat Step 4, repeatedly. At this stage, they need to tweak their proto-types to ensure that they are positioned for the target audience and are in keeping with the brand they created with their brand pyramids. They also need to focus on communicating how the solution works from beginning to end in terms of the user and/or service experience.

Repeated Step 4 Brought to Life: While finishing the business case, the Healthcare Team met with its branding coach to put its brand pyramid together to ensure that the prototype was targeted to the marketers and was in keeping with the healthcare company brand. Team members put together a simple flow chart to show how the tool would be used. First, the marketer creates content. It provides the content to the tool, which gives instant feedback and provides approval to conforming content. Nonconforming content and high-risk content is sent to the legal department separately, and the lawyers then review this material in more depth. The team tweaked its prototype video so that it used real examples of words that marketers use and applied the scale. The team then created another video to show the problem from the marketers' point of view.

Which of the Seven Essential Experiences Applied? The hardest part about this phase is that it is hard. It is why hard work is included in the seventh Essential Experiences. True, it is obvious. But it isn't emphasized enough. By this point, most teams will have worked hard, but it is during this phase that they test their limits for what they can do, how far they can go, how long they can stay awake, and how much feedback they can handle. So although this period involves a great deal of the sixth Essential Experience, Reflecting (Monitoring and Evaluating), it is the hard work that is remembered and, later in Phase 3, celebrated!

Phase 3: Weeks 14–16; Final Mocks, Rehearsal, and ConPosium

The last phase of The 3-4-5 Method is the preparation leading up to the final event and the actual ConPosium (which includes rehearsals). This phase is all about repeating Steps 4 and 5, about determining what needs to be tweaked and reworked. It is also about creating a dynamic presentation and a 30-second commercial designed to sway the target audience of its value.

Final Mocks, Rehearsal, and ConPosium Brought to Life: In this phase, the Healthcare Team took pieces of the two videos they had created to make a 30-second teaser commercial to showcase the benefits of the product. Team members participated in an online final mock meeting and in-person rehearsals right before ConPosium to get feedback. During its final presentation, the team set the stage for its problem through a taped humorous skit employing the healthcare company's marketers and lawyers giving real examples of their concerns. (The skit even involved a healthcare lawyer who was one of the LWOW team leaders who played the hero as an anthropomorphized "Creative License.") Team members rehearsed over and over again (asking for and implementing feedback on voice, presence, cadence, and choreography, for example). Presenting at ConPosium is an altogether different type of presentation than the teams have done in Phase 2. The last time they presented in front of 200 people was at KickOff, and the stakes were not nearly as high. In Phase 2, all of their presentations were short pitches (and virtual), which is a slightly different format and feel than an in-person live performance in front of a panel of judges and an audience of 200+ people. Not many lawyers can say that they presented this way in front of such a diverse audience. This is why, as mentioned in the prior chapter, we are all winners. That said, at ConPosium, we select winning teams in varying categories, one of which is Creativity. You likely won't be surprised: The Healthcare Team was the winner for the creativity category.

Which of the Seven Essential Experiences Applied? As described in the prior chapter, the ConPosium is hard work because it includes a great deal of reflecting and evaluation. This is what the final mocks and rehearsals are all about. And it is a different type of reflection and evaluating because it is about presentation delivery, including the content, look, and feel of the deck and the people (how and what they present). So this is also a time of nurturing of the self and the team. And it is above all else a time for celebration—celebration of learning, failure, and progress.

⟨...Reflection Point⟩ Consider the following topic/challenge: *The Role of In-House Counsel Is Evolving Fast: How Can Lawyers in Law Firms Use Technology to Keep Up?* If you/your team had been given this challenge, how might you have addressed the 5 Steps?

- Step 1: Exploring and Investigating the Challenge, Background, and Big Picture
    - Think through all of the various topics and issues that are subsumed in this challenge and make a list. The list is in some ways endless, including data mining, data privacy, data collection, contract management, calendaring, continuing education, expertise (industry or practice), legal ops, project management, make/buy

decision making, managing the court of public opinion, regulations, compliance, executing NDAs, and contracts.

- What are all of the different types of technologies that might be involved? (consider, for example, AI, big data, cloud storage, social media website technology, content management systems, Wi-Fi, cellular, and bots).
- Think through the various vantage points this challenge could be addressed:
  - How can law firm lawyers help in-house lawyers keep up with their department or internal business clients?
  - How can law firm lawyers keep up with their in-house clients (e.g., match how fast their clients are evolving)?
  - How can a law firm lawyer better meet in-house lawyers' needs?
- What other questions might this topic include?
- What type of research would you do? Where would your start? How might you narrow down the topic?
- Step 2: Finding and Refining the Problem or Opportunity
  - The team that worked on this project identified the following problem: Lawyers need to keep up on the relevant legal news and industry updates; yet it is almost impossible to do so given the time it takes to track and read everything. Essentially, they figured out that both sides—in-house lawyers and law firm lawyers—were facing the same problem.
  - What other problems might they have uncovered? And how might they have uncovered those problems? (For some exercises to help, see the companion handbook to this book called *The 3-4-5 Method of Innovation for Lawyers: A Handbook of Exercises and Best Practices*).
- Step 3: Defining, Understanding, and Empathizing with the Target Audience(s)
  - Assuming that you are on the team that narrowed down the problem to the one identified in Step 2 above, what types of questions might you ask law firm lawyers in an interview to elicit real-life examples of this problem and why it is a problem—what actually does and doesn't happen as a result? In addition, what questions might you ask to understand how the lawyer feels when experiencing the problem?
  - What types of questions might you ask in-house lawyers to learn why they think their outside lawyers should be current on the news

and how that might help them manage their fast-evolving jobs? How might you find out what isn't working and what law firm lawyers aren't doing that in-house lawyers want to be done and how that makes them feel? Alternatively, are any of law firm lawyers meeting (or exceeding) expectations right now on this challenge? If so, what are they doing that is working?

- Step 4: Solving the Problem; Ideating the Solution and Creating a Prototype
  - Where might you find inspiration to solve this problem?
  - What other tools exist in your life that help you manage information? How might they be applied or exapted to solve the narrower problem identified in Step 2 for the target audience identified in Step 3?
- Step 5: Planning, Assessment, and Testing; Build a Business Case and Pitch Your Idea
  - This team created *LEA: Leave it to L.E.A, your Legal Expertise Aggregator*. LEA is an app that helps declutter a lawyer's life by aggregating and curating all of the lawyer's relevant legal news and industry updates in one place.
  - Assess the solution: What types of technology would be needed to create such a solution? How long might that take? What is the minimal viable product that could be tested? How many resources would be needed? What might be a funding model for such a solution? Are competitors doing this already? If so, how? If not, why not? How might this tool be valued by clients? What would make the tool worthwhile?
  - After answering those questions, ask yourself what the ROI would be.
  - What other questions should you ask?

...Reflection Point Imagine presenting on a stage (without notes) in front of 200 people from diverse backgrounds, disciplines, and cultures. Is that vision frightening or invigorating? Why? Should lawyers be trained to present in this fashion? Why or why not? In answering that question, consider how the preparation for that type of presentation would be different from when you present at the firm or office internally or to a client. Also consider how conducting a presentation such as that might help a lawyer grow personally or professionally.

Now consider Ignite style presentations discussed above (20 automated self-moving slides in five minutes). Given clients' demands discussed in Part 1, how might mastering that presentation technique aid lawyers in meetings with clients?

Conclusion

> "*We don't necessarily need a clear, crisp, sharp idea or vision. A hazy one, a sense of vague direction may sometimes be better as we are then more likely to explore along the journey and make serendipitous discoveries.*"
>
> —Pablo Picasso

Given the legal upheaval discussed in this book, people often ask me for my predictions of the future as it relates to the law marketplace and legal education. I usually reply that the direction is up in a way that has never been possible before, up as in *up, up, and away* toward a new level of success.

For the most part in this book, I have defined innovation as lasting incremental change that adds value yet appears small on the surface (i.e., TNT: tiny noticeable things). That definition remains. Clients who fail to demand innovation and lawyers who refuse to step "up" to innovate, to make those kinds of incremental changes in their practice and in how they service their clients and develop business, will not continue to succeed at the same levels as in the past. True, in the near term, they will continue to be tolerated and make money. But in the long term, over time, they will be ousted. Success will belong to those in the legal profession who embrace and hone the mindset, skill set, and behaviors identified in the lower two segments of the Lawyer Skills Delta (from Part 1 of this book) and the Three Rules of Engagement for lawyers: Open Mind, Open Heart, and Open Door as described in Part 2. Success will belong to prospective law school students who attend those law schools that train future lawyers differently from the way they always have, focusing mostly on traditional substantive law training and developing the mind of the issue-spotting lawyer. This is the hope; the good news is that even if I am wrong and the traditional lawyer way of doing things remains tolerated and law schools continue to train as usual, the odds are high that some lawyers, some law firms, some legal departments, and some law schools will still step up in a big, big way.

The four groups I predict will step up in a big big way to affect change in and leverage the future law marketplace are (1) millennial lawyers, (2) women lawyers, (3) new and hungry law schools, and (4) possibly you. Books could be written about each of these groups, but here I will spend only a short time on each.

Millennial Lawyers: A Generation of Unicorns

Since the inception of LawWithoutWalls in 2011, I have taught more than 1,000 millennials (generally defined as people born between 1980 and 2000).[1] Research shows that millennials are less empathetic than prior generations, are overconfident, and are self-absorbed.[2] They yearn for praise, acceptance, and empowerment and have been referred to as the "Me Me Me Generation."[3] Nonetheless, their strength lies in the fact that they will not sacrifice their individuality and differences to get ahead. The authors of a new study of more than 3,500 millennials conducted by Deloitte and the Billie Jean King Leadership Initiative[4] explain that "millennials are refusing to check their identities at the doors of organizations today, and they strongly believe these characteristics bring value to the business outcomes and impact."[5] In keeping with that, the study shows that this generation gets the importance of cognitive diversity and inclusion. Furthermore, they are accepting of differences of all kinds[6] and are 71% more likely to focus on teamwork.[7] When their companies embrace diversity and their leaders lead with inclusion, millennials are more actively engaged at work.[8] So they don't care about just their own uniqueness—they value it in others. Therefore I don't worry so much about the empathy findings or their ability to follow the Open Heart rule of engagement because where their mind goes, their hearts will follow.

Contrary to popular belief, millennials don't care about work-life balance. What they want is something altogether different: They want work-life *integration*. I know from experience that millennials are willing to work—work hard and long—when they care about the work they are doing. They are willing to put in extra hours (at really *odd* hours) if it is a project that not only utilizes but also rewards their passions and creative talents. It doesn't matter what the job is. What matters is that they can bring all of themselves to work, and the whole package is lauded.

Unfortunately, most law schools and law firms often refuse to figure out a way to leverage each millennial's unique talents and preference for a flexible life style. This is a mistake for many reasons, the chief one being that the majority of associates at law firms are millennials. If experts are correct and attrition is at about 20% and it costs law firms almost $300,000 every time a lawyer leaves a firm,[9] motivating millennials is a huge opportunity. Those firms that embrace the Three Rules of Engagement—Open Mind, Open Heart, and Open Door—will be able to hold on to millennials. Offer any millennial the opportunity to go on a 16-week innovation cycle using the 3-4-5 Method, and they will likely jump at the chance because it enables them to utilize their varied talents and to create something new for the firm or organization from the bottom up, whether it is a new process, a new product, or a new service. Some law firms have figured this out (i.e., offering millennials yoga classes, happy hours, and roles on professional development committees and big projects with potential for big impact).[10] For these firms, millennials will be their ticket to the future. And those millennials who can leverage their talents and figure out a way to get their firms and/or schools to utilize and appreciate them for the unicorns that they are will prosper.

Women Lawyers: Even If They Can't Have It All, They Are *All That*

The innovation tournament in law represents a huge opportunity for the advancement of female attorneys. The reason this is so is because, on balance, women are naturally better at the Three Rules of Engagement explained in Part 2 of this book: Open Mind, Open Heart, and Open Door.

First, women are more open-minded. When we talked about the lawyers' crutches in Part 1, we learned that lawyers struggle with a growth mindset in part because they are low on psychological resilience (i.e., they are thin-skinned and defensive). Women generally are more resilient than men. They build psychological resilience by dealing with small-scale stressors over time and learn from dealing with those experiences. Andy Scharlach, a UC Berkeley professor of aging and director of its Center for the Advanced Study of Aging Services, explains that women "have more exposure to the stresses that come from being excluded from the privileges that come automatically to little boys. And that continues throughout women's lives as they carry different burdens and expectations than men. Women still carry more child-rearing responsibilities. They carry more of the emotional load in families. The gender biases that exist either beat you down, or you develop a sense of yourself and others as being okay."[11] Having higher psychological resilience means that you are better able to take critique and therefore are more likely to keep an open mind when receiving feedback and therefore may be better able to improve. As mentioned in Part 2, one of the main tenants of having an open mind is embracing a "Yes and . . ." attitude. Women master the "Yes and . . ." idea of building on each other's ideas at a young age and therefore, when in leadership positions, are naturally better at finding "*the* idea" instead of hanging on to "their own" idea. When IDEO's Tim Brown was working on developing a new Nike product for children, he asked a group of boys and girls 8–10 years old to help ideate. He separated the boys from the girls. The girls came up with four times as many ideas as boys. "The boys, so eager to get their own ideas out there, were barely conscious of the ideas coming from their fellow brainstormers; the girls, without prompting, conducted a spirited but nonetheless *serial* conversation in which each idea related to the one that had come before and became a springboard to the one that came next. They were sparking off one another and getting better ideas as a result."[12]

Another tenant of Open Mind is the ability to work without hierarchies, providing everyone on the team time to talk and contribute and, when in a leadership position, refraining from speaking first. All of these behaviors come easily to women; they are used to not speaking more than others and not speaking first. They are even used to being interrupted. In a recent op-ed, Sheryl Sanburg and Adam Grant, a professor from Wharton, discuss the reality that female executives speak less and are interrupted more than men.[13] Unfortunately, women are literally used to being "manterrupterated" (when a man unnecessarily interrupts a women) and bropropriated (when a man takes credit for a woman's idea).[14]

Another indicator that women are better than men at mastering the Open Mind rule of engagement is that they are better at making associations between things that might not seem obviously connected. According to Helen Fisher in her book *The First Sex*, "Women more regularly think contextually; they take a more holistic view of the issue at hand. That is, they integrate more details of the world around them, details ranging from the nuances of body posture to the position of objects in a room."[15] If Steve Jobs was right and "creativity is just about connecting things," then women leaders are more creative and better able to reach the "adjacent possible" that Steven Johnson promulgates.[16]

Switching to an Open Heart, compared to men, women are generally more able to engage this rule. Historically, they test higher on empathy skills than men do.[17] They often take on caretaking roles—serving as nurses, teachers, therapists.[18] They are more willing to open up to others about the emotional and tough things. And they are better than men at forming closer ties. Unsurprisingly, women are also more likely to join teams as opposed to attempting to be stars or solo artists.[19] As mentioned in Part 2, a recent study by MIT identified three ingredients that go into making the most successful and smartest teams; empathy and having a team with women on it are two of the three.[20] Women are biologically wired to feel empathy. As proof, studies show that women are more likely (than men) to yawn when someone close to them yawns.[21] Moreover, they appear to bounce back easier than men do in the throes of competition.[22]

Moreover, women have richer, wider, stronger networks like the kind described in the third rule of engagement, Open Door, than men do. Their networks are a mixture of people from various parts of their life. They are not categorically from the home or office or from a certain activity.[23] Furthermore, that same MIT study noted above showed that in addition to empathy and diversity, simply having a woman on the team was integral to a team's success.[24] In keeping with that, companies owned by women or that have women on their executive team are valued higher at Series A investment levels and/or outperform other non-blue-chip companies.[25] Furthermore, research shows that female managers are better equipped to manage diverse teams—a key ingredient to innovation. A recent study by Gallup of more than 2.5 million manager-led teams in 195 countries concludes that women are better managers than men and are more likely to contribute to an organization's future success than men.[26] They are better at setting expectations, providing feedback, building relationships with subordinates, motivating people, encouraging teams, and providing opportunities to others for career development.[27] The study includes a section entitled "Why Women Are Better Managers Than Men." Perhaps this is why other research also shows that women CEOs outperform peers three to one in S&P 500 companies.[28]

Finally, as mentioned in Part 3, the largest, most difficult hurdle to innovation—to any type of change—is that change takes time. For women, this may be an advantage because women manage time differently than men.

They make the most of it. Nicole Auerbach, co-founder of Valorem, gives a great talk about why women are best at multiplying time.[29] They are more engaged and engaging, which results in more workers who create more products, services, and new ideas that inevitably spur our economy.[30] They are also more efficient spenders of money and time. There are likely multiple reasons women are better at managing time than men are, including obvious ones such as often being the main person responsible for child rearing even if working full time. There are also some nonobvious reasons, such as studies showing that women are better at tech than men are. Lest you don't believe me, consider a recent study that showed that code written by women (when gender is not disclosed) is approved at a higher rate than code written by men.[31] Another study showed that teen girls, on the whole, outperform boys in technology and engineering literacy.[32] For all of these reasons, in addition to the fact that we are moving to a what Cali Ressler and Jody Thompson call a "Results Only Work Environment" (meaning "each person is free to do whatever they want, whenever they want—as long as they get the work done"[33]), women are poised for an advantage in the law marketplace. This doesn't mean that Anne-Marie Slaughter, one of my first female mentors in the law marketplace, is wrong. Women may never be able to have it all.[34] That said, when it comes to the ability to master the Three Rules of Engagement, they have, and they are *all that*.

New and Hungry Law Schools: Training the Trainers

Far too many academics at law schools do not operate with an Open Mind, Open Heart, or Open Door, particularly when it comes to how we educate future lawyers. They are too tied to Langdell's Socratic case method and the position of being in academia, so much so that they do a disservice to our future profession. Courses that teach the skills in the Lawyer Skills Delta are considered insubstantial and are disdained as being below a professor's work and not worth a professor's time. LawWithoutWalls has been called "fluff" by other academics. I can't change that or them—and believe me, I have tried!—but I will keep trying. Many others are trying too.

The best thing about LawWithoutWalls, however, is the professors and deans from 35 law and business schools and the more than 1,500 legal professionals, entrepreneurs, and business professionals from around the world who have opened up not only their minds, doors, and hearts to LWOW but also their arms (and pockets). These folks? They are hungry. They want new skills from our current and future professionals. They know this goal requires a new way of training. They join LWOW not only because of the innovations created at the intersection of law, business, and technology but also because of the skills honed in the process and because of the community of change agents it creates. It is a continually growing and evolving community of professionals dedicated to changing the way lawyers practice and collaborate with clients to solve problems.

Together we can envision a totally new type of law school one day—one that might be more of a finishing school or a school for law consultants as opposed to just a school for future practicing lawyers (but that's another book, one that I haven't written yet). A rough sketch now is that this new "law" school will be very different from what we consider law school today to be. It likely will not replace the top-tier traditional law schools; instead it will serve as an additional layer, providing skills training for the Lawyer Skills Delta and some practical legal training that is missing from our curriculums (other than that provided by clinics, which can only service a few students at a time). This "new" school will likely use multiple blended methods: blending in-person with virtual interaction, blending lectures with exercises, blending big-name professors with local practitioners, blending law with other disciplines, blending academia with professional services in law and business. Picture it: Deloitte's Advanced Degree in Legal Consulting and Services.

The market is hungry for this new type of "law" school, but for various reasons (including regulatory ones), it won't be developed overnight. In the meantime, the one thing that no law school appears to be doing—and the one thing that could make a real difference in the interim—is training the trainers: the adjuncts, clinical faculty, lecturers, and tenured faculty. The law schools that are not only hungry but also methodically pursuing greatness will start training our trainers. Currently, law faculty receive almost no training on how to teach law school students. Hungry law schools will find a way to train law school faculty in old and new methods of teaching. It is not sufficient to attempt to train our future law school students on the skills in the Lawyer Skills Delta because these skills aren't easily taught by anyone—especially in a classroom format. To blindly think that just anyone can teach these skills, is naïve. It is also naïve to think that it can be or should be taught only by people with traditional law degrees. Given that we know diversity and multidisciplinary interaction is one of the key ingredients to creative problem solving and innovation, it is essential that our trainers come from multidisciplinary and diverse backgrounds.

The top-tier law schools in every country do not *have* to change how they are training future lawyers. Their law school graduates have gotten jobs and will continue to get jobs and somehow will get enough training to prosper financially. (Whether they are adept at providing the kind of full-service client service addressed in Part 1 of this book is another question.) Rather, it is the hungry law schools, those schools ranked in the second and third tier of law schools in their countries, that will effect the most change. Today those hungry schools that are fighting for new ways of training students and attracting untraditional teaching talent to teach (in untraditional ways) the skills in the Lawyer Skills Delta will be those that prosper. Those schools that take a LawWithoutWalls approach—one that is multidisciplinary and blended (virtual/in-person) and that enables academics, business professionals, and lawyers together to co-train aspiring *and* practicing lawyers—will be aligned with marketplace realities.[35] And it is those schools (whether in the traditional category of "law" schools today or add-ons or new ones altogether) that will find a way to build a new market—a new brand—(perhaps in collaboration with a nonacademic organization or company such as a Big Four accounting firm) to provide training that matters. It is those schools that are hungry enough and that collaborate to train the trainers and add new "courses" and types of training to the *existing* curriculum that will prevail.

Possibly You: The Quarterbacks of Our Future

The last group that has the most potential to harness the legal upheaval to their advantage may be you. You are here. You are reading this book. You are in the small segment of the population that wants to transform how lawyers collaborate. And so I see infinite possibility in you: in the people who have asked for prior drafts of this book and copies of my presentations and in the people who have been inspired by my call to action—my mission which is to convince all lawyers to learn *how* to innovate so that they hone the skill set, mindset, and behaviors of innovators even if they do not want to be entrepreneurs and even if they never create or even want to create an innovation in their lifetime. So possibly you will be the intrapreneurs, the potential quarterbacks that harness the right people, the right training, the right networks, the right processes, the right technologies, the right tools, and the right services to create (and bring to life) the vision for law firms and legal departments of the future. Yes, it is as hard to picture as was the "world wide web" in 1991: What in the world could it be? What will it mean? How will it function? What kind of technology will it use? How will it change and impact us, and how can we harness it? "Yes, and . . ." those same questions are here now for you—and the good news is, per the quote at the beginning of this conclusion, that you "don't necessarily need a clear, crisp, sharp idea or vision"; in fact, it is likely "better" that you don't because the point is to continue exploring and making serendipitous discoveries along the way—understanding that "the journey" needs to start now because now is the only time that matters. So I conclude with my favorite quote of all:

"Remember then: there is only one time that is important—Now! It is the most important time because it is the only time when we have any power."

—Leo Tolstoy

APPENDIX A

Recommended Further Reading

Books

1. Johnson, Steven. *Where Good Ideas Come From: The Natural History of Innovation.* New York: Riverhead Books, 2010.

2. Sinek, Simon. *Start with Why: How Great Leaders Inspire Everyone to Take Action.* New York: Penguin Group, 2009.

3. Pink, Daniel H. *To Sell Is Human: The Surprising Truth About Moving Others.* New York: Riverhead Books, 2012.

4. Seelig, Tina. *What I Wish I Knew When I Was 20: A Crash Course on Making Your Place in the World.* New York: HarperOne, 2009.

5. Seelig, Tina. *inGenius: A Crash Course on Creativity.* New York: HarperCollins, 2012.

6. Chabris, Christopher, and Daniel Simons. *The Invisible Gorilla: How Our Intuitions Deceive Us.* New York: Broadway Paperbacks, 2009.

7. Ashton, Kevin. *How to Fly a Horse: The Secret History of Creation, Invention, and Discovery.* New York: Anchor Books, 2015.

8. Heath, Chip, and Dan Heath. *Switch: How to Change Things When Change Is Hard.* New York: Broadway Books, 2010.

9. Fried, Jason, and David Heinemeier Hansson. *Rework.* New York: Crown Business Publishing, 2010.

10. Cross, Rob, and Andrew Parker. *The Hidden Power of Social Networks: Understanding How Work Really Gets Done in Organizations.* Boston: Harvard Business School Press, 2004.

11. Boyd, Drew, and Jacob Goldenberg. *Inside the Box: A Proven System of Creativity for Breakthrough Results.* New York: Simon & Schuster, 2013.

12. Muth, Jon J. *Zen Shorts.* New York: Scholastic Press, 2008.

13. Cline, Ernest. *Ready Player One.* New York: Broadway Books, 2012.

14. Forest, Heather. *Stone Soup.* Little Rock, Arkansas: August House LittleFolk, 1998.

Articles

1. Katzenbach, Jon R., Ilona Steffen, and Caroline Kronley. "Culture Change That Sticks." *Harvard Business Review*, July–August 2012.

2. Christensen, Clayton M., Michael E. Raynor, and Rory McDonald. "What Is Disruptive Innovation?" *Harvard Business Review*, December 2015.

3. Moazed, Alex, and Nicholas Johnson. "Why Clayton Christensen Is Wrong About Uber and Disruptive Innovation." *TechCrunch*, February 27, 2016.

4. Richard, Dr, Larry. "Herding Cats: The Lawyer Personality Revealed." *Altman Weil Report to Management*, 29, no. 11 (2002).

5. Young, Tim. "365 Days, $10 Million, 3 Rounds, 2 Companies, All with 5 Magic Slides." *TechCrunch*, November 2, 2010.

6. Gordon, Leslie A. "Most Lawyers Are Introverted, and That's Not Necessarily a Bad Thing." *ABA Journal*, January 2016.

7. Brown, Tim. "Design Thinking. *Harvard Business Review*, June 2008.

8. Sunstein, Cass R., and Reid Hastie. "Making Dumb Groups Smarter," *Harvard Business Review*, December 2014.

9. Dillon, Bernadette, and Juliet Bourke. "The Six Signature Traits of Inclusive Leadership." Human Capital Consulting, Deloitte Australia, Deloitte University Press, 2017.

10. "5 Whys: Getting to the Root of a Problem Quickly," MindTools, https://www.mindtools.com/pages/article/newTMC_5W.htm.

11. Owyang, Jeremia, and Jaimy Szymanski. "Graphic: Blockchain for Every Industry," NewCo. July 11, 2017, https://shift.newco.co/graphic-blockchain-for-every-industry-dfcbdcfe23ea.

12. Skella, Jamie. "A Blockchain Explanation Your Parents Could Understand," LinkedIn, June 2, 2017, https://www.linkedin.com/pulse/blockchain-explanation-your-mum-could-understand-jamie-skella?_lrsc=ccf22078-11cf-4cda-b83e-3b0a7b91a86e.

APPENDIX B

Descriptions: LawWithoutWalls, LWOW X, and MOVELΔW

What Is LawWithoutWalls (LWOW)?

LWOW is a part-virtual experiential learning program designed for practicing and aspiring lawyers that brings a human-centered design perspective to law. Though LWOW teams create innovations at the intersection of law, business, and technology, LWOW's real value is building collaborative relationships and developing skills such as teaming, communication, leadership, mentoring, project management, innovation, cultural competency, business planning, technology, and networking that are essential to being a successful lawyer today. LWOW builds teams of approximately four law and business professionals (who serve as "Team Leaders," "Topic Experts," and/or "Mentors") along with three students (the "Hackers") from more than 35 law and business schools around the world. Over the course of 16 weeks, lawyer-led multidisciplinary teams co-create a real-time solution to a pressing problem in the legal industry—a Project of Worth—that includes a business case, an interactive presentation, an action/implementation plan, a prototype, an explanatory video demoing the solution, a commercial, and an elevator speech. The program is designed to build a culture of collaboration and engagement while developing skills that are essential for a successful legal career in the 21st century.

LawWithoutWalls transforms how lawyers collaborate with business professionals to solve problems. The projects range from those created to solve laws' business problems to those designed to help in getting access to justice. The overall winner from last year's cycle was a project called Ithaca, a not-for-profit web app that seeks to overcome the difficulties refugees face in obtaining legal assistance. Ithaca connects refugees with lawyers based upon expertise and needs while also providing a platform for the storage and access of legal information and documentation.

Some of the other 2017 winners were as follows:

1. Clear Loan sponsored by Pinsent Masons: A training tool for borrowers and an analytics tool for banks. Clear Loan helps reduce consumer complaints against banks by educating the consumer and helping banks provide standardized evidence of compliance related to borrower complaints during the lending process.

2. LEA sponsored by Eversheds: an app that helps declutter a lawyer's life by aggregating and curating all relevant legal news and industry updates in one place.

The mission of LawWithoutWalls is as follows: (1) to train future lawyers and those who work with lawyers; (2) to retrain current lawyers; and (3) to create innovations at the intersection of law, business, and technology. Currently LWOW sustains itself with sponsors who want to support this mission; as such, we "sell" topics and teams to law firms and legal institutions. Sponsors pick challenges they care about and put their lawyers and clients on teams so that they can hone the mindset, skill set, and behaviors of innovators and transform how lawyers and clients collaborate to solve problems. Recent team and topic sponsors include Avvo, Bupa, Clyde & Co, Eversheds Sutherland, Holland & Knight, HSBC, Interlaw, Janders Dean, Leah Cooper Consulting, Cate Campany, Legal Mosaic, Legal Zoom, LATAM, Linklaters, Lockheed Martin, Microsoft, Pinsent Masons, Spotify, UnitedLex, and White & Case.

What Is LWOW X?

LawWithoutWalls X (LWOW X) is a global, all-virtual program modeled after LawWithoutWalls wherein all projects are focused on solving tomorrow's social justice issues involving youth advocacy, juvenile justice, human rights, and/or access to education and justice for vulnerable client populations. This program is fully funded by Jim Ferraro and his law firm, the Ferraro Law Firm.

The topics and respective winning solutions in 2017 included the following:

- Topic: Underage and Underrepresented: How Can We Protect Youth From Cyberbullying?
- Solution 1: Cybird—Cybird is a fun, interactive, and engaging game to be downloaded by parents on their phone for children between eight and 10 years old (an age when children still play on their parents' phone) to create awareness of cyberbullying.
- Solution 2: Hello Amibot—Amibot is a Facebook Messenger Chatbot that provides LGBTQ+ high school students with first-time comfort and support after they are cyberbullied. By providing first aid, Amibot is your friend and counselor who provides you with a better way to react to cyberbullying and to protect yourself.
- Topic: Friend Rather Than Foe: How Can the Law Enable a Better Life for Migrants Held in Detention?
- Solution: Inlet—When migrants are being held in detention in airports, a gap is created. They can't get in touch with a lawyer, and a lawyer doesn't have access to the information required to file a habeas corpus petition on behalf of the migrant. Inlet is a platform for preemptively submitting personal information necessary for a petition against wrongful detention and automatically connecting that information to a lawyer upon detention to kick-start the petition.

What Is MOVELΔW?

MOVELΔW brings the same approach of LWOW and LWOW X to corporations and law firms. In a two-hour in-person session, a one-day workshop, or a four-month part virtual program, MOVELΔW addresses the developmental needs of lawyers by honing leadership, teamwork, innovation, project management, networking, technology, and cultural competency skills.

For the past three years, MOVELΔW has worked with the learning and development team at Microsoft to create a bespoke experiential learning program modeled after LWOW. Each year six to 10 teams of professionals from Microsoft's Corporate, External, & Legal Affairs (CELA) department go through a four-month innovation cycle and present at the annual summit for their entire department. Microsoft has implemented many of the projects. The fact that many of the projects are being brought to life, demonstrating that the projects are valuable and viable, prompted the leader of learning and development from Microsoft to declare in an article that what he found "most interesting was the number of projects that went on from their proposal presentations to implementation, and even inclusion in a product. An actual link to impact on our business as a direct result of the program."[1]

This would not have been possible (and the program would not have been adopted) if it didn't focus on and achieve real results on changing mindset and behavior and enhancing collaboration across CELA and between CELA and other parts of Microsoft. As the Microsoft partner went on to say, "This program provides what feels like a perfect mix of guided and supported safety with real life stress and challenge, and builds skills in scoping, innovation, research, cross-group teaming, problem solving, storytelling, and presentation. Not just teaching concepts, but forcing you to use them in a real-world environment."[2]

APPENDIX C

Research Methodology and Interview Characteristics

Research Methodology

To explore the topics in this book, I conducted more than 100 interviews of GCs and chief executives from large, international organizations along with heads of innovation and law firm partners from around the world. For most of the interviewes, a "snowball sample" approach was used to find potential respondents.[1] To elicit participation, on average, the interviewees were contacted by e mail one or two times. They were told that the topic was innovation in law. Interview questions were not provided in advance. All interviewees were assured that they and their companies would remain anonymous. These interviews lasted an average of 45 minutes. A large portion of the law firm partner interviews were conducted as part of consulting work I was providing to the firms. These interviews were shorter in length and had a dual purpose: (1) to understand the culture of the firm and (2) to understand the law firm partner's feelings and opinions about innovation. These law firm partners were told both of these purposes and were assured that their comments would remain anonymous at large and within the firm. I utilized a subset of the same questions I used with my other interviews.

Phone or Skype was used to conduct all of the interviews, and they consisted of both closed- and open-ended questions. A codebook was developed consisting of two parts.[2] The first part attempts to measure questions that elicited specific answers to tabulate responses systematically across interviewees. For the most part, the topics were presented in an open-ended fashion; therefore, the second part of the codebook is an analysis of the interview transcripts by certain questions and topics.[3] Various law student research assistants were trained to code the data.

The findings are not statistically significant, and they are not relied on to show or prove any point empirically. The interviews are merely self-reports by senior executives who have their own agendas and stories to tell. To that end, the interviews cannot be used to depict a true picture of how the world is; instead, they depict how "some professionals believe the world is or how it ought to be or how they would like others to believe they see the world."[4] This is sufficient because the research was not designed or used to *prove* anything. Instead, the primary goals of the interviews were to understand how professionals working in the law marketplace define, manage, and think about innovation in legal practice and training. As such, they provide a lens through which to view my theories and to inform my analysis and conclusions.

Interview Characteristics

In sum, I interviewed 107 professionals from 30 law firms, 42 companies, and seven professional service firms located in 13 different countries. The interviewees consisted of the following:

- Forty-four clients (referred to as client Interviewees)
  - These interviewees were mostly GCs but also some chief executives who hired lawyers directly.[5]
- Thirty-one chief innovation officers (referred to as CIO interviewees)[6]
  - These interviewees were individuals in charge of innovation at the law firm. Their titles varied. Some were called chief innovation officers; others were called directors of innovation or heads of innovation; still others had different titles. Some didn't have a title but were recognized as the leader of innovation at the firm nonetheless.
- Twenty-three law firm partners (referred to as law firm partner interviewees)
- Nine senior executives of professional service firms (referred to as PSF interviewees)
  - These interviewees were a mix of senior executives from the Big Four and other professional service and law consulting firms.

Here is a visual depiction of the 107 interviewees by organization type:

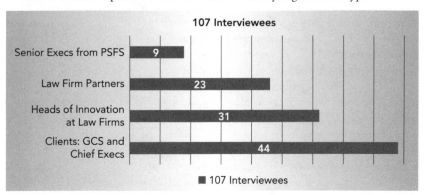

Although my research was global, as depicted in the following chart, most of my interviews were conducted with professionals located at companies or firms in the United States, Australia, and the United Kingdom.

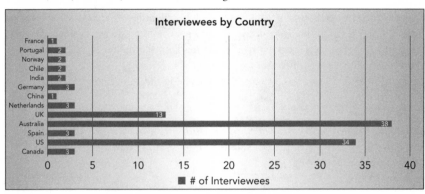

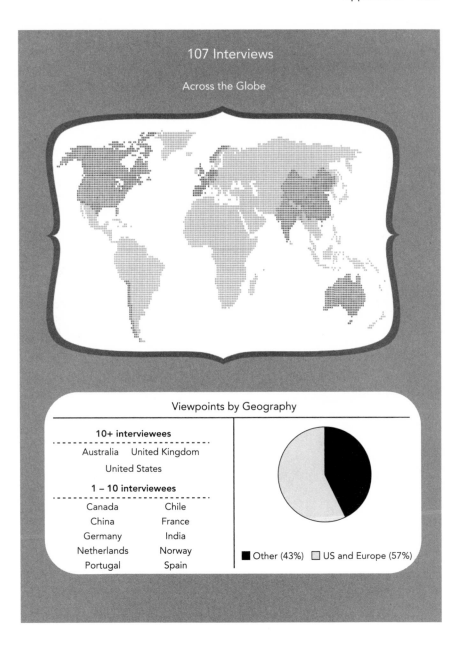

107 Interviews

Across the Globe

Viewpoints by Geography

10+ interviewees

Australia   United Kingdom

United States

1 – 10 interviewees

Canada   Chile

China   France

Germany   India

Netherlands   Norway

Portugal   Spain

■ Other (43%) ☐ US and Europe (57%)

Type	#	Title + Company Description
Client Interviewee	1	Deputy GC, large international airline
Client Interviewee	2	Executive vice president of regulatory strategy, well-known American brokerage firm
Client Interviewee	3	Assistant GC, educational consulting firm
Client Interviewee	4	Assistant GC, international industrial company
Client Interviewee	5	Vice president and senior corporate counsel, global insurance provider from the United States
Client Interviewee	6	Senior vice president and GC, global technology solutions company specializing in language translation
Client Interviewee	7	GC, energy and electric technologies company
Client Interviewee	8	Chief legal officer, American office supplies and business solutions retailer
Client Interviewee	9	Head of knowledge and Development, Compliance and Secretariat, a Big Four Australian bank and financial service provider
Client Interviewee	10	Legal director, worldwide healthcare group based in the United Kingdom
Client Interviewee	11	GC, Australian division of a worldwide healthcare group based in the United Kingdom
Client Interviewee	12	Corporate legal director, cooperative specializing in pension and asset management
Client Interviewee	13	CLO, large Chinese car manufacturer
Client Interviewee	14	Executive vice president and CLO, global insurance provider based in the United States
Client Interviewee	15	GC, international design and consulting firm
Client Interviewee	16	Deputy GC, global insurance company based in the United States
Client Interviewee	17	GC, iconic software and technology company from the United States
Client Interviewee	18	Former chair, Swiss-based financial services corporation specializing in wealth management and investment banking
Client Interviewee	19	GC, American mortgage investment firm

Client Interviewee	20	GC, American nonprofit that designs public competitions for technological development
Client Interviewee	21	GC, British multinational banking and financial services company
Client Interviewee	22	Lead counsel, large global bank headquartered in the United Kingdom
Client Interviewee	23	GC, global music streaming service
Client Interviewee	24	Deputy GC, global network and managed IT service provider that integrates communications products and services for multinational corporations from Germany
Client Interviewee	25	GC, large media and telecommunications company in Australia
Client Interviewee	26	GC, global information technology and consumer electronics company headquartered in the United Kingdom
Client Interviewee	27	GC, online legal technology company that helps clients create legal documents
Client Interviewee	28	GC, global cybersecurity company based in the United States
Client Interviewee	29	VP and associate GC, American multinational enterprise information technology company
Client Interviewee	30	Head of legal, large international airline
Client Interviewee	31	GC, government department of Australia
Client Interviewee	32	Senior legal counsel, global management consulting and professional services company
Client Interviewee	33	Senior corporate counsel, multinational insurance company headquartered in Australia
Client Interviewee	34	Director, government department in Australia
Client Interviewee	35	GC, religious organization in Australia
Client Interviewee	36	Senior vice president, legal affairs and compliance for a large airline
Client Interviewee	37	GC, American chemical distribution company
Client Interviewee	38	Associate GC, American bank holding company specializing in credit cards, auto loans, and banking and savings products
Client Interviewee	39	CEO, a specialist real estate investment management company in Australia

(Continued)

(Continued)

Type	#	Title + Company Description
Client Interviewee	40	General manager, one of Australia's largest insurance companies
Client Interviewee	41	GC, large financial services group based in Norway
Client Interviewee	42	GC, the Chilean division of a French cosmetics company
Client Interviewee	43	VP of legal, EMEA division of American manufacturer and marketer of cosmetics and hair care products.
Client Interviewee	44	GC, Canadian division of a Japanese automobile manufacturer

Type	#	Title + Company Description
CIO Interviewee	1	Practice and clients director, leading Portuguese law firm
CIO Interviewee	2	Quality, organization, and innovation coordinator, leading Portuguese law firm
CIO Interviewee	3	Chair, large Chicago law firm
CIO Interviewee	4	Head of business development and innovation, Spanish-based law firm with more than 30 offices worldwide
CIO Interviewee	5	Head of innovation, a multinational law firm based in London
CIO Interviewee	6	Director of practice innovation, an international corporate law firm from the United States
CIO Interviewee	7	Chief practice management officer, an international law firm headquarted in the northwest United States
CIO Interviewee	8	Executive director of innovation, world-reknowned law firm from Asia
CIO Interviewee	9	Chief information officer, Australian corporate law firm
CIO Interviewee	10	Director of the resources and technology team, leading law firm from the United Kingdom
CIO Interviewee	11	Chief strategy officer, leading London-based law firm
CIO Interviewee	12	Chief information officer, multinational professional services firm from Australia
CIO Interviewee	13	Chief knowledge officer, large American law firm
CIO Interviewee	14	Client relationship director, a multinational Australian law firm

CIO Interviewee	15	Innovation manager, Dutch law firm with offices around Europe and New York
CIO Interviewee	16	National innovation leader, Canada's largest law firms
CIO Interviewee	17	Senior director of professional services, business law firm from California
CIO Interviewee	18	Director of knowledge and innovation, multinational London-based law firm
CIO Interviewee	19	Partner, American law firm with more than two dozen offices worldwide
CIO Interviewee	20	Chief knowledge officer, American law firm with more than two dozen offices worldwide
CIO Interviewee	21	COO, multinational London-based law firm
CIO Interviewee	22	Partner, American law firm with more than two dozen offices worldwide
CIO Interviewee	23	Global head of innovation and business change, a multinational law firm headquarted in London
CIO Interviewee	24	Founder and partner, law firm with five offices in India
CIO Interviewee	25	Head of innovation Europe, one of the world's largest law firms from the United Kingdom
CIO Interviewee	26	Corporate services director, an Australian business law firm
CIO Interviewee	27	The innovation manager and director of innovation, one of Australia's Big Six law firms
CIO Interviewee	28	Partner responsible for innovation, a large Australian law firm
CIO Interviewee	29	Global Chief innovation officer, a London-based law firm with four dozen offices worldwide
CIO Interviewee	30	Head of innovation, a multinational law firm headquarted in both London and Washington, D.C.
CIO Interviewee	31	Innovation and networks leader, a multinational professional services firm from Australia

Type	#	Title + Company Description
Law Firm Partner Interviewee	1	Partner, law firm with offices across the United States and Europe
Law Firm Partner Interviewee	2	Partner, law firm with offices across the United States and Europe
Law Firm Partner Interviewee	3	Partner, law firm with offices across the United States and Europe
Law Firm Partner Interviewee	4	Partner, law firm with offices across the United States and Europe
Law Firm Partner Interviewee	5	Partner, law firm with offices across the United States and Europe
Law Firm Partner Interviewee	6	Partner, law firm with offices across the United States and Europe
Law Firm Partner Interviewee	7	Partner, midtier Australian law firm
Law Firm Partner Interviewee	8	Partner, midtier Australian law firm
Law Firm Partner Interviewee	9	Partner, midtier Australian law firm
Law Firm Partner Interviewee	10	Partner, midtier Australian law firm
Law Firm Partner Interviewee	11	Partner, midtier Australian law firm
Law Firm Partner Interviewee	12	Partner, midtier Australian law firm
Law Firm Partner Interviewee	13	Partner, midtier Australian law firm
Law Firm Partner Interviewee	14	Partner, midtier Australian law firm
Law Firm Partner Interviewee	15	Partner, midtier Australian law firm
Law Firm Partner Interviewee	16	Partner, midtier Australian law firm
Law Firm Partner Interviewee	17	Partner, midtier Australian law firm
Law Firm Partner Interviewee	18	Deputy chief executive partner, top-tier Australian law firm
Law Firm Partner Interviewee	19	Chief executive partner, top-tier Australian law firm
Law Firm Partner Interviewee	20	Partner, top-tier Australian law firm
Law Firm Partner Interviewee	21	Partner, top-tier Australian law firm
Law Firm Partner Interviewee	22	Deputy chief executive partner, top-tier Australian law firm
Law Firm Partner Interviewee	23	Partner, New York City–based law firm

Type	#	Title + Company Description
PSF Interviewee	1	Director, consultany firm with expertise in growth and strategy projects
PSF Interviewee	2	Director of legal transformation, consulting firm specializing in legal practice management
PSF Interviewee	3	Partner and head of technology, global consultancy firm that provides advice across a wide range of business ventures
PSF Interviewee	4	Independent consultant, UK-based consulting firm
PSF Interviewee	5	Director, Big Four global consulting firm
PSF Interviewee	6	Chief financial officer, top-tier Australian law firm
PSF Interviewee	7	Executive director, Big Four global consultancy firm
PSF Interviewee	8	Former CEO, professional services firm located in the United States.
PSF Interviewee	9	Partner and head of legal, Big Four global consulting firm

NOTES

Part I

1. Simon Sinek, *Start with Why: How Great Leaders Inspire Everyone to Take Action* (New York: Penguin Group, 2009).

Chapter 1

1. J. D. Salinger, *The Catcher in the Rye* (Boston: Little, Brown and Company, 1991) 122.
2. *See generally,* World Economic Forum, The Future of Jobs, Employment, Skills and Workforce Strategy for the Fourth Industrial Revolution, Global Challenge Insight Report [hereinafter WEF Report] (January 2016) preface.
3. WEF Report at Part I, Chapter 1, 3 (explaining that "only a minority of the world's global workforce of more than three billion people is directly employed by large and emerging multinational employers, these companies often act as anchors for smaller firms and local entrepreneurship ecosystems" and "have the potential to transform local labour markets through indirect employment and by setting the pace for changing skills and occupational requirements"). *See also id.* at 5.
4. *See, e.g.,* Adam Fletcher, *Honey We Shrunk Your Job: The Future of Work,* CREATIVEMORNINGS, March 2, 2016, Berlin host Jürgen Siebert, accessed March 29, 2016, https://creativemornings.com/talks/adam-fletcher/1.
5. WEF Report, *supra* note 3, at 3–5.
6. Kate Taylor, *Fast-Food CEO Says He's Investing in Machines Because the Government Is Making It Difficult to Afford Employees,* BUSINESS INSIDER, March 16, 2016, http://www.businessinsider.com/carls-jr-wants-open-automated-location-2016-3.
7. *Skype Translator Unveils the Magic to More People Around the World,* MICROSOFT (blog), http://blogs.skype.com/2015/10/01/skype-translator-unveils-the-magic-to-more-people-around-the-world.
8. *See, e.g.,* www.23andMe.com, a website to find out what your DNA can tell you about your health, accessed December 5, 2017, https://www.23andme.com/service.
9. *Printing a Human Kidney—Anthony Atala,* TED-ED, accessed December 5, 2017, http://ed.ted.com/lessons/printing-a-human-kidney-anthony-atala.
10. Maggie Clark, *States Take the Wheel on Driverless Cars,* USA TODAY, July 29, 2013, accessed March 29, 2016, https://www.usatoday.com/story/news/nation/2013/07/29/states-driverless-cars/2595613/; Victoria Ho, *These Futuristic Driverless Pods Will Run On Singapore's Roads by End of the Year,* MASHABLE.COM, accessed April 20, 2016, https://mashable.com/2016/04/20/driverless-pods-singapore/#JL_mikz1egqc (stating that Singaporeans will be transported by autonomous lithium battery run pods by 2017).
11. Danielle Muoio, *Tesla Is Pushing the Insurance Industry to Prepare for Massive Disruption,* BUSINESS INSIDER FRANCE, May 25, 2107, www.businessinsider.fr/us/how-tesla-self-driving-cars-are-changing-insurance-industry-2017-5/?_lrsc=af38f3d5-c08a-4edf-8d5f-76024af40f4f.

12. Arion McNicoll, *How Google's CalicoAims to Fight Aging and 'Solve Death,'* CNN, October 3, 2013, accessed March 29, 2016, https://www.cnn.com/2013/10/03/tech/innovation/google-calico-aging-death/.

13. Zoe Corbyn, *Live for Ever: Scientists Say They'll Soon Extend Life 'Well Beyond 120',* THE GUARDIAN, January 11, 2015, accessed March 29, 2016, https://www.theguardian.com/science/2015/jan/11/-sp-live-forever-extend-life-calico-google-longevity.

14. Rebecca Boyle, *With an Artificial Memory Chip, Rats Can Remember and Forget at the Touch of a Button,* POPULAR SCIENCE, June 17, 2011, accessed March 29, 2016,http://www.popsci.com/technology/article/2011-06/artificial-memory-chip-rats-can-remember-and-forget-touch-button; *see also* Tracy Staedter, *Matrix-Style Brain Implant Could Boost Memory,* GROUP NINE, https://www.seeker.com/matrix-style-brain-implant-could-boost-memory-1770250895.html See<er, September 15, 2015 (reporting that "small electrode arrays placed in brain regions known to be associated with memory were used to improve patients' memories").

15. Ashley Feinberg, *An 83,000-Processor Supercomputer Can Only Match 1% of Your Brain,* GIZMODO, accessed December 5, 2017, https://gizmodo.com/an-83-000-processor-supercomputer-only-matched-one-perc-1045026757 (explaining that the Japanese and German scientists were able to mimic just 1 percent of one second's worth of human brain activity—the prediction is that within the next decade, we'll be able to use computers to represent the entire brain "at the level of the individual nerve cell and its synapses").

16. *See AlphaGo Zero: Learning from Scratch,* DEEPMIND, accessed April 24, 2018, https://deepmind.com/blog/alphago-zero-learning-scratch/.

17. *See* Lauren F. Friedman, *IBM's Watson Supercomputer May Soon Be the Best Doctor in the World,* BUSINESS INSIDER, April 22, 2014, accessed April 24, 2018, http://www.businessinsider.com/ibms-watson-may-soon-be-the-best-doctor-in-the-world-2014-4.

18. Dentons, accessed March 28, 2016, https://www.dentons.com/en/whats-different-about-dentons/connecting-you-to-talented-lawyers-around-the-globe/news/2015/may/dentons-launches-nextlaw-labs-creates-legal-business-accelerator; *see also* www.nextlawlabs.com.

19. *How Watson Helps Lawyers Find Answers in Legal Research,* MEDIUM, COGNITIVE VOICES, January 4, 2017, https://medium.com/cognitivebusiness/how-watson-helps-lawyers-find-answers-in-legal-research-672ea028dfb8.

20. *See* Ray Kurzweil, *The Singularity Is Near: When Humans Transcend Biology* (New York: Penguin Group, 2005) 134–36; *see* Vinge Vernor, *The Coming Technological Singularity: How to Survive in the Post-Human Era,* NASA. Lewis Research Center, Vision 21: Interdisciplinary Science and Engineering in the Era of Cyberspace, pp. 11–22 (SEE N94-27358 07-12) March 1993.

21. Irving John Good, *Speculations Concerning the First Ultraintelligent Machine,* *Advances in Computers,* Volume 6, eds. Franz L. Alt and Morris Rubinoff (Harahan,

Academic Press, 1965), 31–88, https://doi.org/10.1016/S0065-2458(08)60418-0; also available at http://www.aeiveos.com/%257Ebradbury/Authors/Computing/Good-IJ/SCtFUM.html, accessed January 22, 2018.

22. Adam Fletcher, *The Freedom Figure: How to Work Less, Live More, and Thrive in the Digital Age* (Seattle: CreateSpace Independent Publishing Platform, 2016).

23. Aebra Coe, *Will a Robot Lawyer Take Your Job? What AI Means for You*, LAW360, May 31 2017, accessed June 2, 2017, https://www.law360.com/technology/articles/930096/will-a-robot-lawyer-take-your-job-what-ai-means-for-you?nl_pk=0b4f7f93-5efc-420e-94f0-98e085b43c37&utm_source=newsletter&utm_medium=email&utm_campaign=technology&read_more=1.

24. Mark A. Cohen, *The Latest Legal Delivery Collaboration: LISA and Billy—They're Robots*, LEGAL MOSAIC, accessed September 11, 2017, https://legalmosaic.com/2017/09/11/the-latest-legal-delivery-collaboration-lisa-and-billy-theyre-robots/#.

25. Ernest Cline, *Ready Player One* (New York: Broadway Books, 2012) 93–99.

26. Angela Johnston, *Robotic Seals Comfort Dementia Patients but Raise Ethical Concerns*, KALW Local Public Radio, August 17, 2015, accessed November 29, 2017, http://kalw.org/post/robotic-seals-comfort-dementia-patients-raise-ethical-concerns#stream/0.

27. Sophia was created by David Hanson of Hanson Robotics and given citizenship by Saudi Arabia. *See* Zara Stone, *Everything You Need to Know About Sophia, The World's First Robot Citizen*, FORBES, November 7, 2017, accessed November 29, 2017, https://www.forbes.com/sites/zarastone/2017/11/07/everything-you-need-to-know-about-sophia-the-worlds-first-robot-citizen/#338167746fa1.

28. Adam Conner-Simons and Rachel Gordon, *Detecting Emotions with Wireless Signals*, MIT NEWS, September 20, 2016, accessed May 31, 2017, http://news.mit.edu/2016/detecting-emotions-with-wireless-signals-0920.

29. Daniel Susskind and Richard Susskind, *The Future of the Professions* (Oxford, Oxford University Press, 2015), 251–52.

30. Francie Diep, *Long Distance Relationships May Benefit from "Hug Shirts," Other Technologies*, THE HUFFINGTON POST, April 12, 2012, accessed March 29, 2017, https://www.huffingtonpost.com/2012/02/12/long-distance-relationshi_n_1271210.html; *see also* http://cutecircuit.com/the-hug-shirt/.

31. A few years ago, University of Miami School of Law Professor Michael Froomkin started a conference series called We Robot, designed to engage people from various disciplines about the legal and policy questions relating to robots. This conference began at the University of Miami in 2012 and has since then been hosted by Stanford, the University of Washington, and Yale, accessed November 20, 2017, http://www.werobot2017.com/.

32. WEF Report, *supra* note 3, at Table 3, 9 ; *id.* at 6.

33. *Id.* at 6, 9.

34. Jeanne C. Meister and Karie Willyerd, *Are You Ready to Manage 5 Generations of Workers?* HARVARD BUSINESS REVIEW, October 16, 2009; WEF Report Part I, at 8.

35. For a discussion regarding creating a culture of compliance, *see* Michele DeStefano, *Creating a Culture of Compliance: Why Departmentalization May Not Be the Answer*, 10 HASTINGS BUSINESS L.J. 71 (2014).
36. Jennifer M. Ortman et al., *An Aging Nation: The Older Population in The United States: Population Estimates and Projections*, UNITED STATES CENSUS BUREAU, https://www.census.gov/prod/2014pubs/p25-1140.pdf, accessed January 21, 2018, (discussing the aging population based on the 2012 National Projections by the U.S. Census Bureau and stating that "[i]n 2050, the population aged 65 and over is projected to be 83.7 million, almost double its estimated population of 43.1 million in 2012"); *Demographic Profile of the Older Population*, WORLD POPULATION AGEING 1950–2050, accessed January 21, 2018, http://www.un.org/esa/population/publications/worldageing19502050/pdf/90chapteriv.pdf (showing that in 1950, one in fifteen persons aged 60 or older was 80 or above and projecting that in 2050, this will increase to one in five).
37. Jeanne C. Meister and Karie Willyerd, *Are You Ready to Manage 5 Generations of Workers?* HARVARD BUSINESS REVIEW, October 16, 2009; Dan Bursch and Kip Kelly, *Managing the Multigenerational Workplace*, UNC Kenan-Flagler Business School Executive Development White Paper, at 2, accessed December 5, 2017, www.kenan-flagler.unc.edu/~/media/Files/documents/executive-development/managing-the-multigenerational-workplace-white-paper.pdf.
38. EY Executive Summary of Study *Younger Managers Rise in the Ranks, Managing the Generational Mix and Preferred Workplace Perks*, accessed December 5, 2017, www.ey.com/us/en/issues/talent-management/talent-survey-managing-the-generational-mix-and-preferred-workplace-perks; *see also* EY Survey Data, accessed December 5, 2017, http://www.ey.com/Publication/vwLUAssets/EY-Survey_shows_younger_managers_rising_in_the_ranks/%24FILE/Executive-Summary-Generations-Research.pdf; Bursch et al, *supra* note 38, 2–3. [Hereinafter EY Exec Summary].
39. Susan A. Murphy, *Leading a Multigenerational Workforce*, AARP, (2007), accessed December 5, 2017, https://assets.aarp.org/www.aarp.org_/articles/money/employers/leading_multigenerational_workforce.pdf,. 2017).
40. Rob Asghar, *Study: The War of Generations Results in Lost Productivity*, FORBES, February 5, 2014, accessed April 10, 2016, http://www.forbes.com/sites/robasghar/2014/02/05/study-the-war-of-generations-results-in-lost-productivity/ [reporting results from a survey of 1,350 workers and managers conducted by the American Society for Training and Development (ASTD); Bursch, *supra* note 37.
41. *See* EY Exec Summary of Study *supra* note 38; *see supra* note 38; *see also* Bursch, *supra* note 37; Diane Brady, *In the Corner Office, Life Doesn't Suck for Generation X*," BLOOMBERG BUSINESSWEEK, September 3, 2013), accessed April 10, 2016, http://www.bloomberg.com/news/articles/2013-09-03/in-the-corner-office-life-doesnt-suck-for-generation-x).
42. The Council of Economic Advisers, Executive Office of the President, *15 Economic Facts About Millennials*, White House Report, October 2014 at 3–5, accessed

December 5, 2017, https://obamawhitehouse.archives.gov/sites/default/files/docs/millennials_report.pdf; Richard Fry, *Millennials Surpass Gen Xers as the Largest Generation in U.S. Labor Force*, May 11, 2015, accessed December 5, 2016, http://www.pewresearch.org/fact-tank/2015/05/11/millennials-surpass-gen-xers-as-the-largest-generation-in-u-s-labor-force/ft_15-05-04_genlaborforcecomposition-2/.

43. *See* EY Exec Summary of Study *supra* note 38 at 3 and 6.

44. *See* EY Exec Summary of Study *supra* note 38 at 3.

45. 15 Economic Facts, *supra* note 43, at 10–11.

46. EY Study, *Global Generations: A Global Study On Work-Life Challenges Across Generations*; Detailed Findings at 12, accessed December 5, 2017, http://www.ey.com/Publication/vwLUAssets/EY-global-generations-a-global-study-on-work-life-challenges-across-generations/%24FILE/EY-global-generations-a-global-study-on-work-life-challenges-across-generations.pdf; Kathy Gurchiek, *Millennials Drive Change in Workplace*, SHRM (blog), September 4, 2013, https://blog.shrm.org/millennials-drive-change-in-workplace; Harrison Kratz, *Maximizing Millennials: The Who, How, and Why of Managing Gen Y*, UNC KENAN-FLAGLER BUSINESS SCHOOL (blog), June 24, 2013, https://onlinemba.unc.edu/blog/geny-in-the-workplace/.

47. *See, e.g.,* research conducted by North Carolina State University's ERM Initiative and Protivit, *Executive Perspectives on Top Risks for 2016: Key Issues Being Discussed in the Boardroom and C-Suite*, accessed December 5, 2017, https://erm.ncsu.edu/az/erm/i/chan/library/NC-State-Protiviti-Survey-Top-Risks-2016.pdf; Hazel Bradford, *Chief Compliance Officers Prepare for Closer SEC Scrutiny*, PENSIONS & INVESTMENTS, January 11, 2016, accessed April 10, 2016, http://www.pionline.com/article/20160111/PRINT/301119976/chief-compliance-officers-prepare-for-closer-sec-scrutiny; Grant Thornton LLP 2014 Corporate General Counsel Survey, *Resource-Strapped In-House Counsel Battle Regulations, Cybercrime and Litigation* (on file with author).

48. Sarbanes-Oxley Act of 2002, Pub. L. No. 107-204, 116 Stat. 745 [codified in sections of 11, 15, 18, 28, and 29 U.S.C. (2002)].

49. Dodd-Frank Wall Street Reform and Consumer Protection Act, Pub. L. No. 111-203 124 Stat. 1376 (2010) (codified as amended in scattered sections of 7, 12, 15, 18, and 31 U.S.C.).

50. Ben Bedell, *Probes of White-Collar Crime to Target Corporate Leaders*, NY L.J. (September 11, 2015).

51. *Managing Risk Better in 2013: Is What's Old, New Again?*, INTELLIGIZE 3, June 2013, https://www.intelligize.com, on file with author (reporting that there was a 28% increase in enforcement actions by the SEC based on FCPA violations from 2006 to 2012); Susan Lorde Martin, *Compliance Officers: More Jobs, More Responsibility, More Liability*, 29 NOTRE DAME J.L. ETHICS & PUB. POL'Y 169 (2015).

52. Valentina Pasquali, *Compliance Goes Global: The Unavoidable Costs of Increasing Regulation*, GLOBAL FINANCE, May 4, 2015.

53. *Id.*

54. *See supra* 35.

55. Client Interviewee 31.

56. Law Firm Partner Interviewee 23.

Chapter 2

1. Law Firm Partner Interviewee 11.

2. Thomas Connelly, *Deutsche Bank Refuses to Pay for External Legal Work Completed by Trainees and Newly-Qualified Lawyers*, LEGAL CHEEK, March 22, 2017, accessed December 5, 2017, https://www.legalcheek.com/2017/03/deutsche-bank-refuses-to-pay-for-external-legal-work-completed-by-trainees-and-newly-qualified-lawyers/ NEWS.

3. Suzi Ring, *Fixed-Fee Spin-Off Radiant Moves into Litigation with Double Partner Hire*, LEGAL WEEK, April 4, 2012, accessed October 1, 2017, www.legalweek.com/sites/legalweek/2012/04/04/fixed-fee-spin-off-radiant-moves-into-litigation-with-double-partner-hire/.

4. Katy Dowell, *Deloitte Prepares to Take on the UK Legal Market*, THE LAWYER, June 9, 2014, accessed September 30, 2017, https://www.thelawyer.com/issues/online-june-2014/deloitte-prepares-to-take-on-the-uk-legal-market/.

5. EY, accessed September 30, 2017,www.ey.com/uk/en/services/tax/law.

6. Elizabeth Olson, *PwC, the Accounting Giant, Will Open a Law Firm in the U.S.*, THE NEW YORK TIMES, September 22, 2017, accessed September 30, 2017, https://www.nytimes.com/2017/09/22/business/dealbook/pwc-law-firm-ilc.html?mcubz=1.

7. Emily Maltby and Sarah E. Needleman, *Dot-Com Bubble's Equity Swaps Are Back: Short of Cash, Start-Ups Opt to Pay for Professional Services by Offering Stakes to Website Designers, Marketers, Law Firms*, THE WALL STREET JOURNAL, September 5, 2012, accessed December 5, 2017, https://www.wsj.com/articles/SB10000872396390443589304577633552964792854.

8. *Dentons Signs Relationship with WeWork Labs in New York*, DENTONS, February 22, 2016, accessed June 4, 2016, https://www.dentons.com/en/whats-different-about-dentons/connecting-you-to-talented-lawyers-around-the-globe/news/2016/february/dentons-signs-relationship-with-wework-labs-new-york.

9. Roksana Slavinsky, *Dentons and WeWork Form Partnership*, BISNOW DC, February 19, 2016, accessed June 4, 2017, https://www.bisnow.com/washington-dc/news/washington-dc-legal/dentons-and-wework-labs-form-partnership-56227.

10. William Peacock, *Should You Swap Legal Services for Interest in Client's Business?* FINDLAW (blog), August 16, 2013, blogs.findlaw.com/strategist/2013/08/should-you-swap-legal-services-for-interest-in-clients-business.html.

11. Bureau of Labor Statistics' Business Employment Dynamics, table 7, accessed January 22, 2018, https://www.bls.gov/bdm/us_age_naics_00_table7.txt; Keith Speights, *What Percentage of Businesses Fail in Their First Year?*, THE MOTLEY FOOL, May 3, 2017, accessed January 22, 2018, https://www.fool.com/careers/2017/05/03/what-percentage-of-businesses-fail-in-their-first.aspx.

12. Michele DeStefano, *Compliance and Claim Funding, Testing the Borders of Lawyers' Monopoly and the Unauthorized Practice of Law*, 82 FORDHAM L. REV. 2961 (2014); Michele DeStefano, *Claim Funders and Commercial Claim Holders: A Common Interest or a Common Problem?* 63 DEPAUL L. REV. 305 (2014); Michele DeStefano, *Nonlawyers Influencing Lawyers: Too Many Cooks in the Kitchen or Stone Soup?* 80 FORDHAM L. REV. 2791 (2012).

13. DeStefano, *supra* note 12.

14. Vicky Waye et al., *Innovation in the Australian Legal Profession*, INTERNATIONAL JOURNAL OF THE LEGAL PROFESSION 2017.

15. *Id.*

16. *Id.*

17. Dirk Naumann, *The Legal Tech-Train Is Rolling—Better Get on Board!*," INTERNATIONAL IN-HOUSE COUNSEL JOURNAL, 10, no. 39.

18. *Lawyered Up: Deals to Legal Tech Up in 2016*, CB INSIGHTS (blog), March 17, 2017, https://www.cbinsights.com/blog/legal-tech-startup-funding-deals-dollars/ (highlighting a $12 million investment in legal research company casetext).

19. *The 2017 Alternative Legal Service Study: Understanding the Growth and Benefits of New Legal Service Providers*, Report by Thompson Reuters and Georgetown Law, the University of Oxford Saïd Business School, accessed December 5, 2017, http://legalsolutions.thomsonreuters.com/law-products/solutions/legal-outsourcing-services/outsourcing-insights/alternative-legal-service-provider-study-2017.

20. Joe Borstein, *Alt.legal: Follow the White Rabbit: Alternative Legal Service Providers (ALSPs) Are Transforming the Business and Practice of Law*," ABOVE THE LAW, April 12, 2017, accessed January 28, 2018, https://abovethelaw.com/2017/04/alt-legal-follow-the-white-rabbit/.

21. Alternative Legal Service Study, *supra* note 19.

22. Naumann, *supra* note 17.

23. BODHALA, accessed November 30, 2107, https://www.bodhala.com/.

24. Miriam Rozen, *This Startup Helps Clients Dish on Their Law Firms. Will the Firms Listen?* THE AMERICAN LAWYER, June 1, 2017, accessed June 3, 2017, https://www.americanlawyer.com/id=1202788172424/This-Startup-Helps-Clients-Dish-on-Their-Law-Firms-Will-the-Firms-Listen?kw=This%20Startup%20Helps%20Clients%20Dish%20on%20Their%20Law%20Firms.%20Will%20the%20Firms%20Listen?et=editorial&bu=The%20American%20Lawyer&cn=20170602&src=EMC-Email&pt=Am%20Law%20Daily.

25. In Australia, it appears that big law firms are more likely to be engaged in innovative activity than smaller firms. *See supra* note 14.

26. *Id.*

27. Jason Clay, *The Rise of the Extrapreneur: Making Cross-Sector Collaboration Happen*, June 21, 2013, THE GUARDIAN, accessed January 20, 2018, https://www.theguardian.com/sustainable-business/rise-of-extrapreneur-cross-sector-collaboration; *see also* Madalina Dobraca, TAG ARCHIVES: ENTREPRENEUR, accessed January 20, 2018, www.madalinadobraca.com/tag/entrepreneur/.

28. Susan Adams, *Clayton Christensen On What He Got Wrong About Disruptive Innovation*, FORBES, October 3, 2016, accessed June 3, 2017, https://www.forbes.com/sites/forbestreptalks/2016/10/03/clayton-christensen-on-what-he-got-wrong-about-disruptive-innovation/#7a732ac7391b.

29. David B. Wilkins, 113th Sibley Lecture, accessed September 30, 2017, https://www.youtube.com/watch?v=4CqYJHkjAlQ at 2:53.

30. Ray Worthy Campbell, *Rethinking Regulation and Innovation in the U.S. Legal Services Market*, 9 N.Y.U. J. L. & BUS. 1 (2012); Brian Sheppard, *Incomplete Innovation and the Premature Disruption of Legal Services*, 2015 MICH. ST. L. REV. 1797.

31. Alternative Legal Service Study, *supra* note 19.

32. Casey Ross and Ike Swetlitz, *IBM Pitched Its Watson Supercomputer as a Revolution in Cancer Care. It's Nowhere Close*, STAT, September 5, 2017, accessed December 5, 2017, https://www.statnews.com/2017/09/05/watson-ibm-cancer.

33. Kurt Gray, *AI Can Be a Troublesome Teammate*, HARVARD BUSINESS REVIEW, July 20, 2017, accessed December 5, 2017, https://hbr.org/2017/07/ai-can-be-a-troublesome-teammate.

34. Client Interviewee 25.

35. Client Interviewee 29.

36. Client Interviewee 30.

37. Daniel Kahneman, *Thinking Fast and Slow* (New York: Farrar, Straus and Giroux, 2011).

38. D. H. Lawrence, *Women in Love*, ed. Charles Ross (New York: Penguin Books, 1989) 409.

39. Adams, *supra* note 85.

40. Eric Chin, *Bigger. Better. Both? Applying Clayton Christensen's Theories to BigLaw vs NewLaw*, BEATONCAPITAL, January 12, 2015, accessed December 5, 2017, www.beatoncapital.com/2015/01/applying-clayton-christensens-theories-biglaw-vs-newlaw/.

41. Lee McIntyre Routledge, *Respecting Truth: Willful Ignorance in the Internet Age* (London, Routledge, 2015).

Chapter 3

1. Client Interviewee 42.

2. Henrik Kniberg, Making Sense of MVP (Minimum Viable Product)—and Why I Prefer Earliest Testable/Usable/Lovable, CRISP'S BLOG FROM THE CRISP CONSULTANTS (blog), January 25, 2016, https://blog.crisp.se/2016/01/25/henrikkniberg/making-sense-of-mvp. Note: I was first introduced to this chart by a presentation delivered by Professor David Wilkins at Harvard Law School in one of the Executive Education programs we both teach.

3. Client Interviewee 30 ("It sounds trite, but I am amazed how many times it is missed in practice.").

4. Client Interviewee 33.

5. Client Interviewee 39.

6. Max Hübner, *The Case of PGGM: The Transformational Legal Department*, accessed December 5, 2017, https://www.pggm.nl/wat-vinden-we/Documents/the-case-of-pggm_the-transformational-legal-department.pdf.

7. Client Interviewee 30.

8. Client Interviewee 9.

9. Hübner, *supra* note 6.

10. Reena SenGupta, *Legal Success Comes from Turning Orthodoxies on Their Heads*, FINANCIAL TIMES, June 2, 2016, accessed October 1, 2017, https://www.ft.com/content/48a7b0a2-2069-11e6-aa98-db1e01fabc0c; *see also* HERBERT SMITH FREEHILLS, accessed October 1, 2017, https://www.herbertsmithfreehills.com/news/herbert-smith-freehills-wins-financial-times-top-asia-pacific-innovation-award.

11. Jamie Smyth, *Australian Law Firms—Up from Down Under: Fierce Competition Has Made Them Inventive at Home and Ambitious Overseas*, FINANCIAL TIMES, June 1, 2017, accessed December 5, 2017, https://www.ft.com/content/734c3c98-2922-11e7-bc4b-5528796fe35c.

12. Law Firm Partner Interviewees confirm this over and over again. *See, e.g.*, Law Firm Partner Interviewee 23 ("At the end of the day, what they want you to do is run their business and tell them, confidently what to do . . . with instantaneous responsiveness.").

13. Client Interviewee 29.

14. Steven Walker, *6 Things Modern GCs Really Want: From Their Law Firms*, LINKEDIN, November 27, 2017, https://www.linkedin.com/pulse/6-things-modern-gcs-really-want-from-law-firms-steven-walker/?trackingId=t0FwMBJIN7G7xanbDRbB%2BQ%3D%3D, accessed December 4, 2017, (making a similar point, "Once again, this is an opportunity for law firms. Many GCs would welcome guidance from their trusted partner law firms on technology they might look at. Firms are in a unique position to provide expertise and communicate a point of view; they are vendor-agnostic and have a history of service delivery for established clients, putting them in an excellent position to support their clients on technology strategies and requirements. Such services may not be core to today's law firms and may even seem incongruous or beyond their current capabilities, but they are most certainly going to be core to the Big 4 and the new generation of alternative legal service providers.").

15. Client Interviewee 29.

16. Leo Staub, "8 Steps to Management Excellence in Law Firms, The Comprehensive St. Gallen Approach," University of St. Gallen, 2014 (pointing out that the "strategic challenge" for the lawyer is to "stabilize this sporadic contact with the client" and "develop a significantly more intensive, and above all more permanent, relationship with the client").

17. "Thumbs-up smiley face" and "Thumbs-down smiley face" icons are by iconsmind.com, GB, from the Noun Project, accessed April 25, 2018, https://thenounproject.com/search/?q=thumbs%20up%20face&i=68448.

18. Tiffani Alexander, *Q&A with the EIC: GC Summit Chairs*, ACC DOCKET, May 5, 2017, accessed December 5, 2017, www.accdocket.com/articles/gc-summit-chairs.cfm.

19. Walker, *supra* note 14.

20. Client Interviewee 25.

21. Richard Susskind, *Tomorrow's Lawyers: An Introduction to Your Future* (Oxford, Oxford University Press, 2013) 109–20.

22. *Supra* note 17.

23. Heidi K. Gardner, *When Senior Managers Won't Collaborate*, HARVARD BUSINESS REVIEW, March 2015; Heidi K. Gardner, *Smart Collaboration: How Professionals and Their Firms Succeed by Breaking Down Silos* (Boston: Harvard Business Review Press, 2016) 8; Henry N. Nassau, *Collaboration as Superpower: Optimizing Value to Lead in the Future*, NEW YORK L.J., April 24, 2017, accessed September 17, 2017, https://www.newyorklawjournal.com/id=1202784074939/Collaboration-as-Superpower-Optimizing-Value-to-Lead-in-the-Future?mcode=0&curindex=0&curpage=ALL.

24. Nassau, *supra* note 23.

25. Alexander, *supra* note 18.

26. Client Interviewee 22.

27. Daniel H. Pink, *To Sell Is Human: The Surprising Truth About Moving Others* (New York: Riverhead Books, 2012) 5; Tina Seelig, *What I Wish I Knew When I Was 20: A Crash Course on Making Your Place in the World* (New York: HarperOne, 2009); Tina Seelig, *inGenius: A Crash Course on Creativity* (New York: HarperCollins Publishers, 2012).

28. Client Interviewee 23.

29. Client Interviewee 9.

30. Jamie Condliffe, *What Skills Will You Need to Be Employable in 2030?*, MIT TECHNOLOGY REVIEW, THE DOWNLOAD, September 28, 2017, accessed October 8, 2017, https://www.technologyreview.com/the-download/608981/what-skills-will-you-need-to-be-employable-in-2030/ (discussing research by Nesta, the British innovation foundation, and the University of Oxford to determine what skills will be most desirable in 2030 when robots and AI have taken even more tasks and jobs).

31. Client Interviewee 23.

32. *Supra* note 17.

33. Client Interviewee 1.

34. Steven Johnson, *Where Good Ideas Come From: The Natural History of Innovation* (New York: Riverhead Books, 2010) 159–61.

35. Michael Mankins et al., *Strategy in the Age of Superabundant Capital*," HARVARD BUSINESS REVIEW, March–April 2017.

36. Client Interviewee 25.

37. *Id.*

38. *Id.*

39. Client Interviewee 30.
40. Client Interviewee 29.
41. Client Interviewee 32.
42. *Supra* note 17.
43. Charles Sanders Peirce, Collected Papers (1931–1958), Vol. VI, par. 191, accessed December 10, 2017, https://en.wikiquote.org/wiki/Charles_Sanders_Peirce.
44. *Jacobellis v. Ohio*, 378 U.S. 184 (1964) (holding that the Constitution protected all obscenity except "hard-core pornography"); in his concurrence, Justice Potter Stewart wrote: "I shall not today attempt further to define the kinds of material I understand to be embraced within that shorthand description; and perhaps I could never succeed in intelligibly doing so. But I know it when I see it, and the motion picture involved in this case is not that." *Id.* Lawyers remain confused about what is and is not "obscene" pornography, and the doctrine remains vague in defining it. *See, e.g., Movie Day at the Supreme Court or "I Know It When I See It": A History of the Definition of Obscenity*, FINDLAW, accessed July 16, 2017, http://corporate.findlaw.com/litigation-disputes/movie-day-at-the-supreme-court-or-i-know-it-when-i-see-it-a.html.
45. Client Interviewee 29.
46. Client Interviewee 22.
47. PSF Interviewee 10.
48. Cris Bewick, https://crisbeswick.com/.
49. Melanie Lasoff Levs, *Call to Action: Sara Lee's General Counsel: Making Diversity a Priority*, MINORITY CORPORATE COUNSEL ASSOCIATION, DIVERSITY & THE BAR, accessed December 8, 2017, archive.mcca.com/index.cfm?fuseaction=page.viewpage&pageid=803.
50. Erin Geiger Smith, *Wal-Mart Will Slash Firms That Don't Have Flex-Time Policies*, BUSINESS INSIDER, October 27, 2009, accessed December 5, 2017, www.businessinsider.com/wal-mart-will-slash-firms-that-dont-have-flex-time-policies-2009-10.
51. Lisa Kirby and Caren Ulrich Stacy, *Client Call for Greater Diversity at Fever Pitch*, LAW.COM, July 25, 2017, accessed July 17, 2107, https://www.law.com/sites/almstaff/2017/07/17/client-call-for-greater-diversity-at-fever-pitch/.
52. Client Interviewee 25.
53. *The Main Themes from Dare to Disagree—A Ted Talk from Margaret Heffernan*, NVMS, October 12, 2016, accessed December 9, 2017, https://nvms.us/2016/10/12/the-main-themes-of-dare-to-disagree-a-ted-talk-from-margaret-heffernan/.
54. Client Interviewee 11.
55. *Supra* note 17.
56. Client Interviewee 39.
57. Client Interviewee 31.
58. Client Interviewee 33.
59. Client Interviewee 9.
60. Client Interviewee 32.

61. Client Interviewee 28.
62. Client Interviewee 33.
63. Client Interviewee 25.
64. Client Interviewee 11.
65. Law Firm Partner Interviewee 10.
66. This is a Russian proverb for the English saying "so near yet so far." *See, e.g., Top 40 Russian Idoms, Proverbs, & Sayings. Part 4.* LinguaJunkie.com, March 15, 2015, accessed April 18, 2018, https://www.linguajunkie.com/russian/top-russian-idioms-proverbs-sayings-part; Speech Improvement Now, December 26, 2016, last visited April 18, 2018, https://www.speechimprovementnow.com/russian-proverbs-idiomatic-expressions-english/.
67. The GC of a global music streaming service explained that it is common within legal departments to find "silo operations and teams that don't work together and people not used to measuring their own success to how they contribute to the success of others and, as a result, lawyers are doing their own thing and creating conflict within the legal department and with other divisions like finance and accounting." Client Interviewee 23.
68. Client Interviewee 27.
69. Client Interviewee 20.
70. Law Firm Partner Interviewee 19.
71. Law Firm Partner Interviewee 10.
72. PSF Interviewee 6.
73. Subir Chowdhury, *The Difference: When Good Enough Isn't Enough* (New York: Crown Business Publishing, 2017).
74. Nassau, *supra* note 23.
75. Chowdhury, *supra* note 79; *id.* at 36–37 (describing the difference as "a caring mindset" made up of four "STAR principles": "Being Straightforward," "Being Thoughtful," "Being Accountable," and "Having Resolve.").

Chapter 4

1. "Man in the Mirror," written by Glen Ballard and Siedah Garrett, sung by Michael Jackson, fourth single from album *Bad* (1987).
2. *See, e.g.,* Peter F. Drucker, *Managing Oneself* (Cambridge, Harvard Business Press, 2008).
3. *Id.*; Paul J. Brouwer, *The Power to See Ourselves,* Harvard Business Review, November 1964, accessed December 7, 2107, https://hbr.org/1964/11/the-power-to-see-ourselves.
4. J. P. Flaum, Managing Partner, Green Peak Partners, *When It Comes to Business Leadership, Nice Guys Finish First: A Green Peak Partners Study Shows That Conventional Wisdom Is Wrong—And That Leaders Who Possess Strong Soft Skills Perform Better at Driving Hard Results,* accessed January 21, 2018, http://greenpeakpartners.com/uploads/Green-Peak_Cornell-University-Study_What-predicts-success.pdf.
5. *Id.*

6. Jack Zenger and Joseph Folkman, *We Like Leaders Who Underrate Themselves*, Harvard Business Review, November 10, 2015 (writing about data describing 69,000 managers as seen through the eyes of 750,000 respondents); *see also* Jack Zenger, *Humble Versus Egocentric Leaders: When Lacking Self-Awareness Helps*, Forbes, November 19, 2015, accessed December 7, 2017, https://www.forbes.com/sites/jackzenger/2015/11/19/humble-versus-egocentric-leaders-when-lacking-self-awareness-helps/#1555d1025bf4.

7. David Dunning et al., *Why People Fail to Recognize Their Own Incompetence*, Current Directions in Psychological Science, SAGE Journals Volume 12, Issue 3, 83–87, doi: 10:1111/1467/8721-01235 (2003).

8. Oliver Sheldon et al., *Emotionally Unskilled, Unaware, and Uninterested in Learning More: Reactions to Feedback about Deficits in Emotional Intelligence*, J. Appl. Psychol., 99(1), 125–37, January 2014, http://dx.doi.org/10.1037/a0034138.

9. *Id.*

10. Benjamin Franklin, *Poor Richard's Almanac*, "There are three things extremely hard, Steel, a Diamond, and to know one's self." (1750).

11. Brouwer, *supra* note 3.

12. *Id.*

13. *Id.*

14. Client Interviewee 35.

15. Client Interviewee 20.

16. Client Interviewee 24.

17. Dr. Larry Richard, "Herding Cats: The Lawyer Personality Revealed," *Altman Weil Report to Management*, 29, no. 11 (2002) (showing that rainmaking partners score higher on empathy and resilience than service partners).

18. Stephen Poor, *An Audience of Lawyers: A Guide to Managing Change within the Cynical, Competitive, and Critical*, Rethink the Practice, June 24, 2015, accessed December 7, 2017, https://medium.com/rethink-the-practice/an-audience-of-lawyers-34c43156a17.

19. Dr. Larry Richard, *The Lawyer Personality: Why Lawyers Are Skeptical*, What Makes Lawyers Tick? (blog), February 11, 2013, https://www.lawyerbrainblog.com/2013/02/the-lawyer-personality-why-lawyers-are-skeptical/; *see also supra* note 17; *see also* Jathan Janove, *Can Risk-Averse Lawyers Learn to Embrace Change? An Interview with Dr. Larry Richard*, Ogletree Deakins (blog), January 12, 2016, https://ogletree.com/shared-content/content/blog/2016/january/can-risk-averselawyers-learn-to-embrace-change-an-interview-with-dr-larry-richard.

20. Richard, *supra* note 17; *see also* Janove, *supra* note 19.

21. Richard, *supra* note 19.

22. William Shakespeare, ed. William J. Rolfe, *Shakespeare's King Henry the Sixth, Part II* (New York: Harper & Brothers, 1895), Act IV, Scene II, p. 107.

23. Jacob Gershman, *To Kill or Not to Kill All the Lawyers? That Is the Question: Attorneys Object to Interpretation of Shakespeare's Line; 'Not a Slur,'* The Wall Street Journal, August 18, 2014, accessed December 7, 2107, https://www.wsj.com/articles/

shakespeare-says-lets-kill-all-the-lawyers-but-some-attorneys-object-1408329001; Debbie Vogel, '*Kill the Lawyers,' A Line Misinterpreted,* The New York Times, June 17, 1990, accessed December 7, 2107, http://www.nytimes.com/1990/06/17/nyregion/ l-kill-the-lawyers-a-line-misinterpreted-599990.html?mcubz=1; Howard Troxler, *Don't Kill the Lawyers, Just the Frivolous Lawsuits,* St. Petersburg Times, July 10, 2002, accessed December 7, 2017, www.sptimes.com/2002/07/10/Columns/ Don_t_kill_the_lawyer.shtml; Seth Finkelstein, *The First Thing We Do, Let' s Kill All the Lawyers—It's a Lawyer Joke,* The Ethical Spectacle, July 1997, accessed December 7, 2017, www.spectacle.org/797/finkel.html.

24. Ernest Hemingway, *The Sun Also Rises* (New York: Sribner 1926, paperback edition 2006) 185.

25. Andrew Miller, *Oxygen* (Stirlingshire, Hodder Headline 2001) 104.

26. Richard, *supra* note 17.

27. Janove, *supra* note 19.

28. Law Firm Partner Interviewee 23.

29. Leslie A. Gordon, *Most Lawyers Are Introverted, and That's Not Necessarily a Bad Thing,* ABA Journal, January 2016, accessed December 7, 2017, www. abajournal.com/magazine/article/most_lawyers_are_introverted_and_thats_not_ necessarily_a_bad_thing.

30. Janove, *supra* note 19.

31. Richard, *supra* note 17.

32. Julie Beck, *This Article Won't Change Your Mind: The Facts on Why Facts Alone Can't Fight False Beliefs,* The Atlantic, March 13, 2017.

33. Adam D. Galinsky et al., *Power and Perspectives Not Taken,* SAGE Journals, Psychological Science, December 1, 2006.

34. Law Firm Partner Interviewee 23.

35. Shana Lebowitz, *Dan Pink Shares 2 Simple Strategies for Motivating Employees,* Business Insider, January 13, 2016, accessed December 7, 2017, http://www .businessinsider.com/dan-pink-on-how-to-boost-team-performance-2016-1.

36. Client Interviewee 24.

37. Client Interviewee 27.

38. Robert Eli Rosen et al., *The Framing Effects of Professionalism: Is There a Lawyer Cast of Mind? Lessons from Compliance Programs,* 40 Fordham Urb. L.J. 297 (2013).

39. *You Sending THE WOLF?,* accessed December 7, 2017, https://www.youtube.com/ watch?v=OzNvicZWZ_A; *Winston Wolf—I Solve Problems,* accessed December 7, 2017, https://www.youtube.com/watch?v=ANPsHKpti48.

40. Law Firm Partner Interviewee 12.

41. Law Firm Partner Interviewee 23.

42. Tiffani Alexander, *Q&A with the EIC: GC Summit Chairs,* ACC Docket, May 5, 2017, accessed December 7, 2017, www.accdocket.com/articles/gc-summit-chairs.cfm.

43. *See, e.g.,* Mark A. Cohen, *Who Will Train Tomorrow's Lawyers and How Will They Learn?* Legal Mosaic, September 28, 2017, accessed December 7, 2017, https://legalmosaic. com/2017/09/28/who-will-train-tomorrows-lawyers-and-how-will-they-learn/; *see*

also Robin Wellford Slocum, *An Inconvenient Truth: The Need to Educate Emotionally Competent Lawyers*, 45 CREIGHTON L. R. 827, 828 (August 2012).

44. Richard Susskind, *Tomorrow's Lawyers: An Introduction to Your Future* (Oxford, Oxford University Press, 2013) 135–36.

45. Client Interviewee 23.

46. Law Firm Partner Interviewee 8.

47. Client Interviewee 29.

48. Law Firm Partner Interviewee 10.

49. Aristotle, *Nichomachean Ethics*, trans. W. D. Ross 350 B.C. E. Provided by The Internet Classics Archive by Daniel C. Stevenson, Web Atomics, accessed January 22, 2018, classics.mit.edu/Aristotle/nicomachaen.2.ii.html.

50. Tina Seelig, *What I Wish I Knew When I Was 20: A Crash Course on Making Your Place in the World* (New York: HarperOne, 2009) 20.

51. Client Interviewee 11.

Chapter 5

1. Client Interviewee 25.

2. Client Interviewee 9.

3. Client Interviewee 30.

4. Heidi K. Gardner, *When Senior Managers Won't Collaborate*, HARVARD BUSINESS REVIEW, March 2015; Heidi K. Gardner, *Smart Collaboration: How Professionals and Their Firms Succeed by Breaking Down Silos* (Boston: Harvard Business Review Press, 2016) 72–78.

5. *Id.*

6. Client Interviewee 9.

7. Failcon, accessed December 7, 2017, www.thefailcon.com/.

8. Walter Frick, *Research: Serial Entrepreneurs Aren't Any More Likely to Succeed*, HARVARD BUSINESS REVIEW, February 20, 2014, accessed December 7, 2017, https://hbr.org/2014/02/research-serial-entrepreneurs-arent-any-more-likely-to-succeed (It was almost the opposite. Even after accounting for education and industry experience, they concluded that founders that had previously failed were more likely to fail than first-time entrepreneurs.).

9. Kenneth A. Grady, *Why Your Law Firm Can't Innovate: The Rise of the Innovation Killers*, THE ALGORITHMIC SOCIETY, June 1, 2017, accessed December 7, 2017, https://medium.com/the-algorithmic-society/why-your-law-firm-cant-innovate-58524ca2ec9.

10. Client Interviewee 17.

11. Client Interviewee 9. Note: A tick is a positive thing such as a check mark.

12. Client Interviewee 11.

13. Client Interviewee 41.

14. Client Interviewee 9.

15. Client Interviewee 16.

16. Tim Brown, *Change by Design: How Design Thinking Transforms Organizations and Inspires Innovation* (New York: HarperCollins Publishers, 2009) 138–39.

17. Portia Crowe, *IT'S OFFICIAL: Intel Is Buying the Autonomous-Driving Company Mobileye for $15.3 Billion*, BUSINESS INSIDER, March 13, 2017, accessed December 7, 2017, www.businessinsider.com/intel-mobileye-acquisition-report-2017-3.

18. Robert Musil, *The Man Without Qualities, Vol. I: A Sort of Introduction and Pseudoreality Prevails into the Millennium* (New York: Vintage Books, 1996) 62.

19. There is debate about who this quotation should be attributed to, but it is often attributed to Winston Churchill. *See, e.g.*, THE QUOTE INVESTIGATOR, accessed April 18, 2018, https://quoteinvestigator.com/2013/03/13/attitude-little-big/04-18-18.

20. Madeleine L'Engle, *A Wrinkle in Time* (New York: Square Fish, 2007) 95.

21. Bernadette Dillon and Juliet Bourke, "The Six Signature Traits of Inclusive Leadership: Thriving in a Diverse New World," Human Capital Consulting, Deloitte Australia, Deloitte University Press, 2017 (identifying the six essential traits of inclusive leaders as courage, cognizance, commitment, curiosity, cultural intelligence, and collaboration); Daniel Goleman, *What Makes a Leader?* HARVARD BUSINESS REVIEW, January 2004, https://hbr.org/2004/01/what-makes-a-leader; Sunnie Giles, *The Most Important Leadership Competencies, According to Leaders Around the World*, HARVARD BUSINESS REVIEW, March 15, 2016, https://hbr.org/2016/03/the-most-important-leadership-competencies-according-to-leaders-around-the-world; Katherine Graham-Leviss, *The 5 Skills That Innovative Leaders Have in Common*, HARVARD BUSINESS REVIEW, December 20, 2016; Bill McBean, *The 5 Characteristics of Great Leaders*, FAST COMPANY, January 24, 2013, accessed December 7, 2017, https://www.fastcompany.com/3004914/5-characteristics-great-leaders; Olivia Fox Cabane and Judah Pollack, *Your Brain Has A 'Delete' Button—Here's How to Use It*, FAST COMPANY, May 11, 2016.

22. Law Firm Partner Interviewee 10.

23. Michele DeStefano, *The Chief Compliance Officer: Should There Be a New "C" in the C-Suite?* HARVARD LAW SCHOOL'S THE PRACTICE, July 2016, accessed December 8, 2017, https://thepractice.law.harvard.edu/article/the-chief-compliance-officer/; Michele DeStefano, *Creating a Culture of Compliance: Why Departmentalization May Not Be the Answer*, 10 HASTINGS BUSINESS L.J. 71 (2013).

24. Law Firm Partner Interviewee 18.

25. DeStefano, *supra* note 23.

26. Jon R. Katzenbach et al., *Cultural Change That Sticks*, HARVARD BUSINESS REVIEW, July–August 2012, https://hbr.org/2012/07/cultural-change-that-sticks.

27. Jason Fried and David Heinemeier Hansson, *Rework* (New York: Crown Business Publishing, 2010) 249.

28. *See* FT INNOVATIVE LAWYERS 2013, FINANCIAL TIMES, AWARDS WINNERS, October 3, 2013; accessed December 8, 2017, https://www.eiseverywhere.com//ehome/67065/147754/.

29. Nathan Cisneros, et al., *Vieira de Almeida (VdA): Legal Innovation Pioneers in Portugal*, Product number: HLS 15-15 (November 24, 2015); *see also Innovating to Grow:*

Building an Integrated Firm in Portugal, Harvard Law School's THE PRACTICE, Volume 3, Issue 1, November 2016, accessed December 8, 2017, https://thepractice.law. harvard.edu/article/innovating-to-grow/.

30. Mary Doria Russell, *Children of God* (New York: Villard Books, 1998) 225.

31. They were all discoveries or inventions that were made independently but almost simultaneously by multiple inventors or scientists. It's the theory of multiples.

32. Brown, *supra* note 16, at 138–139 and 161–165.

33. Shirley Gregor and Alan Hevner, *The Knowledge Innovation Matrix (KIM): A Clarifying Lens for Innovation*, INFORMING SCIENCE: THE INTERNATIONAL JOURNAL OF AN EMERGING TRANSDISCIPLINE, 17, 217–39, www.inform.nu/Articles/Vol17/ISJv17p217-239Gregor0800.pdf.

34. Greg Satell, *How to Manage Innovation*, FORBES, March 7, 2013, accessed December 8, 2017, https://www.forbes.com/sites/gregsatell/2013/03/07/how-to-manage-innovation-2/#4ac6d8744785.

35. Hutch Carpenter, *The Four Quadrants of Innovation: Disruptive vs Incremental* WORDPRESS (blog), December 1, 2009, https://bhc3.com.

Part II

1. I developed this mnemonic in LawWithoutWalls in 2014. As I was writing this book, I went online to see whether anyone else has used it (as lawyers, we are trained to footnote everything). Unsurprisingly, it has been used before but not in this context. For example, it is the motto for the United Methodist Church faith.

2. CIO Interviewee 18.

3. Bernadette Dillon and Juliet Bourke, "The Six Signature Traits of Inclusive Leadership: Thriving in a Diverse New World," Human Capital Consulting, Deloitte Australia, Deloitte University Press, 2017; Juliet Bourke, "Innovation, High Performance, and Diversity: Putting the Puzzle Pieces Together," Deloitte.com 2017.

4. Richard Wiseman, *The As If Principle, The Radically New Approach to Changing Your Life* (New York: Simon & Schuster, 2014) 177.

Chapter 6

1. Behance Team, *10 Laws of Productivity*, 99U, accessed December 8, 2017, http://99u.com/articles/6585/10-laws-of-productivity.

2. Ingrid Wickelgren, *Speaking Science: Why People Don't Hear What You Say*, SCIENTIFIC AMERICAN, November 8, 2012, accessed December 8, 2107, https://www.scientificamerican.com/article/bring-science-home-speaking-memory/; Rebecca Lake, *Listening Statistics: 23 Facts You Need to Hear*, CREDIT DONKEY, September 17, 2015, accessed December 8, 2017, https://www.creditdonkey.com/listening-statistics.html; *but see*, Will Thalheimer, *Debunk This: People Remember 10 Percent of What They Read*, ASSOCIATION FOR TALENT DEVELOPMENT, March 12, 2015, accessed December 8, 2017, https://www.td.org/insights/debunk-this-people-remember-10-percent-of-what-they-read (arguing that Edgar Dale's

"the Cone of Experience," which depicted that people remember 10% of what they read, 20% of what they hear, 30% of what they see, 50% of what they see and hear; 70% of what they say and write; 90% of what they do is completely false."); *see also People Remember 10%, 20% . . . Oh Really?*, WORK-LEARNING RESEARCH, 2002, accessed December 8, 2017, https://www.worklearning.com/2006/05/01/people_remember/ (arguing that the Cone Experience is inaccurate).

3. Simon Sinek, *Start with Why: How Great Leaders Inspire Everyone to Take Action* (New York: Penguin Group, 2009); Simon Sinek, *How to Listen*, ASKMEN, accessed December 8, 2017, https://www.askmen.com/money/career_300/364_how-to-listen-simon-sinek ("There is a difference between listening and waiting for your turn to speak.").

4. This is likely why Daniel Pink contends that you will do better at sales if you follow three rules: hear offers, make your partner look good, and say "yes and." Daniel H. Pink, *To Sell Is Human: The Surprising Truth About Moving Others* (New York: Riverhead Books, 2012) 88–89.

5. Cass R. Sunstein and Reid Hastie, *Making Dumb Groups Smarter*, HARVARD BUSINESS REVIEW, December 2014.

6. Anita Williams Woolley et al., *Evidence for a Collective Intelligence Factor in the Performance of Human Groups*, 330, Issue 6004, 686–88, (October 29, 2010), doi: 10.1126/science.1193147.

7. Anita Woolley et al., *Why Some Teams Are Smarter Than Others*, THE NEW YORK TIMES, January 16, 2015, accessed December 7, 2017,https://www.nytimes.com/2015/01/18/opinion/sunday/why-some-teams-are-smarter-than-others.html; *see also* Charles Duhigg, *What Google Learned From Its Quest to Build the Perfect Team*, THE NEW YORK TIMES, February 28, 2016, accessed December 7i, 2017, https://www.nytimes.com/2016/02/28/magazine/what-google-learned-from-its-quest-to-build-the-perfect-team.html; Cameron Herold, *Why Leaders Should Speak Last in Meetings*, THE GLOBE AND MAIL, September 19, 2016, accessed December 7, 2107, https://www.theglobeandmail.com/report-on-business/careers/leadership-lab/why-leaders-should-speak-last-in-meetings/article31934105/; Mike Myatt, *Why Most Leaders Need to Shut Up and Listen*, FORBES, February 9, 2012, accessed December 7, 2017, https://www.forbes.com/sites/mikemyatt/2012/02/09/why-most-leaders-need-to-shut-up-listen/#4df4c8586ef9; Mark Williams, *Why Leaders Should Have the Last Word in ALL Meetings*, MTD (blog), February 24, 2016, http://www.mtdtraining.com/blog/the-3-main-benefits-of-the-leader-closing-every-meeting.htm.

8. Woolley et al., *supra* note 7.

9. Steven Spear, *Learning to Lead at Toyota*, HARVARD BUSINESS REVIEW, May 2004.

10. *Id.*

11. Law Firm Partner Interviewee 2.

12. Amy Edmondson, *Psychological Safety and Learning Behavior in Work Teams*, ADMINISTRATIVE SCIENCE QUARTERLY, June 1999), accessed December 7, 2017,

http://web.mit.edu/curhan/www/docs/Articles/15341_Readings/Group_Performance/Edmondson%20Psychological%20safety.pdf.

13. Steven Johnson, *Where Good Ideas Come From: The Natural History of Innovation* (New York: Riverhead Books, 2010) 243 (using YouTube as an example of a good idea that led to better ideas on the Internet); *id.* at 22 ("If there is a single maxim that runs through this book's arguments, it is that we are often better served by connecting ideas than we are by protecting them.")

14. Mary Kay Ash, Founder of Mary Kay Cosmetics.

15. Carol S. Dweck, *Mindset: The New Psychology of Success* (New York: Ballantine Books, 2006) 12; Marina Krakovsky, *The Effort Effect*, STANFORD ALUMNI MAGAZINE, March/April 2007, accessed December 8, 2017, https://alumni.stanford.edu/get/page/magazine/article/?article_id=32124.

16. Dr. Larry Richard, *The Lawyer Personality: Why Lawyers Are Skeptical*," WHAT MAKES LAWYERS TICK? (blog), February 11, 2013, https://www.lawyerbrainblog.com/2013/02/the-lawyer-personality-why-lawyers-are-skeptical; *see also* Dr. Larry Richard, "Herding Cats: The Lawyer Personality Revealed," *Altman Weil Report to Management*, 29, no. 11 (2002) (utilizing the Caliper Profile on over 1,000 lawyers).

17. Marcie Borgal Shunk, *Fixed Mindset or Growth Mindset? How Learning Mindsets May Be Stifling Law Firm Change*, LAWVISION INSIGHTS (blog), September 1, 2014, lawvisiongroup.com/fixed-mindset-or-growth-mindset-how-learning-mindsets-may-be-stifling-law-firm-change/#.WisJQrQ-eF0.

18. Dr. Larry Richard's research on the personalities of lawyers shows that having low resilience and being averse to risk contributes to a resistance to change. Dr. Larry Richard, "Herding Cats: The Lawyer Personality Revealed," *Altman Weil Report to Management*, 29, no. 11 (2002).

19. Shunk, *supra* note 17. If a lawyer is known for being excellent, he or she may not believe a client when provided negative feedback or s/he might blame the other lawyers on the teams (e.g., the associates). *Id.* This comports with the research by Dr. Larry Richard that shows that lawyers are more likely to be skeptical and to look for who might be at fault. Dr. Larry Richard, *The Lawyer Personality: Why Lawyers Are Skeptical*, WHAT MAKES LAWYERS TICK? (blog), February 11, 2013, https://www.lawyerbrainblog.com/2013/02/the-lawyer-personality-why-lawyers-are-skeptical/.

20. Melanie Curtin, *How Open Minded Are You? Science Says This Simple Eye Test Will Tell You*," INC.COM, June 14, 2017, accessed December 8, 2017, https://www.inc.com/melanie-curtin/how-open-minded-are-you-science-says-this-simple-eye-test-will-tell-you.html.

21. Dweck, *supra* note 15, at 217–18; Krakovsky, *supra* note 15.

22. Matt Weinberger, *Satya Nadella Says This Book Gave Him the 'Intuition' He Needed to Revamp Microsoft*," BUSINESS INSIDER, August 4, 2016, accessed December 7, 2017, http://www.businessinsider.com/microsoft-ceo-satya-nadella-on-growth-mindset-2016-8.

23. Mark Swatzell, *Achieving Business Impact through Experiential Learning*, LINKEDIN, March 27, 2017, accessed October 1, 2017, https://www.linkedin.com/pulse/achieving-business-impact-through-experiential-mark-swatzell/.

24. Darren Orf, *10 Awesome Accidental Discoveries*, POPULAR MECHANICS, June 27, 2013, accessed December 8, 2017, http://www.popularmechanics.com/science/health/g1216/10-awesome-accidental-discoveries/; Katie Kalvaitis, *Penicillin, An Accidental Discovery Changed the Course of Medicine*, HEALIO, ENDOCRINE TODAY, August 2008, accessed December 8, 2017, https://www.healio.com/endocrinology/news/print/endocrine-today/%7B15afd2a1-2084-4ca6-a4e6-7185f5c4cfb0%7D/penicillin-an-accidental-discovery-changed-the-course-of-medicine.

25. *See, e.g.*, Daven Hiskey, *Post-It Notes Were Invented by Accident*, TODAY I FOUND OUT, FEED YOUR BRAIN, November 9, 2011, accessed December 7, 2017, www.todayifoundout.com/index.php/2011/11/post-it-notes-were-invented-by-accident/.

26. Nick Glass and Tim Hume, *The "Hallelujah Moment" Behind the Invention of the Post-it Note*, CNN, April 4, 2013, accessed April 24, 2018, https://www.cnn.com/2013/04/04/tech/post-it-note-history/index.html. Note: Alan Amron claims that he discovered Post-it notes before 3M did. *See, e.g.*, Allan Smith, *Guy Sues 3M after a 40-year Battle Over Who Invented an Everyday Product*, BUSINESS INSIDER, January 28, 2016, accessed December 8, 2017, http://www.businessinsider.com/post-it-notes-at-the-heart-of-a-40-year-battle-2016-1.

27. Frank McCourt, *Angela's Ashes: A Memoir* (New York: Scribner Publishing, 1996) 288; *see also* Wikiquote (citing dialogue from the film version), accessed January 22, 2018).

28. Richard Wiseman, *The Luck Factor: Four Simple Principles That Will Change your Luck—and Your Life* (New York: Arrow Books, 2004); Richard Wiseman, *Be Lucky—It's an Easy Skill to Learn*, THE TELEGRAPH, January 9, 2003, accessed, December 7, 2017, https://www.telegraph.co.uk/technology/3304496/Be-lucky-its-an-easy-skill-to-learn.html.

29. Christopher Chabris and Daniel Simons, *The Invisible Gorilla: How Our Intuitions Deceive Us* (New York: Broadway Paperbacks, 2009).

30. Daniel Simons, *Failures of Awareness: The Case of Inattentional Blindness*, NOBA, accessed April 16, 2018, http://nobaproject.com/modules/failures-of-awareness-the-case-of-inattentional-blindness; *see also*, Craig E. Geiss, *Inattentional or Change Blindness*, accessed April 15, 2018, http://www.cti-home.com/wp-content/uploads/2014/01/Inattentional-Blindness.pdf.

31. Geiss, *supra* note 30.

32. Ed Yeates, *Fire Alarm Uses Parent's Voice to Wake Children*, KSL.COM, accessed April 15, 2018, https://www.ksl.com/?nid=148&sid=526053.

33. *The Monkey Business Illusion*, https://www.youtube.com/watch?v=IGQmdoK_ZfY; *see also* LIVE SCIENCE, accessed January 21, 2018, http://www.livescience.com/6727-invisible-gorilla-test-shows-notice.html. The authors also point out that sometimes we can't even see something we are looking for even when we are looking right at it. Chabris and Simons, *supra* note 29, at 9–19.

34. Chabris and Simons, *supra* note 29 at 38–39 ("Focused attention allows us to avoid distraction and use our limited resources more effectively; we don't want to be distracted by everything around us.").

35. Guillaume Hervet et al., *Is Banner Blindness Genuine? Eye Tracking Internet Text Advertising*, Applied Cognitive Psychology. 25, no. 5: 708–16, doi:10.1002/acp.1742; Xavier Drèze and François-Xavier Hussherr, *Internet Advertising: Is Anybody Watching?* Journal of Interactive Marketing, 17, no. 4: (September 2003), 8–23, doi:10.1002/dir.10063.

36. Chabris and Simons, *supra* note 29, at 241.

37. *Id.* at 37.

38. Wiseman, *supra* note 28.

39. Johnson, *supra* note 13, at 174.

40. *Id.*

41. *Id.*

42. *Id.*

43. Bec Oakley, *Ten Things for Parents to Love About Minecraft*, MineMum, accessed December 7, 2017, minemum.com/minecraft-parents-things-to-love.

44. Jeff Dyer et al., *The Innovator's DNA: Mastering the Five Skills of Disruptive Innovators* (Boston: Harvard Business Review Press, 2011) 23–27.

45. Kurt Kohlsteadt, *Blue Light Special: Colored Streetlamps Precede Decline in Crime*, Web Urbanist, April 19, 2016, accessed December 7, 2017, https://weburbanist.com/2016/04/19/blue-light-special-colored-streetlamps-precede-decline-in-crime/; Cameron Allan McKean, *How Blue Lights on Train Platforms Combat Tokyo's Suicide Epidemic*, Next City, March 20, 2014, accessed December 7, 2017, https://nextcity.org/daily/entry/how-blue-lights-on-train-platforms-combat-tokyos-suicide-epidemic (explaining that track-jumping suicides actually form "a bigger threat to Tokyo's citizens than natural disasters and traffic fatalities combined.").

46. Dyer et al., *supra* note 44, at 31–32.

47. *See, e.g.*, Alan Watts, *The Watercourse Way*, The Unbound Spirit, accessed December 17, 2017, https://theunboundedspirit.com/short-story-the-taoist-farmer/; *see also* www.katinkahesselink.net/tibet/zen.html.

48. Jon. J. Muth, *Zen Shorts* (New York: Scholastic Press, 2008); Leslie Green, *Maybe . . . and What If?* Trust Life Today, July 18, 2011, accessed January 7, 2018, trustlifetoday.com/tag/jon-j-muth/; *see also* a video wherein Jon Muth reads the story aloud from his book, accessed October 1, 2017, https://vimeo.com/17468634.

Chapter 7

1. Antoine de Saint-Exupéry, *The Little Prince* (New York: Harcourt Brace Jovanovich,) 70.

2. Daniel Susskind and Richard Susskind, *The Future of the Professions* (Oxford, Oxford University Press, 2015) 251.

3. Charles Duhigg, *What Google Learned From Its Quest to Build the Perfect Team*, The New York Times Magazine, February 28, 2016, accessed December 7, 2017,

https://www.nytimes.com/2016/02/28/magazine/what-google-learned-from-its-quest-to-build-the-perfect-team.html; Anita Williams Woolley et al., *Evidence for a Collective Intelligence Factor in the Performance of Human Groups*, 330, Issue 6004, 686, doi: 10.1126/science.1193147; doi: 10.1126/science.1193147.

4. Woolley et al., *supra* note 3.
5. David Engel et al., *Reading the Minds in the Eyes or Reading Between the Lines? Theory of Mind Predicts Collective Intelligence Equally Well Online and Face-To-Face*, PLOS, December 16, 2014, https://doi.org/10.1371/journal.pone.0115212 (providing strong empirical support for the conclusion that the ability to read others' mental states whether via text-based online interactions or other cues is as important to group effectiveness in online environments).
6. Cass R. Sunstein and Reid Hastie, *Making Dumb Groups Smarter*, HARVARD BUSINESS REVIEW, December 2014.
7. Duhigg, *supra* note 3.
8. Billie Tarascio, *A Woman's Edge in the Modern Legal World*, LAW PRACTICE TODAY, February 14, 2017, accessed December 8, 2017, www.lawpracticetoday.org/article/womans-edge-modern-legal-world/?utm_source=February17&utm_medium=email&utm_campaign=February17LPTemail.
9. Dr. Larry Richard, "Herding Cats: The Lawyer Personality Revealed," *Altman Weil Report to Management*, 29, no. 11 (2002).
10. *Id.*
11. *Id.*
12. *Id.*
13. Sigal G. Barsade, *The Ripple Effect: Emotional Contagion and Its Influence on Group Behavior*, SAGE JOURNALS, ADMINISTRATIVE SCIENCE QUARTERLY, http://web.mit.edu/curhan/www/docs/Articles/15341_Readings/Affect/Barsade_2002_The_ripple_effect.pdf.
14. *Id.*
15. Andrew M. Perlman, *Unethical Obedience by Subordinate Attorneys: Lessons from Social Psychology*, HOFSTRA L. REV., 36, Issue 2, Article 13, 2007.
16. Lauren Young, *Watch These Awkward Elevator Rides from an Old Episode of Candid Camera*, ATLAS OBSCURA, September 30, 2016, accessed December 8, 2017, https://www.atlasobscura.com/articles/watch-these-awkward-elevator-rides-from-an-old-episode-of-candid-camera.
17. *WYFFT: Would You Fall For That—Elevator*, accessed December 8, 2017, https://www.youtube.com/watch?v=dDAbdMv14Is.
18. Barsade, *supra* note 13.
19. L. Nummenmaa et al, "Emotions Promote Social Interaction by Synchronizing Brain Activity Across Individuals," Proceedings of the National Academy of Sciences, 2012; doi: 10.1073/pnas.1206095109; L. Nummenmaa et al., "Synchronous Brain Activity Across Individuals Underlies Shared Psychological Perspectives"; doi: 10.1016/j.neuroimage.2014.06.022, https://www.ncbi.nlm.nih.gov/pubmed/24936687; Aalto University *Synchronized Brains: Feeling Strong*

Emotions Makes People's Brains "Tick Together," SCIENCE DAILY, May 24, 2012, accessed December 8, 2017, https://www.sciencedaily.com/releases/2012/05/120524112342.htm.

20. Nancy J. Adler, "Communicating Across Cultural Barriers," *International Dimensions of Organizational Behavior* (Boston: PWS-KENT Publishing Company, 1991) 63–91.

21. Anaïs Nin, *Seduction of the Minotaur* (Athens, Ohio, The Swallow Press, 1962). Nin credited this statement to the Talmud. In 2005, *Newsweek* cited this same quote as an English translation of a comment with the Talmud. Marc Gellman, *How We See Sharon—and Israel*, NEWSWEEK, January 8, 2006, accessed December 7, 2017, http://www.newsweek.com/how-we-see-sharon-and-israel-108309. However, there is debate about whether the meaning of the Talmud matched the meaning that Nin meant when she wrote the statement. *See, e.g.*, Quote Investigator, accessed December 7, 2017, https://quoteinvestigator.com/2014/03/09/as-we-are/.

22. Adler, *supra* note 20.

23. *Id.*

24. Philip C. Burger and Bernard M. Bass, *Assessment of Managers: An International Comparison* (New York: Free Press, 1979) (conducting a study of managers from fourteen different countries and finding that managers assumed that their peers were more like them than they actually were).

25. Christopher Chabris and Daniel Simons, *The Invisible Gorilla: How Our Intuitions Deceive Us* (New York: Broadway Paperbacks, 2009) 86–92.

26. Kahlil Gibran, *The Ultimate Collection—21 Books in One Volume (Illustrated): Including Spirits Rebellious, The Prophet, The Broken Wings, The Madman, The . . . Nation, I Believe in You and Many Others* (Kindle version, 2015).

27. Teresa Amabile et al., *IDEO's Culture of Helping*, HARVARD BUSINESS REVIEW, January–February 2014 ("Research across many kinds of companies finds that those with higher rates of helping have lower employee turnover, enjoy greater customer satisfaction, and are more profitable."); *see also* Amy C. Edmondson et al., *Speeding Up Team Learning*, HARVARD BUSINESS REVIEW, October 2001; *see also* Margaret Heffernan, *The Secret Ingredient That Makes Some Teams Better Than Others*, IDEAS.TED.COM, May 5, 2015, accessed December 9, 2017, https://ideas.ted.com/the-secret-ingredient-that-makes-some-teams-better-than-others/.

28. Teresa Amabile et al., *IDEO's Culture of Helping*, HARVARD BUSINESS REVIEW, January–February 2014.

29. Shel Silverstein, *Helping—Poem by Shel Silverstein*, POEM HUNTER, accessed December 9, 2017, https://www.poemhunter.com/poem/helping-2/; *see also Help— Free To Be . . .*, accessed December 9, 2017, https://www.youtube.com/watch?v=X6r0MVQANjI.

30. Steven Spear, *Learning to Lead at Toyota*, HARVARD BUSINESS REVIEW, May 2004.

31. Client Interviewee 25.

32. Silverstein, *supra* note 29.

33. Margaret Hagan was one of my first students in LawWithoutWalls. Through her experience in our program, she rediscovered her passion for drawing and illustrating and found a path to connect her design background with law.

34. *Forget the Pecking Order at Work*, TEDWOMEN 2015, May 2015, accessed December 8, 2017, https://www.ted.com/talks/margaret_heffernan_why_it_s_time_to_forget_the_pecking_order_at_work.

35. William M. Muir and Heng Wei Cheng, *Genetics and the Behaviour of Domestic Animals*, Chapter 9: Genetics and the Behaviour of Chickens: Welfare and Productivity, (San Diego: Academic Press) 2.

36. *Happy and Passive Means More Productive Animals*, PURDUE UNIVERSITY NEWS, August 2, 2005, accessed April 24, 2018, https://news.uns.purdue.edu/html4ever/2005/050802.Muir.behavior.html.

37. Deborah L. Rhode, *Lawyers as Leaders* (Oxford, Oxford University Press, 2013) 1 ("Although leadership development is now a forty-five-billion-dollar industry, and an Amazon search reveals close to 88,000 leadership books in print, the topic is largely missed in legal education."). *See also* John Dean, *Teaching Lawyers, and Others, To Be Leaders*, VERDICT, November 1, 2013, accessed December 7, 2017, https://verdict.justia.com/2013/11/01/teaching-lawyers-others-leaders (explaining that former attorneys are the dominant profession in the U.S. Congress and the House of Representatives, and U.S. Presidency is the legal profession); *cf.* Nick Robinson, *The Decline of the Lawyer Politician*, 65(4) BUFFALO L. R. 657 (August 2017) (showing that there is a slow, gradual decline of lawyers in Congress and the U.S. Presidency since the 1960s).

38. *See, e.g.*, Christine E. Parker et al., *The Two Faces of Lawyers: Professional Ethics and Business Compliance with Regulation*, 22 GEO. J. L. ETHICS 201 (2009).

39. *See* David Kershaw and Richard Moorhead, *Where Were the Lawyers When Lehman Crashed?*" THE TIMES, January 24, 2013, https://www.thetimes.co.uk/article/where-were-the-lawyers-when-lehman-crashed-9p9tdgcgfpx, accessed December 8, 2017); LINCOLN SAV. & LOAN ASS'N V. WALL, 743 F. Supp. 901, 920 (D.D.C. 1990) (Sporkin, J.) ("Where were these professionals, a number of whom are now asserting their rights under the Fifth Amendment, when these clearly improper transactions were being consummated?"); *See* Deborah L. Rhode, *Legal Ethics: Moral Counseling*, 75 FORDHAM L. REV. 1317 (2006); *see, e.g.*, U.S. Securities and Exchange Commission Chairman, Christopher Cox, Address to the 2007 Corporate Counsel Institute, March 8, 2007, accessed December 8, 2017, https://www.sec.gov/news/speech/2007/spch030807cc.htm.

40. *How to Start a Movement*, TED, February 2010, accessed December 8, 2017, https://www.ted.com/talks/derek_sivers_how_to_start_a_movement.

41. Derek Sivers, *First Follower: Leadership Lessons from Dancing Guy*, February 11, 2010, accessed December 8, 2017, https://www.youtube.com/watch?v=fW8amMCVAJQ.

42. Boris Groysberg et al., *The Risky Business of Hiring Stars*, HARVARD BUSINESS REVIEW, May 2004.

43. Coates et al., *Hiring Teams, Firms, and Lawyers: Evidence of the Evolving Relationships in the Corporate Legal Market*, 36 LAW & SOC. INQUIRY 999 (Fall 2011) (analyzing interview and survey data from 166 chief legal officers of S&P 500 companies from 2006–2007).

44. Rachel Moloney, *Freshfields Loses Entire Paris Real Estate Team to Jones Day*, THE LAWYER, February 22, 2017, accessed December 8, 2017, https://www.thelawyer.com/issues/online-february-2017/freshfields-loses-paris-real-estate-jones-day/?cmpid=dnews_3128729.

45. Mark A. Bellis et al., *Dying to Be Famous: Retrospective Cohort Study of Rock and Pop Star Mortality and Its Association with Adverse Childhood Experiences*, BRITISH MEDICAL JOURNAL, BMJ OPEN, accessed December 8, 2017, http://bmjopen.bmj.com/content/2/6/e002089.full; Emily Leaman, *Study: Musicians in Bands Live Longer Than Solo Acts Or, Why It's Better to Be a Beatle Than a Bieber*, BEWELL PHILLY, PHILADELPHIA MAGAZINE, December 20, 2012, accessed December 8, 2017, https://www.phillymag.com/be-well-philly/2012/12/20/study-musicians-bands-live-longer-solo-acts/.

46. Bellis et al., *supra* note 45.

47. *Id.*

48. ROLLING STONE, *Read Bruce Springsteen's E Street Band Induction Speech*, April 11, 2014, accessed December 8, 2017, https://www.rollingstone.com/music/news/read-bruce-springsteens-e-street-band-induction-speech-20140411.

49. Adler, *supra* note 20, at 63–91.

50. There are six *F*s in the sentence.

51. Adler, *supra* note 20, at 63–91.

52. *Id.*

53. Annabel Fenwick Elliott, *The Science Behind Why People Who Prefer the Window Seat Are More Selfish*, THE TELEGRAPH, October 20, 2017, accessed April 25, 2018, https://www.telegraph.co.uk/travel/comment/window-versus-aisle-debate/ (reporting that airline statistics and studies by Expedia and Quartz show that "it's almost an even split" between window and aisle seat preferences).

54. *Id.*

55. *Id.*

56. *Id.*

57. Client Interviewee 25.

58. Coates, *supra* note 43.

Chapter 8

1. William Blake, *The Marriage of Heaven and Hell*, composed between 1790 and 1793 and found in his works (New York: Dover Publications, 1994).

2. Aldous Huxley, *The Doors of Perception* (New York: Harper Perennial Modern Classics 2009).

3. Heather Forest, *Stone Soup* (Little Rock, Arkansas: August House LittleFolk) 1998.

4. Steven Johnson, *Where Good Ideas Come From: The Natural History of Innovation* (New York: Riverhead Books, 2010) 60.

5. Jonah Lehrer, *How to Be Creative*, THE WALL STREET JOURNAL, March 12, 2012, accessed December 8, 2017, https://www.wsj.com/articles/SB100014240529702 03370604577265632205015846.

6. https://www.broadinstitute.org/about-us, accessed April 16, 2018.

7. Eric Niiler, *Human Embryo Editing Gets the OK—But No Superbabies*, WIRED, February 148, 2017, accessed December 8, 2017, https://www.wired.com/2017/02/human-embryo-editing-gets-ok-no-superbabies/?mc_cid=cba7edaccd&mc_eid=34b5220f4a.

8. Dr. Felix Maringe et al., *Leadership, Diversity and Decision Making*, Centre for Excellence in Leadership 13, March 2007, accessed January 21, 2018, https://www.lancaster.ac.uk/media/lancaster-university/content-assets/documents/lums/lsis/r9.pdf.

9. Samuel R. Sommers, *On Racial Diversity and Group Decision Making: Identifying Multiple Effects of Racial Composition on Jury Deliberations*, 90 J. PERSONALITY & SOC. PSYCHOL. 597, 598 (2006); *see also* Dr. Felix Maringe et al., *supra* note 8 (explaining that the advantages of diverse groups "include an increase in the quality of group performance through creativity of ideas, cooperation, and the number of perspectives and alternatives considered"); *id.* at 13 ("Since then, numerous writers have suggested that diverse teams may be advantageous to organisations, especially in performing decision making tasks.").

10. *See* Anthony Lising Antonio et al., *Effects of Racial Diversity on Complex Thinking in College Students*, SAGE JOURNALS, PSYCHOLOGICAL SCIENCE, August 1, 2004, accessed January 20, 2018, journals.sagepub.com/doi/abs/10.1111/j.0956-7976.2004.00710.x?url_ver=Z39.88-2003&rfr_id=ori:rid:crossref.org&rfr_dat=cr_pub%3dpubmed.

11. Sommers, *supra* note 9 at 597, 601–07.

12. *Id.*

13. Warren E. Watson et al., *Cultural Diversity's Impact on Interaction Process and Performance: Comparing Homogeneous and Diverse Task Groups*, 36 ACAD. MGMT. J. 590, 596–98 (1993).

14. *See* Marvin E. Shaw, *Group Dynamics: The Psychology of Small Group Behavior*, 219–27 (New York: McGraw-Hill Book Company, 1981) (finding that gender and personality diversity can also improve problem solving).

15. Lu Hong and Scott E. Page, *Groups of Diverse Problem Solvers Can Outperform Groups of High-Ability Problem Solvers*, 101 PNAS, 16385, 16385–389 (2004).

16. Scott E. Page, *The Difference: How the Power of Diversity Creates Better Groups, Firms, Schools, and Societies* (Princeton: Princeton University Press, 2007) xxix.

17. Johnson, *supra* note 4, at 58.

18. *See, e.g.*, Doris Tirone, *Lazy Government Employees*, GovLoop, January 14, 2011, accessed December 8, 2017, https://www.govloop.com/community/blog/lazy-government-employees/

19. *See* Marc Gobe, *Brandjam: Humanizing Brands Through Emotional Design* (New York: Allworth Press, 2007); *see also* Thomas Lockwood, ed., *Design Thinking:*

Integrating Innovation, Customer Experience, and Brand Value (New York: Allworth Press, 2009) Chapter 10: Marc Gobe, Let's Brandjam to Humanize Our Brands, pp. 109–20.

20. Roya Behnia, *"Legal Kaizens" and Getting Lawyers to Solve Simple Problems Together*, ABA, Legal Rebels, November 2, 2011, accessed December 8, 2017, www. abajournal.com/legalrebels/article/getting_lawyers_to_solve_simple_problems_ together/ (explaining that the Japanese word *kaizen*, "[r]oughly translated as 'improvement for the better,'" is a collaboration method that "get[s] employees to solve simple problems together").

21. Johnson, *supra* note 4, at 170–71.

22. Behnia, *supra* note 20.

23. *See* Carsten K.W. De Dreu and Laurie R. Weingart, *Task Versus Relationship Conflict, Team Performance, and Team Member Satisfaction: A Meta-Analysis*, 2003, web.mit.edu/curhan/www/docs/Articles/15341_Readings/Negotiation_and_ Conflict_Management/De_Dreu_Weingart_Task-conflict_Meta-analysis.pdf.

24. Susan E. Jackson et al., "Understanding the Dynamics of Diversity in Decision-Making Teams," in *Team Effectiveness and Decision Making in Organizations*, 1st edition, Richard A. Guzzo, Eduardo Salas, & Associates (San Francisco, Pfeiffer Publishing, 1995) 204, 214 accessed January 22, 2018, https://smlr.rutgers.edu/sites/default/files/documents/ faculty_staff_docs/UnderstandingTheDynamicsofDiversityInDecisionMakingTeams. pdf, on file with author; Martin Ruef, *Strong Ties, Weak Ties and Islands: Structural and Cultural Predictors of Organizational Innovation*, 11 Indus. & Corp. Change, 427 (2002) 433 (hypothesizing that "[a]ctors embedded in a diverse set of network ties are more likely to be innovative than actors relying on homogenous ties").

25. Vivian Hunt et al., *Why Diversity Matters*, McKinsey & Company, January 2015, accessed December 8, 2017, https://www.mckinsey.com/business-functions/ organization/our-insights/why-diversity-matters.

26. Thomas Barta et al., *Is There a Payoff from Top-Team Diversity*, McKinsey & Company, April 2012, accessed December 8, 2017, https://www.mckinsey.com/ business-functions/organization/our-insights/is-there-a-payoff-from-top- team-diversity http://www.mckinsey.com/business-functions/organization/our- insights/is-there-a-payoff-from-top-team-diversity.

27. *See* Rick Palmore, *A Call to Action: Diversity in the Legal Profession*, Association of Corporate Counsel, October 2004, accessed December 8, 2017, http://www .acc.com/vl/public/Article/loader.cfm?csModule=security/getfile&pageid= 16074&recorded=1; *see also* Melanie Lasoff Levs, *Call to Action: Sara Lee's General Counsel: Making Diversity a Priority*, Minority Corporate Counsel Association, Diversity & The Bar, accessed December 8, 2017, http://archive.mcca.com/index. cfm?fuseaction=page.viewpage&pageid=803.

28. *Wal-Mart Requires Diversity in its Law Firms: Commitment to Participation Already Making an Impact*, Walmart.com, December 9, 2005, accessed December 8, 2017, https://corporate.walmart.com/_news_/news-archive/2005/12/09/wal-mart- requires-diversity-in-its-law-firms. *See also* Christopher J. Whelan and Neta Ziv,

Privatizing Professionalism: Client Control of Lawyers' Ethics, 80 Fordham L. Rev. 2577, 2596–98 (2012).

29. *See, e.g.,* Flor M. Colon, *Better Decision Making Through Diversity*, Wayback Machine, Summer 2009, accessed January 19, 2018, https://web.archive.org/web/20101018122053/www.diversityisnatural.com/colon/_.

30. FT Innovative Lawyers 2013, Financial Times, Awards Winners, October 3, 2013, accessed December 8, 2017, https://www.eiseverywhere.com//ehome/67065/147754/.

31. Deborah L. Rhode, *Law Is the Least Diverse Profession in the Nation. And Lawyers Aren't Doing Enough to Change That*, The Washington Post, May 27, 2015, accessed December 8, 2017, https://www.washingtonpost.com/posteverything/wp/2015/05/27/law-is-the-least-diverse-profession-in-the-nation-and-lawyers-arent-doing-enough-to-change-that/?utm_term=.4b6efb872707; *see also* Deborah Rhode, *The Trouble with Lawyers* (Oxford: Oxford University Press: 2015) 60.

32. *See* Rhode, *Law Is the Least Diverse Profession in the Nation, supra* note 31; *see* Rhode, *The Trouble with Lawyers, supra* note 31 at 60–96.

33. Lisa Kirby and Caren Ulrich Stacy, *Client Call for Greater Diversity at Fever Pitch*, Law.com, July 25, accessed July 17, 2017, https://www.law.com/sites/almstaff/2017/07/17/client-call-for-greater-diversity-at-fever-pitch/.

34. Levs, *supra* note 27.

35. Martin Ruef, *Strong Ties, Weak Ties and Islands: Structural and Cultural Predictors of Organizational Innovation*, 11 Indus. & Corp. Change, 427, 429–30, 432, and 443 (2002) ("[T]he propensity of individual entrepreneurs to break with convention is both encouraged by social relations—which may bring disparate ideas, routine or technologies to an entrepreneur's attention—and discouraged by social relations—which may introduce pressures for conformity or concerns about trust.").

36. Rob Cross and Andrew Parker, *The Hidden Power of Social Networks: Understanding How Work Really Gets Done in Organizations* (Boston: Harvard Business School Press, 2004) 81–83 ("Research has shown that people with more diverse, entrepreneurial networks tend to be more successful.").

37. *Id.*

38. Mark S. Granovetter, *The Strength of Weak Ties*, 78 Am. J. Soc. 1360, 1361–66 (1973), https://sociology.stanford.edu/sites/default/files/publications/the_strength_of_weak_ties_and_exch_w-gans.pdf.

39. Richard Ogle, *Smart World: Breakthrough Creativity and the New Science of Ideas* (Boston: Harvard Business School Press, 2007) 87–88.

40. Roger Guimerà et al., *Team Assembly Mechanisms Determine Collaboration Network Structure and Team Performance*, Science 697, 697–702 (2005) Issue 5722; doi: 10.1126/science.1106340.

41. *Eagles, Hotel California* (Asylum Records, 1977), (vinyl, cassette, and 8-track cartridge), fifth studio album, Asylum Records, December 8, 1976, written by Glenn Lewis Frey, Don Felder, and Donald Hugh Henley.

42. *See, e.g.*, Bruno Ribeiro, *The Real Meaning Behind Hotel of California*, ENGLISH STUDIO, accessed April 17, 2018, https://englishstudio.com/blog/real-meaning-behind-hotel-california/; Chris, S., *5 Famous Hidden Song Meanings that are Total B.S.*, CRACKED, October 05, 2011, accessed April 17, 2018, www.cracked.com, http://www.cracked.com/article_19454_5-famous-hidden-song-meanings-that-are-total-b.s..html.

43. Heidi K. Gardner, *Smart Collaboration: How Professionals and Their Firms Succeed by Breaking Down Silos* (Boston: Harvard Business Review Press,2016) 37–38.

44. Michele DeStefano Beardslee, *The Corporate Attorney-Client Privilege: Third Rate Doctrine for Third Party Consultants*, 62 S.M.U. L. REV. 727, 746 (2009); Michele DeStefano, *Taking the Business Out of Work Product*, 79 FORDHAM L. REV. 1869, 1898 (2011); Michele DeStefano, *Claim Funders and Commercial Claim Holders: A Common Interest or a Common Problem?* 63 DEPAUL L. REV. 305, 305–06 (2014).

45. Michele DeStefano, *Nonlawyers Influencing Lawyers: Too Many Cooks in the Kitchen or Stone Soup?* 80 FORDHAM L. REV. 2791, 2808–14 (2012).

46. Model Rules of Professional Conduct, Rule 5.4, cmt. 1 (demonstrating that its restrictions are designed to "protect the lawyer's professional independence of judgment").

47. *See* Model Rules of Professional Conduct, Rule 5.4(a)–(b) (2009). Some contend that this Model Rule is unconstitutional. *See, e.g.*, Renee Newman Knake, *Democratizing the Delivery of Legal Services: On the First Amendment Rights of Corporations and Individuals*, 73 OHIO ST. L.J. 1 (2012), http://papers.ssrn.com/sol3/papers.cfm?abstract_id=1800258 (arguing that recent Supreme Court decisions make blanket prohibitions on outside ownership of law firms unconstitutional).

48. Alexia Garamfalvi, *In a First, Law Firm Goes Public*, LEGAL TIMES (May 22, 2007), on file with author (archived and currently available at LexisNexis in "The National Law Journal (Online)" database). *See* Legal Services Act, 2007, c. 29, pt. 5 (U.K.) (enabling equity investment in law firms in England and Wales by nonlawyer investors). For a comprehensive history of the Act, *see generally* Christopher J. Whelan, *The Paradox of Professionalism: Global Law Practice Means Business*," 27 PENN ST. INT'L L. REV. 465 (2008).

49. *Report and Recommendation of the District of Columbia Bar Special Committee on Multidisciplinary Practice*, DC BAR, accessed April 21, 2012, http://www.dcbar.org/inside_the_ bar/structure/reports/special_committee_on_multidisciplinary_practice/background.cfm (accessed April 21, 2012) (report on file with author).

50. *See* Bruce A. Green, *The Disciplinary Restrictions on Multidisciplinary Practice: Their Derivation, Their Development, and Some Implications for the Core Values Debate*, 84 MINN. L. REV. 1115, 1128–32 (2000).

51. Dr. Larry Richard, "Herding Cats: The Lawyer Personality Revealed," *Altman Weil Report to Management*, 29, no. 11 (2002).

52. *See* John C. Coates et al., *Hiring Teams, Firms, and Lawyers: Evidence of the Evolving Relationships in the Corporate Legal Market*, 36 LAW & SOC. INQUIRY 999, 1000, 1011, 1017–18 (2011).

53. Susan Cain, *Quiet: The Power of Introverts in a World That Can't Stop Talking* (New York: Crown Publishing Group, 2013) 7–11, 61.

54. Daniel H. Pink, *To Sell Is Human: The Surprising Truth About Moving Others* (New York: Riverhead Books, 2012) 90.

55. Dr. Seuss, *Oh, The Places You'll Go* (New York: Random House, 1990).

56. Ray Oldenburg, *The Great Good Place: Cafés, Coffee Shops, Community Centers, Beauty Parlors, General Stores, Bars, Hangouts and How They Get You Through the Day* (New York: Marlowe & Company, 1989) 42.

57. Johnson, *supra* note 4, at 162–63.

58. *Id.*

59. Lisa Bannon, *Mattel's Project Platypus Aims To Inspire Creative Thinking*, THE WALL STREET JOURNAL, June 6, 2002, accessed April 17, 2017, https://www.wsj.com/articles/SB1023305181289347920.

60. Tina Seelig, *inGenius: A Crash Course on Creativity* (New York: HarperCollins Publishers, 2012) 95–102.

61. https://www.broadinstitute.org/about-us, accessed December 8, 2017.

62. Lehrer, *supra* note, at 5.

63. David A. Graham, *Silly Ideas That Made Millions*, NEWSWEEK, December 16, 2010, accessed December 8, 2017, http://www.newsweek.com/silly-ideas-made-millions-69107.

64. Todd Spangler, *Twitter Posts First-Ever Profit on Strong Q4 Results as User Growth Stalls*, VARIETY, February 8, 2018, (explaining that Twitter was launched in 2006 and as of 2018, it had more than 300 million monthly active users), accessed April 25, 2018, http://variety.com/2018/digital/news/twitter-q4-2017-earnings-monthly-users-1202691803/.

65. Hugh MacLeod, *Ignore Everybody: And 39 Other Keys to Creativity* (New York: Portfolio Press, 2009).

66. Lehrer, *supra* note 5.

67. *Id.* (reporting that "[w]hen people are exposed to a short video of stand-up comedy, they solve about 20% more of insight puzzles").

68. Anthony Rivas, *How Drinking Alcohol Makes You More Creative: Drink Up For More "Aha!" Moments*, MEDICAL DAILY, March 11, 2014, accessed December 8, 2017, http://www.medicaldaily.com/how-drinking-alcohol-makes-you-more-creative-drink-more-aha-moments-271026; Cassie Shortsleeve, *Why Drinking Boosts Creativity*, MEN'S HEALTH, March 9, 2015, accessed December 8, 2017, https://www.menshealth.com/health/drinking-creativity; Leo Widrich, *Why We Have Our Best Ideas in the Shower: The Science of Creativity*, LIFE HACKING (blog), February 28, 2013, https://blog.bufferapp.com/why-we-have-our-best-ideas-in-the-shower-the-science-of-creativity; David Hindley, *Running, An Aid to the Creative Process?* THE GUARDIAN (blog), October 30, 2014, https://www.theguardian.com/lifeandstyle/the-running-blog/2014/oct/30/running-writers-block-creative-process.

69. Mihaly Csikszentmihalyi, *Flow: The Psychology of Optimal Experience* (New York: Harper Perennial Modern Classics, 2008).

Part III

1. William Shakespeare, *Hamlet* (New York: Bantam Books 1980), Act 2, Scene 2, p. 72, lines 205–06.

2. This message, innovate or die, is often communicated in the law marketplace. *See, e.g.*, Richard Susskind, *The End of Lawyers? Rethinking the Nature of Legal Services* (Oxford: Oxford University Press, 2010); Stephen Fairley, *3 Areas Where Your Law Firm Needs to Innovate . . . or Die*, THE RAINMAKER BLOG, September 28, 2015, https://www.therainmakerblog.com/2015/09/articles/lead-conversion/3-areas-where-your-law-firm-needs-to-innovate-or-die/; Bas Boras Visser, *CC Innovation Head Warns Partners to Innovate or Die*, THE GLOBAL LEGAL POST, September 25, 2015, accessed December 8, 2017, http://www.globallegalpost.com/global-view/cc-innovation-head-warns-partners-to-innovate-or-die-94516177/. It is also often said outside about other professions and industries. *See, e.g.*, Greg Satell, *How to Manage Innovation*, FORBES, March 7, 2013, accessed December 8, 2017, https://www.forbes.com/sites/gregsatell/2013/03/07/how-to-manage-innovation-2/#29e588bc4785.

3. *See, e.g.*, Alastair Ross, *Innovating Professional Services: Transforming Value and Efficiency* (Burlington, Vermont: Gower Publishing Company, 2015) (raising awareness among leaders of professional service firms of the opportunities for, challenges in creating, and best practices in innovation by professional service firms); David Galbenski written with David Barringer, *Legal Visionaries: How to Make Their Innovations Work For You* (CreateSpace Independent Publishing Platform, 2013) (attempting to inspire lawyers to change their old structure by telling stories of visionaries that have enacted change in the law marketplace); David Galbenski with David Barringer, *Unbound: How Entrepreneurship Is Dramatically Transforming Legal Services Today* (David J. Galbenski, 2009) (synthesizing trends affecting the law marketplace and urging those in the legal industry to refresh their business plans to meet the needs of the new legal marketplace).

Chapter 9

1. Don Norman, *The Design of Everyday Things: Revised and Expanded Edition* (New York: Basic Books, 2013); Don Norman, *Emotional Design: Why We Love (or Hate) Everyday Things* (New York: Basic Books, 2007); William Lidwell, Kritina Holden, and Jill Butler, *Universal Principles of Design* (Beverly, Massachusetts: Rockport Publishers, 2010); Francesca (Franki) Simonds, *Human Centered Design vs Design Thinking vs Service Design vs UX . . . What Do They All Mean?* LINKEDIN, June 8, 2016, accessed December 8, 2017, https://www.linkedin.com/pulse/human-centred-design-vs-thinking-service-ux-what-do-all-simonds.

2. Dimiter Simov-Jimmy and Ina Ivanova, *User-Centered Design Versus Design Thinking*, SLIDESHARE, LINKEDIN, June 12, 2013, accessed December 8, 2017, https://www.slideshare.net/dsimov/usercentered-design-versus-design-thinking.

3. David M. Kelley, the founder of IDEO (a consulting and design firm) and a professor at Stanford University, is generally credited with popularizing this method in the corporate world. Tim Brown, *The Making of a Design Thinker*, METROPOLIS, October 1, 2009, ("David Kelley . . . said that every time someone came to ask him about design, he found himself inserting the word thinking to explain what it is that designers do. The term design thinking stuck.").

4. Thomas Lockwood, ed., *Design Thinking: Integrating Innovation, Customer Experience, and Brand Value* (New York: Allworth Press, 2009) xi. Thomas Lockwood is a former president of the Design Management Institute (DMI), a nonprofit institute aimed at advancing design in management and business.

5. *See, e.g.*, Tom Kelley with Jonathan Littman, *The Art of Innovation: Lessons in Creativity from IDEO, America's Leading Design Firm* (New York: Doubleday, 2001); Richard Florida, *The Rise of the Creative Class—Revisited: Revised and Expanded*, (New York: Basic Books, 2014); Daniel H. Pink, *A Whole New Mind: Why Right-Brainers Will Rule the Future* (New York: Riverhead Books, 2006); Tim Brown, *Change by Design: How Design Thinking Transforms Organizations and Inspires Innovation* (New York: HarperCollins Publishers, 2009); Lockwood, ed., *supra* note 4.

6. Brown, *supra* note 5, pp. 15–17.

7. Lockwood, ed., *supra* note 4, pp. 35–45.

8. Lockwood, ed., *supra* note 4, Chapter 4: Heather M. A. Fraser, "Designing Business: New Models for Success," pp. 35–45, and Chapter 17: Chris Bedford and Anson Lee, "Would You Like Service with That?" pp. 197–204.

9. Brown, *supra* note 5, at 184.

10. Lockwood, *supra* note 4, vii–xvii.

11. Daniel H. Pink, *To Sell Is Human: The Surprising Truth About Moving Others* (New York: Riverhead Books, 2012) 89.

12. Ranjay Gulati, *Reorganize for Resilience: Putting Customers at the Center of Your Business* (Boston: Harvard Business Review Press, 2009).

13. Bruce Turkel, *All About Them: Grow Your Business by Focusing on Others* (Boston: Da Capo Press, 2016).

14. Pink, *supra* note 11 at 72.

15. Christiaans, H.H. C.M., "Creativity in Design: The Role of Domain Knowledge in Designing" (PhD thesis, Delfit University of Technology, Delfit, The Netherlands (1992).

16. Tina Seelig, *inGenius: A Crash Course on Creativity* (New York: HarperCollins Publishers, 2012) 19–30.

17. Pink, *supra* note 11 at 5; Tina Seelig, *What I Wish I Knew When I Was 20: A Crash Course on Making Your Place in the World* (New York: HarperOne, 2009); Tina Seelig, *see supra* note 16.

18. Sir James Dyson created the bagless vacuum cleaner because he was frustrated with the smell from the dust, the lack of power, and the loud noise of traditional vacuum clears. *See, e.g.*, Shoshana Davis, *Vacuum Inventor James Dyson on Desire*

to *"Change the World,"* CBS News, January 14, 2014, accessed December 8, 2017, https://www.cbsnews.com/news/why-vacuums-sir-james-dyson-on-the-story-behind-his-invention/.

19. Seelig, *supra* note 17 at 23.

20. To view this exercise, see my forthcoming book *The 3-4-5 Method of Innovation for Lawyers: A Handbook of Exercises and Best Practices.*

21. I hadn't heard of any human-centered design approaches to innovation that included celebration as we have in LWOW since its inception in 2010. Two years ago, however, I was introduced to the concept of Dragon Dreaming, and I was pleasantly surprised to learn that it includes celebration as an important component to creating projects. *See What is Dragon Dreaming and Why is it Important? An Interview with John Croft,* Dragon Dreaming (blog), October 14, 2008, dragondreamingtraining.blogspot.com/2008/10/what-is-dragon-dreaming-and-why-is-it.html (explaining that it "is a process pioneered in Western Australia, to assist individuals, community organisations, and ecologically responsible businesses [to] develop, undertake and complete outrageously successful projects").

22. Many writers have been accredited for saying this, including Stephen King. *See, e.g.,* Forrest Wickman, *Who Really Said You Should "Kill Your Darlings,"* Slate (blog), October 18, 2013, accessed December 8, 2017, www.slate.com/blogs/browbeat/2013/10/18/_kill_your_darlings_writing_advice_what_writer_really_said_to_murder_your.html.

23. Stephen Poor, *An Audience of Lawyers: A Guide to Managing Change within the Cynical, Competitive, and Critical,* Rethink the Practice, June 24, 2015, accessed December 7, 2017, https://medium.com/rethink-the-practice/an-audience-of-lawyers-34c43156a17.

24. Lockwood, *supra* note 4, at vii–xvii.

25. Nicky Leijtens, *Design Thinking and the Future of Law: Finding the Balance between Knowledge, Processes, and the Use of Technology,* Knowledge Management Design Thinking, December 2015, accessed December 8, 2017, https://www.nautadutilh.com/siteassets/documents/design_thinking_and_the_future_of_law.pdf.

26. Phil Charron, *Divergent Thinking vs Convergent Thinking,* Think Company (blog), October 26, 2011, https://www.thinkcompany.com/2011/10/divergent-thinking-vs-convergent-thinking/.

27. Tim Brown, *What Does Design Thinking Feel Like?* Design Thinking (blog), September 7, 2008, https://designthinking.ideo.com/?p=51.

28. Brown, *supra* note 5, at 92.

29. Poor, *supra* note 23.

30. Cass R. Sunstein and Reid Hastie, *Making Dumb Groups Smarter,* Harvard Business Review, December 2014.

31. *Definition of Red Team,* Financial Times/Lexicon, accessed December 8, 2017, http://lexicon.ft.com/Term?term=red-team.

32. For a review of DiSC, see https://discprofile.com/what-is-disc/overview/, accessed December 9, 2017. Other personality tests can be used as well, including Myers-Briggs and a new assessment tool created by Suzanne M. Johnson Vickberg and Kim Chrisfort. *See* Suzanne M. Johnson Vickberg and Kim Christfort, *Pioneers, Drivers, Integrators, and Guardians*, Harvard Business Review, March–April 2017 (explaining the assessment as dividing people into pioneers, guardians, drivers, and integrators).

33. Kevin Ashton, *How to Fly a Horse: The Secret History of Creation, Invention, and Discovery* (New York: Anchor Books) 2015.

34. Tim Brown, *Design Thinking*, Harvard Business Review, June 2008.

35. Alina Bradford, *What Is Science*, Live Science, August 4, 2017, accessed April 25, 2018, https://www.livescience.com/20896-science-scientific-method.html.

36. Brown, *supra* note 5, at 176.

Chapter 10

1. Robert Frost, "In the Home Stretch," in *Mountain Interval* (Alexandria, United Kingdom, Chadwyck-Healey, 1924) lines 190–91.

2. Tom Robbins, *Jitterbug Perfume* (New York: Bantam Books, 1984).

3. *See, e.g.*, Piercarlo Valdesolo et al., *The Rhythm of Joint Action: Synchrony Promotes Cooperative Ability*, Journal of Experimental Social Psychology, July 2010, (finding that synchronous rocking enhances connectedness), accessed December 8, 2017, http://www.sciencedirect.com/science/article/pii/S0022103110000430; Sebastian Kirschner and Michael Tomasello *Joint Music Making Promotes Prosocial Behavior in 4-Year-Old Children*, Evolution and Human Behavior, April 24, 2010, accessed December 8, 2017, http://citeseerx.ist.psu.edu/viewdoc/download?doi=10.1.1.467.7835&rep=rep1&type=pdf.

4. Scott Wiltermuth and Chip Heath, *Synchrony and Cooperation*, Psychological Science, January 2009, accessed December 8, 2017, https://www.ncbi.nlm.nih.gov/pubmed/19152536.

5. Selin Kesebir (2011), *The Superorganism Account of Human Sociality: How and When Human Groups Are Like Beehives*, Personality and Social Psycholology Review, August 2012, accessed December 8, 2017, https://www.ncbi.nlm.nih.gov/pubmed/22202149.

6. Dr. Larry Richard, "Herding Cats: The Lawyer Personality Revealed," *Altman Weil Report to Management*, 29, no. 11 (2002).

7. David Rock, *SCARF: A Brain-Based Model for Collaborating with and Influencing Others*, NeuroLeadership Journal, accessed December 8, 2017, https://www.epa.gov/sites/production/files/2015-09/documents/thurs_georgia_9_10_915_covello.pdf. (explaining that SCARF stands for S status, C certainty, A autonomy, R relatedness, F, Fairness).

8. Shaun Temby, *10 Things That Law Firms Are Saying That Kill Innovation*, LinkedIn, June 6, 2016, accessed December 8, 2017, https://www.linkedin.com/pulse/10-things-law-firms-saying-kill-innovation-shaun-temby.

9. Leonard Cohen, *The Lyrics of Leonard Cohen: Enhanced Edition* (Omnibus Press, August 2011), song "Anthem" from album *The Future*.

10. *A Conference Call in Real Life*, accessed December 8, 2017, https://www.youtube.com/watch?v=DYu_bGbZiiQ.

11. Haruki Murakami, *Norwegian Wood* (New York: Vintage Books, 2000) 115.

12. *See, e.g.,* Daniel Oberhaus, *First-Ever LSD Microdosing Study Will Pit the Human Brain Against AI*, MOTHERBOARD, May 9, 2017, (explaining that microdosers claim that microdosing enhances creativity and business executives claim that Bulletproof Coffee helps people think smarter), accessed December 8, 2017, https://motherboard.vice.com/en_us/article/gvzvex/first-ever-lsd-microdosing-study-will-pit-the-human-brain-against-ai; Michael J. Coren, *A Doctor Is Helping Silicon Valley Execs Live Their Best Life for $40k a Year*, QUARTZ, May 28, 2017, accessed December 8, 2017, https://qz.com/967362/maloof/ last; Courtney Rubin, *Bulletproof Coffee: The New Power Drink of Silicon Valley*, FAST COMPANY, July 3, 2014, accessed December 8, 2017, https://www.fastcompany.com/3032635/bulletproof-coffee-the-new-power-drink-of-silicon-valley.

13. Cass R. Sunstein and Reid Hastie, *Making Dumb Groups Smarter*, HARVARD BUSINESS REVIEW, December 2014.

14. Kevin Ashton, *How to Fly a Horse: The Secret History of Creation, Invention, and Discovery* (New York: Anchor Books, 2015) 23.

15. Tim Young, *365 Days, $10 Million, 3 Rounds, 2 Companies, All with 5 Magic Slides*, TECHCRUNCH, November 2, 2010.

16. *Id.*

17. Ashton, *supra* note 14.

Chapter 11

1. Ursula K. Le Guin, *The Left Hand of Darkness* (New York: Ace Books, 2000) 220.

2. Master's degree in law and business.

3. Le Guin, *supra* note 1, at 70.

4. Mary Doria Russell, *Children of God* (New York: Villard Books, 1998) 210.

5. Louis de Bernieres, *Corelli's Mandolin* (New York: Vintage Books,1995) 3.

6. This may seem chauvinistic, but our research showed that the main purchasing decision makers were moms, not dads, at the time, so that was our focus.

7. *Apple Jacks Cereal Ad—1994*, accessed December 8, 2017, https://www.youtube.com/watch?v=BXKUwWsI4ng; *Apple Jacks Ad—Baseball*, accessed December 8, 2017, https://www.youtube.com/watch?v=YTw1e9iLTew; *Apple Jacks Commercial*, accessed December 8, 2017, https://www.youtube.com/watch?v=nsFO9JwFclM.

8. Thomas MacMillan, *Alternative Courts Can Transform Offenders, Not Just Punish Them*, NATION SWELL, December 4, 2014, accessed November 29, 2017, http://nationswell.com/alternative-courts-effective-reforming-offenders. In some drug courts, for example, defendants can choose to undergo supervised treatment monitored by the court instead of receiving probation or a prison sentence. *Id.*

They are required to come to the court regularly to have two-way conversations with the judge that include personal questions as well as praise and encouragement. *Id.*

9. Chip Heath and Dan Heath, *Switch: How to Change Things When Change is Hard* (New York: Broadway Books, 2010) 28–48.

10. Drew Boyd and Jacob Goldenberg, *Inside the Box: A Proven System of Creativity for Breakthrough Results* (New York: Simon & Schuster, 2013).

11. Margaret Boden, *Creativity and Unpredictability*, SEHR, June 4, 1995, accessed December 8, 2017, https://web.stanford.edu/group/SHR/4-2/text/boden.html.

12. Jeff Dyer et al., *The Innovator's DNA: Mastering the Five Skills of Disruptive Innovators* (Boston: Harvard Business Review Press, 2011) 41–63 (identifying associating as one of the five skills of disruptive innovators).

13. The term was originally coined by evolutionary biologists Stephen Jay Gould and Elizabeth S. Vrba to describe a change in the biology of a species other than adaptation. *See* Stephen Jay Gould and Elizabeth S. Vrba, *Exaptation—A Missing Term in the Science of Form*, PALEOBIOLOGY, http://www2.hawaii.edu/~khayes/Journal_Club/fall2006/Gould_&_Vrb_1982_Paleobio.pdf.

14. Others have made similar points as it relates to technology today. *See, e.g.,* Nicholas Dew *et al.*, *The Economic Implications of Exaptation*, J. EVOL. ECON. 2004, accessed December 8, 2017, https://link.springer.com/article/10.1007/s00191-003-0180-x. ("[N]ew markets develop as the result of the application of an existing technology to a new domain of use. . . . When an entrepreneur flips a technology into an adjacent possible market this is truly an exaptation of the technology, not an adaptation.")

15. Allyson Reedy, *The Butcher Training Army Special Forces to Stay Healthy*, SOUTHWEST: THE MAGAZINE, July 2017, accessed December 8, 2017, https://issuu.com/southwestmag/docs/july2017/52.

16. Bryan Nelson, *Spider Drinks Graphene, Spins Web That Can Hold the Weight of a Human*, MOTHER NATURE NETWORK, September 1, 2017, accessed December 4, 2017, https://www.mnn.com/green-tech/research-innovations/stories/spider-spins-web-can-hold-weight-human-after-drinking-graphene; Andrew Masterson, *Scientists Have Spiders Producing Enhanced Web That Can Hold a Human*, THE SYDNEY MORNING HERALD, August 23, 2017, accessed December 4, 2017, http://www.smh.com.au/technology/sci-tech/nanotech-super-spiderwebs-are-here-20170822-gy1blp.html.

17. Tim Carmody, *Why Graphene Won Scientists the Nobel Prize*, SHARE, October 5, 2010, accessed December 4, 2017, https://www.wired.com/2010/10/graphene/; *see also* Press Release, *The Royal Swedish Academy of Sciences*, October, 5, 2010, accessed *December 4, 2017*, https://www.nobelprize.org/nobel_prizes/physics/laureates/2010/press.html.

18. Sigmund Freud, *Thoughts for the Time on War and Death*, 1915, PANARCHY.ORG, accessed December 10, 2017, https://www.panarchy.org/freud/war.1915.html.

19. For an article supporting the value of performing premortems, see Gary Klein, *Performing a Project Premortem*, HARVARD BUSINESS REVIEW, September 2007.

Conclusion

1. I have taught over 500 millennials in LawWithoutWalls and another 500 in my substantive courses including Professional Responsibilty, Civil Procedure, and Law, Innovation and Tech.

2. Ray Williams, *Is the "Me Generation" Less Empathetic?* FINANCIAL POST, June 13, 2010, http://business.financialpost.com/executive/careers/is-the-me-generation-less-empathetic.

3. Joel Stein, *Millennials: The Me Me Me Generation*, TIME MAGAZINE, May 9, 2013, accessed November 26, 2017, http://time.com/247/millennials-the-me-me-me-generation/.

4. *The Radical Transformation of Diversity and Inclusion: The Millennial Influence*, DELOITTE, accessed November 26, 2017, https://www2.deloitte.com/us/en/pages/about-deloitte/articles/radical-transformation-of-diversity-and-inclusion.html.

5. Lydia Dishman, *The New Rules of Work: Millennials Have A Different Definition of Diversity and Inclusion*, FASTCOMPANY, May 18, 2015, accessed November 21, 2017, https://www.fastcompany.com/3046358/millennials-have-a-different-definition-of-diversity-and-inclusion.

6. Stein, *supra* note 3.

7. Dishman, *supra* note 5.

8. *The Radical Transformation of Diversity and Inclusion: The Millennial Influence*, *supra* note 4 ("83 percent of millennials are actively engaged when they believe the organization *fosters* an inclusive culture," compared to only "60% of millennials [who] are actively engaged when they believe the organization does not have an inclusive culture.").

9. Billie Tarascio, *A Woman's Edge in the Modern Legal World*, LAW PRACTICE TODAY, February 14, 2017, accessed December 8, 2017, http://www.lawpracticetoday.org/article/womans-edge-modern-legal-world/?utm_source=February17&utm_medium=email&utm_campaign=February17LPTemail.

10. *Id.*

11. Frank Browning, *Survival Secrets: What Is It About Women That Makes Them More Resilient Than Men?*, CALIFORNIA MAGAZINE, April 29, 2015, accessed December 8, 2017, https://alumni.berkeley.edu/california-magazine/just-in/2015-04-30/survival-secrets-what-it-about-women-makes-them-more.

12. Tim Brown, *Change by Design: How Design Thinking Transforms Organizations and Inspires Innovation* (New York: HarperCollins Publishers, 2009) 79.

13. Sheryl Sandberg and Adam Grant, *Speaking While Female: Sheryl Sandberg and Adam Grant on Why Women Stay Quiet at Work*, THE NEW YORK TIMES, January

12, 2015, accessed December 8, 2017, https://www.nytimes.com/2015/01/11/opinion/sunday/speaking-while-female.html?smid=tw-share&_r=0).

14. Jessica Bennett, *How Not to Be "Manterrupted' in Meetings,"* Time Magazine, January 20, 2015, accessed December 8, 2017, http://time.com/3666135/sheryl-sandberg-talking-while-female-manterruptions/.

15. Helen Fisher, *The First Sex: The Natural Talents of Women and How They Are Changing the World* (New York: Random House, 1999).

16. Steven Johnson, *Where Good Ideas Come From: The Natural History of Innovation* (New York: Riverhead Books, 2010) 23–42.

17. Tarascio, *supra* note 9.

18. *Id.*

19. *See, e.g.,* Peter Kuhn and Marie Claire Villeval, *Do Women Prefer a Co-operative Work Environment?* November 19, 2011, accessed December 8, 2017, http://legacy.iza.org/en/papers/158_10052012.pdf (demonstrating that women are more likely than men to select team-based compensation); Jamie Doward and Grace Harper, *Women Compete Better When They Are In Teams,* Research Finds, The Guardian, September 10, 2011, accessed December 8, 2017, https://www.theguardian.com/world/2011/sep/11/women-equality-competition-gender.

20. Anita Williams Woolley et al., *Evidence for a Collective Intelligence Factor in the Performance of Human Groups,*330, Issue 6004 (2010): 686–88, doi: 10.1126/science.1193147, 29 Oct 2010; Anita Woolley et al., *Why Some Teams Are Smarter Than Others,* The New York Times, January 16, 2015, accessed December 7, 2017, https://www.nytimes.com/2015/01/18/opinion/sunday/why-some-teams-are-smarter-than-others.html; Young Ji Kim et al., *What Makes a Strong Team? Using Collective Intelligence to Predict Team Performance in* League of Legends, CSCW 2017, February 25–March 1, 2017, Portland, Oregon, accessed December 8, 2017, http://mitsloan.mit.edu/shared/ods/documents/?DocumentID=2710 (finding that cognitive intelligence is positively correlated with the presence of a female team member).

21. Steve Connor, *Women More Likely to Yawn Because They Feel Greater Empathy Than Men, Study Says,* Independent, February 3, 2016, accessed December 8, 2017, http://www.independent.co.uk/news/science/women-more-likely-to-yawn-because-they-feel-greater-empathy-than-men-study-says-a6849956.html.

22. Alison Beard, *Women Respond Better Than Men to Competitive Pressure,* Harvard Business Review, Nov–Dec 2017, 1, 4 (finding that although men are physically stronger than women on average, when it comes to mental toughness as it relates to competitive pressure, women outperform men, and highlighting a University of St. Gallen study of more than 8,200 games from Grand Slam tennis matches and bronze medal judo fights from 2009 to 2014 that found that women respond better than men to competitive pressure).

23. Browning, *supra* note 11.
24. Woolley et al., *supra* note 20.
25. Lisa Calhoun, *30 Surprising Facts About Female Founders*, INC.COM, July 6 2015, accessed December 8, 2017, https://www.inc.com/lisa-calhoun/30-surprising-facts-about-female-founders.html.
26. *State of the American Manager: Analytics and Advice for Leaders* Gallup Study 2014, 26–28.
27. *Id.*; *see also* Kimberly Fitch and Sangeeta Agrawal, *Why Women Are Better Managers Than Men*, BUSINESS JOURNAL, October 16, 2014, accessed November 26, 2017, http://news.gallup.com/businessjournal/178541/why-women-better-managers-men.aspx (reporting findings form Gallup study 2014).
28. Ellie Martin, *Why Women Entrepreneurs Can Do More With Less*, ENTREPRENEUR.COM, August 16, 2016, accessed December 8, 2017, https://www.entrepreneur.com/article/280088#; *see also The 2015 State of Women-Owned Businesses Report*, Commissioned by American Express OPEN, A Summary of Important Trends, 1997–2015 (showing that between 2007 and 2015, net 340,000 jobs were added by women-owned businesses versus men-owned businesses that shed 1.2 million jobs) http://www.womenable.com/content/userfiles/Amex_OPEN_State_of_WOBs_2015_Executive_Report_finalsm.pdf.
29. Nicole Auerbach, Co-founder, Valorem, *Tick Tock, Women Should Bash the Clock*, REINVENT LAW CHANNEL, accessed January 22, 2018, http://www.reinventlawchannel.com/nicole-auerbach-tick-tock-women-should-bash-the-clock.
30. *See supra* note 26; Victor Lipman, *Are Women Really, As This Major Research Says, Better Managers Than Men?,"* FORBES, April 16, 2015, accessed December 8, 2017, https://www.forbes.com/sites/victorlipman/2015/04/16/are-women-really-as-this-major-research-says-better-managers-than-men/#6d11fb047f0c.
31. Julia Carrie Wong, *Women Considered Better Coders—But Only If They Hide Their Gender*, THE GUARDIAN, February 12, 2106, accessed December 8, 2017, https://www.theguardian.com/technology/2016/feb/12/women-considered-better-coders-hide-gender-github.
32. Rebecca Klein, *Girls Understand Technology Better Than Boys on This Test*, HUFFINGTON POST, May 18, 2106, accessed December 8, 2017, https://www.huffingtonpost.com/entry/naep-technology-girls_us_5739f461e4b08f96c183abc2 (reporting results from the National Assessment for Educational Progress, aka, the Nations Report Card).
33. Cali Ressler and Jody Thompson, *Why Managing Sucks and How to Fix It: A Results-Only Guide to Taking Control of Work, Not People* (Hoboken, New Jersey: John Wiley & Sons, 2013) 7.
34. Anne-Marie Slaughter, *Why Women Still Can't Have It All*, THE ATLANTIC, July–August 2012, accessed December 8, 2017, https://www.theatlantic.com/magazine/archive/2012/07/why-women-still-cant-have-it-all/309020.
35. For an article supporting a LawWithoutWalls-like collaborative approach and discussing the misalignment between the realities of the legal marketplace

and how lawyers are trained, see Scott A. Westfahl and David B. Wilkins, *The Leadership Imperative: A Collaborative Approach to Professional Development in the Global Age of More for Less*, 60 STANFORD L. REV. 1667 (2017).

Appendix B

1. Mark Swatzell, *Achieving Business Impact through Experiential Learning*, LINKEDIN, March 27, 2017, accessed May 31, 2017, https://www.linkedin.com/pulse/achieving-business-impact-through-experiential-mark-swatzell.
2. *Id.*

Appendix C

1. In snowball sampling. initial participants provide connections to other potential interviewees who might be willing to be interviewed by the researcher. For a more detailed description, see Leo A. Goodman, *Snowball Sampling*, ANNALS MATHEMATICAL STAT., 32, 148, 148–49 (1961) (defining snowball sampling); Charles Kadushin, *Power, Influence, and Social Circles: A New Methodology for Studying Opinion Makers*, 33 AM. SOC. REV., no. 5 (1968): 685, 694–96 (discussing the strengths and weaknesses of snowball sampling); *see also* Jean Faugier and Mary Sargeant, *ampling Hard to Reach Populations*, J. ADVANCED NURSING, 26 (1997): 790; Sarah H. Ramsey and Robert F. Kelly, *Using Social Science Research in Family Law Analysis and Formation: Problems and Prospects*, 3 S. CAL. INTERDISC. L.J., (1994): 631, 642. Legal scholars often base research on snowball samples. *See, e.g.,* Kimberly Kirkland, *Ethics in Large Law Firms: The Principle of Pragmatism*, 35 U. MEM. L. REV., (2004): 631 (utilizing a snowball sample of twenty-two lawyers practicing in ten large law firms to investigate "how bureaucratic legal workplaces shape lawyers' ethical consciousness").
2. This could be called quasi-content analysis, which is a type of analysis often used for analyzing transcripts, political speeches, advertisements, and judicial opinions. *See, e.g.,* Klaus Krippendorff, *Content Analysis: An Introduction to Its Methodology* (Thousand Oaks, California: Sage Publications 2004).
3. This approach is similar in some ways to that taken by Nelson and Nielsen. *See* Robert L. Nelson and Laura Beth Nielsen, *Cops, Counsel, and Entrepreneurs: Constructing the Role of Inside Counsel in Large Corporations*, 34 LAW & SOC'Y REV. no. 4 (2000): 457, 470.
4. *See* Christine Parker, *The Ethics of Advising on Regulatory Compliance: Autonomy or Interdependence?* J. BUS. ETHICS, 28, no. 4: 339, 341. In other areas of study, examination of narratives is a method used successfully (e.g., critical legal studies literature). Furthermore, the number of interviews in this study generally exceeds the number of interviews utilized to research other topics in the legal profession.
5. For the most part, I interviewed the highest-ranking legal officer at the company, usually having the title GC. However, in some situations, I interviewed the deputy GC. Also, in two situations, I interviewed the top two legal officers.

6. The titles of these interviewees varied. Often, they held the title Chief Innovation Officer or Head of Innovation. However, sometimes, they were identified as the leader of innovation in their firm but held a different title (e.g., Chief Information Officer).

Acknowledgments

1. The Beatles, "With a Little Help From My Friends," title of song from *Sgt. Pepper's Lonely Hearts Club Band* (Parlophone, June 1, 1967) (vinyl, LP, album, mono), written by Lennon-McCartney (June 1, 1967); *see also*, *The Beatles Lyrics: The Songs of Lennon, McCartney, Harrison and Starr*, 2nd edition, (Hal Leonard, May 1, 1992).

"With a little help from my friends."

The Beatles[1]

The truth is, I don't get by "with a *little* help from my friends." I get by because I have so much help from friends of all kinds, old and new. Without their help, I would not have been able to do the research for this book, let alone write it. Nor would I have been able to bring LawWithoutWalls to life and grow it over the past eight years. So this section is about giving thanks to those who have helped me "get by."

To My Family

I start by thanking my three incredible, supportive children: My oldest son, Master Jasper, for knocking on my bedroom door (ever so lightly) late, late in the night as he was getting home, checking on me because I was still up writing. He'd place his hand on my shoulder, and I could feel him sending me good energy to help me keep plowing through. My daughter, Reading (aka Sweet Pea), for always knowing exactly what to say or text *just when* I needed it most, when I was experiencing writer's block, when I was in tears because I couldn't possibly get it all done (book, classes, presentations, Kickoffs, ConPosiums, fund-raising, travel, and parenting). She picked me up, and she picked up where I left off, even learning how to cook my youngest son's favorite dinners just right because he is such a finicky eater. (She now cooks paninis better than I do, that's for sure!) And finally, I thank my youngest son, Trip, my *favorite* third baby, who was always there to relax with me in front of some inane TV show when I needed a break and who always understood when the answer to his question "Mom, are we doing anything this weekend?" was "No, sugar, I have to write."

My next thanks are to my significant other, Ian. Thank you, Ian, for believing in me, for working alongside me in the office every Sunday (and many other weeknights well in to the early morning), for providing breaks with snacks and wine (lots of wine) and laughs (lots of laughs), and for giving me that harsh-and-from-love advice when things were tough and complicated and hard. Thank you, Hayden and Connor, Ian's warmer-than-warm teenage sons, who feel like my own after all these years, who supported me, and who went to the office every Sunday with me and their dad for what we called "Study Hall" even though there were times they stayed hours after they were done with their homework and ready to go.

Likely, the only way I really survived was because of my mom. This is not an exaggeration. Thank you, Mom, for knowing how to say *"Yes, and . . ."* and for saying *"Yes, and . . ."* to me over and over (and over) again whether it was to grocery shop the day before Thanksgiving, take my children to their doctor's appointments and activities, or spend time with them on the weekends when I could not.

I thank my sister, Des, who, in addition to treating my children like her own and inviting them to her house every weekend, refrained from judgment when I wasn't with my children. Instead, she always told me how much she admired my ambition. I also thank my ex-husband, Bill, not only for being the reason LawWithoutWalls has its name but also for being so understanding and flexible and willing to swap different days and nights with me to watch the children, helping me out when I needed to travel for LWOW or MOVELΔW or conduct *just one more* interview for my book.

To My Friends and Mentors

I thank the friends from my past who joined me on my quest to create what is now called LawWithoutWalls. I thank Jon Callaghan, my closest friend from college, who taught me how to think and act like an entrepreneur and who gave LawWithoutWalls its powerful, punchy acronym: LWOW (pronounced L-WOW). I thank Eric Satz for joining us as as one of our first venture capitalists in LWOW. And I thank Phyllis Dealy and Anita James Ritchie, such unique, multitalented women, for playing multiple roles in LWOW to teach our community new and different skills. And I thank all of the other friends from my past who served in various roles from thought leaders on webinars to mentors and pitch coaches.

I thank the new friends I made through LawWithoutWalls and MOVELΔW, who have supported me and helped make LawWithoutWalls and MOVELΔW what they are today. Thank you, Ray Abadin, Richard Barlow, Jeff Carr, Mark Cohen, Leah Cooper, Anna Pope Donovan, Jim Ferraro, Alisa Fiddes, Chad Fischer, Tristan Forrester, Horacio Gutierrez, Fred Headon, David Halliwell, Karen Hough, Renee Knake, Imogen Lee, Lisa Leong, Alessandro Philip Maiano, Stephen Makin, Rick Matasar, Paul McCormack, Alastair Morrison, Justin North, James Peters, Hendrik Schneider, John Stewart, Peter Sudbury, Mark Swatzell, Mari Cruz Taboada, and Scott Westfahl, to name a few.

I thank my mentors who were early adopters of LWOW, without whom LWOW would not exist at all or be nearly as robust. Thank you, David Wilkins, for believing in me and jumping into LWOW for that reason only. Thank you, as well, for guiding me these past 15 years in my work and life decisions, for supporting my candidacy for every role I've ever attempted to play, and mostly for being *there* for me at odd times from whatever time zone you were in to listen and give me advice and send love. Thank you, Ida Abbot, Soledad Atienza, Ray Campbell, Elizabeth Chambliss, John Flood, Jordan Furlong, Dame Hazel Genn, Bruce Green, Bill Henderson, Martha Minow, Deborah Rhode, Scott Rogers, Rob Rosen, Susan Sneider, Leo Staub, and Laurel Terry for joining LWOW before it was clear what it was and for providing advice to me (both personal and professional) along the way as I attempted to help drive its growth and mine. Thank you James Batham, Kevin Doolan, and Moray McLaren for selling LWOW better than I could, for providing active guidance year after year to me and the community, and for holding me up when things were tougher than tough. Thank you, Georgie Angones, for guiding me and helping me fund raise to support LWOW every year. Thank you, Richard Susskind, for presenting at the very first LWOW KickOff in 2011, for supporting me, and for continuing to give me the gift of feedback. Some big thanks also go to the people who mentored me pre-LWOW, without whom I would never have become a professor, including John Coates, Anne-Marie Slaughter, and Judge William Young.

To My Book Advisers and Contributors

Thank you to the people who have been advisers and readers of this book. Thank you, Heidi Gardner and Deborah Epstein Henry, for giving me so much useful advice for how to go about getting a book published. Thank you to John Palmer of Ankerwycke Publications and his dedicated copy editors, who together have proven false everything I have ever heard about how tough the book editing process is.

My deepest thanks and gratitude also go to all of the colleagues who provided insights that I have woven throughout the book and the 100+ interviewees who gave me not only their time but also their voices to help me me say everything better than I could have myself. I also owe a great deal of gratitude to my 12 research assistants (among the top 15 students in my 2017 Civil Procedure class) who thanklessly checked every source cited in the book: Alyssa Altonaga, Lauren Alvarez, Taylor Fox, Gil Greber, Jacob Hensch, Brendan W. Mehler, Theodore Obrien, Jose Paez, Brenno Lim Ribeiro, Leanne Roca, Casey Soares, and Trevor Youshak.

Perhaps ironically, words cannot express my gratitude to my editor, my Aries friend, Stuart Horwitz of Book Architecture, who helped me pick the right words and find the right balance between my voice and the cacophony of voices I was representing. Stuart was a tireless partner, helping me rewrite and restructure, fearless in his edits, and cuts, and pushbacks. This book is so much better because of him.

To LWOW and Beyond!

LWOW wouldn't exist today if it weren't for two people: Peter Lederer and Trish White. When I told them I wanted to create a program that was altogether different, that broke down the hierarchies that existed between education and practice, law and business, students and academics and lawyers, schools of different ranks, people from different countries and different disciplines, they said, "Great. Bring us a proposal, and we will help you build it." And that's what they have done, thanklessly, for the past eight years. With their advice, their support, their creative input, and their pushing (indeed, sometimes very hard when I needed it badly), they helped me create what we now know as LawWithoutWalls. Thank you both for being fearless and constant in your support and engagement with me and LWOW.

A big thanks also goes to everyone in LWOW today and yesterday: those who have served on the LWOW leadership team (including Hakim Lakhdar and Lauren Madigan); those from MiamiLaw who have given all kinds of support to LWOW (including Ellen Greenfield and the entire UM IT/AV team, Peggy Hollander, Lisa Iglesias, Tamara Lave, Jose Marcos, Madeleine Plasencia, Laurie Silvers, Annette Torres, and Cheryl Zuckerman); and those who volunteer their time, who come back year after year to play new and old roles in new and old ways to help us together create a new vision for law's future and create a community of change agents. Thank you to our students who put their hearts and souls (and grit) into LWOW each year and who return as alumni to spread the LWOW culture as alumni advisers and leaders, such as Amir Singh Dhillon, Salvador Gomez, Maria Pedrique, Lachlan Robb, Felix Schulte-Strathaus, and Zachary Windham.

My final thanks go to the only person who is indispensable in *both* LWOW and my life, and that is Erika Concetta Pagano. She is more than a colleague, and she is more than a friend. She is "my millennial" who teaches me something new every day; who pushes me in every way; and who supports me no matter how crazy I am, how hard I push back, or how high I ask her to reach. She is the most exceptional young woman with whom I have ever worked. She has that perfect combination of intellect and creativity, of humility and confidence, of doing and inspiring. She is a leader, a mentor, a project manager, a teacher, a trainer, and a creator all in one. Thank you, Erika. Without you and all of your help, I would not (even a little bit) get by.

ABOUT THE AUTHOR

"The world is full of magic things, patiently waiting for our senses to grow sharper."

—W. B. Yeats[1]

My first paying job was as a mini magician when I was 12 years old. One of the tricks I learned was how to pull a pigeon out of hat. The first time I pulled off this magic trick at a children's birthday party, I saw the eyes of those skeptical children and . . . aah, I felt it: my calling.

And no, my calling wasn't to be the next David Copperfield. It was to change the way people see, think, and behave. After attending Dartmouth College, I went into advertising and marketing for eight years. My job as an account executive at Leo Burnett in Chicago was to help write creative strategies so that commercials would motivate consumers to buy products (such as Frosted Flakes)—to change their behavior, in other words. After four years, I moved to Levi Strauss & Co. as a marketing manager, researching urban youth to help create new products that would restimulate the brand and change the way people viewed Levi's and ultimately to get them to buy the product.

I then decided to move from the world of cereal and jeans to a world of principles and ethics—to things that mattered more (i.e., the law). And even though the intellectual and moral stakes were higher, being a lawyer is not that different from being an advertising executive or a marketing manager. In the law, we impact how people see the world and behave and how they think.

After getting my degree at Harvard Law School (HLS), I practiced as a special master on a patent law case, then returned to HLS where Professor David Wilkins hired me to work with him as the associate research director of the Center on the Legal Profession. In addition to being involved in launching the HLS Executive Education Program with Professor Ashish Nanda, we worked on a project studying purchasing decisions by GCs, specifically the make-buy decision. It was then that I realized I was "home." I had found a way to merge my background in marketing, advertising, and market research with law, the legal profession, and legal education. After working as a Climenko Fellow and Lecturer on Law at HLS for a couple more years, I decided to go back to my childhood home, Miami, to follow my calling.

For the past eight years through MOVELΔW (my consultancy) and Law-WithoutWalls, an experiential learning program designed to transform how law and business professionals collaborate, I have led more than 190 multidisciplinary teams with lawyers on a four-month journey of collaborative, creative problem solving. Based on others' human-centered approaches to innovation and some of my own, I lead each team through an innovation cycle. Each of these teams starts with a problem in legal education or practice, and at the end, team members have a practicable solution: a business case with a branded prototype and commercial. But the point is not the solution; the point is changing mindsets, skill sets, and behaviors by teaching team members to open their minds, their hearts, and their doors. This overcomes the typical lawyers' temperament and training that bar us from reaching our true collaborative and creative potential.

Lawyers have been given a bad rap when it comes to creativity, collaboration, and innovation; it is simply not true that lawyers are not creative or that the practice of law is not a creative practice. The challenge of applying creativity to our field is that lawyers are taught to use the same legal thinking they have engaged in before, the same reasoning, the same processes, and the same opinions (precedents) to solve new problems. What we need is a new kind of thinking, a new theoretical framework, a new method designed not only to create innovation in law but also to hone new skills, mindsets, and behaviors. For any method or framework to resonate, however, it needs to be catered to lawyers—how they work, think, and are trained. I wrote this guide do just that, and I hope you enjoy it.

LIST OF FIGURES

INDEX